3 7847 00004305

GQ 500 J63 2017
Johnston, Janis Clark,
Midlife maze : a map to
recovery and rediscovery...
Gen.Col.

DATE DUE

			PRINTED IN U.S.A.

Midlife Maze

Midlife Maze

A Map to Recovery and Rediscovery after Loss

Janis Clark Johnston

ROWMAN & LITTLEFIELD
Lanham • Boulder • New York • London

Published by Rowman & Littlefield
A wholly owned subsidiary of The Rowman & Littlefield Publishing Group, Inc.
4501 Forbes Boulevard, Suite 200, Lanham, Maryland 20706
www.rowman.com

Unit A, Whitacre Mews, 26-34 Stannary Street, London SE11 4AB

British Library Cataloguing in Publication Information Available

Library of Congress Cataloging-in-Publication Data Available
ISBN 978-1-4422-7269-9 (cloth : alk. paper)
ISBN 978-1-4422-7270-5 (electronic)

♾™ The paper used in this publication meets the minimum requirements of American National Standard for Information Sciences—Permanence of Paper for Printed Library Materials, ANSI/NISO Z39.48-1992.

Printed in the United States of America

To Lois Treasure Whitacre Clark,
a mother for all ages,

and to everyone who grapples with loss

Contents

Acknowledgment of Gratitude

I am indebted to a mainstay, my mother, Lois Treasure Whitacre Clark, for both my birth and her unwavering support throughout my life. Mom and my late father, Robert Dale Clark, taught the value of lifelong learning. Mom took me to the public library as a child. Every week I checked out ten books. Our home was filled with books – my home is filled with books. While today I find many learning opportunities in person and online, I continue to read many books from public libraries.

Mom also taught the value of making a difference. If there is one notion to capture my mother's peace-in-the-world actions over her 94 years, it is Henry David Thoreau's words, offered gender free: If a man or a woman does not keep pace with their companions, perhaps it is because they hear a different drummer. Let each step to the music which he or she hears, however measured or far away. Human behavior, in daily drumbeats, suggests that people lean toward pessimism or optimism. Mom leans not only on her walker these days, but she leans toward optimism. Her ability as a difference drummer, every day making a difference in small steps, inspires me. Her present-moment living is an example of how to make our world a better place.

Two more mainstays are my children, Ryan Clark Johnston and Megan Gale Johnston, who taught me more about present-moment living than they might guess. While each generation models a way to live for future generations, children have a tremendous influence in shaping parental behavior. My beloved late husband, Mark Emmett Johnston, and I were truly blessed as parents to have their child guidance. Their incredible childhood creativity stoked my desire to meet my own need for creativity. I continue to reap many insights from my wise children.

I am very grateful to Dick Schwartz for his Internal Family Systems (IFS) therapy training. As I adapted IFS to work with children in my family therapy private practice, I found that adult clients also benefited from drawing personality maps to understand and change their behavior. I am equally grateful to Francine Shapiro for her development of Eye Movement Desensitization and Reprocessing (EMDR) therapy. Shapiro's integrative psychotherapy is powerful in treating PTSD and bereavement. This book complements diverse therapeutic approaches to loss and grieving.

Midlife Maze was a seed ready to sprout when Bill O'Hanlon's online course on book writing reached my email treasure chest. Bill's expert coaching helped to germinate this book. His straightforward feedback led me out of an initial haze of crisscrossing ideas. His sound advice was just what I needed to organize my thoughts. Thanks to Deborah Malmud for her online course in publishing.

My first reader, Melanie Weller, made poignant suggestions; I am so appreciative of her fruitful support of this work. Other generous readers added fertilizer to the growing manuscript: Frieda Brown, Jean D'Amico, Alice Epstein, Gail Gehrig, Marnie Gielow, Mary Rose Lambke, Theresa Lebeiko, Celia Schulhoff, Ann Solari-Twadell, Joan Suchomel, Annie Tolle, Carol Wade and LeeLee Ward. Gini Williams asked all the right questions about glitches in my book proposal.

I am truly blessed to have the support of an extended community. I am forever grateful to my book group for 25 years of sharing tea and talk about great books, my mahjong group for creating incredible food and fun, my tai chi and yoga partners for savoring balance and breath, my gym exercise buddies for enduring belly and brain workouts, my gardening volunteer companions for expanding plant awareness and appreciation, and my church and meditation community for giving compassion and clarity.

Since I thoroughly enjoyed working with Suzanne I. Staszak-Silva, senior acquisitions editor at Rowman and Littlefield, on my first book, *It Takes a Child to Raise a Parent,* I am grateful for another opportunity to learn from her editorial expertise. Also, special thanks go to the Rowman & Littlefield team, including Kathryn M. F. Knigge, Anita Singh, and Indrani Samaddar among others.

Ongoing thanks to numerous friends who shared heartfelt stories of loss and recovery. And especially, I am deeply grateful for countless client families who were not afraid to air their sadness and pour out raw passion regarding their significant losses. I have been privileged to walk by their side in rediscovering meaning after loss. I am honored to have their trust. They taught me much of what I know about a healthy grieving process. Each one of us has something to teach another.

Introduction

Janis Clark Johnston

Midway upon the journey of my life I found myself in a dark wood, where the right way was lost.

> – Dante, Middle Ages Italian poet, *The Divine Comedy*

Born between 1946 and 1964, the baby boomers bloomed, well most of them. The generation following the boomers (born between 1965 and 1981), Generation X, germinated and grew, well most of them. Have you found yourself wilting in midlife, and wondering what you might do to flourish in your remaining years? Have you lost your way in the midlife maze due to a significant loss? Did you lose your job or desired career advancement? Did you separate or divorce? Did your last child leave home? Did your family experience a virtual storm of bankruptcy or lose your life savings to Bernie Madoff's fraudulent Ponzi scheme? Or did a real storm – a tornado or hurricane – demolish your home? Did you or someone in your family experience the loss of good health? Or did you weather the death of a family member, partner, or friend? Your loss story is personal. Your path through winding passages in the midlife maze is unique. *The most important encouragement for your grieving process is to know this simple fact: grieving is a natural healing response to loss rather than a pathological experience.*

MIDLIFE: THE AFTERNOON OF LIFE

The afternoon knows what the morning never suspected.

> – Swedish proverb

1

The "change" for midlife women is not the only change. Ready or not, many changes flood midlife. Denial of the need to change is common. Denial of time to grieve changes brought by loss is especially common. Who has any time? Midlifers are on the cusp of handling mortgages/rents that are too high, juggling career/lifetime decisions, and perhaps navigating the throes of parenting. Middle-aged adults cope with the "afternoon" of their lives as well as the "morning" of children's lives if they are parents, teachers, and/ or coaches. Most baby boomers view themselves as still young, in spite of advancing numbers on their birthdays. Some boomers consider themselves more as the lunch bunch along with Gen Xers, rather than the afternoon nap crowd. However, loss has a way of letting you know that there is no free lunch.

While no one wants loss to enter his or her life during midlife, there is tremendous learning from a grieving process. This book views broken dreams as "fertilizer" for new dreams. Many stories of loss – from my caseload of middle-aged clients, my family and friends who have suffered great loss, and famous midlifers who go public with their losses – will show how grieving can evolve into a threshold of new beginnings. Research and theories that support my tools for creativity after loss come from a cross section of experts from psychology, sociology, anthropology, medicine, and health care. Middle age is the longest developmental stage, but it is called the "last uncharted territory in human development" by psychologist Orville Brim.

FROM UNCHARTED LOSS TO PURPOSE

Dr. Brim directed the John D. and Catherine T. MacArthur Foundation longitudinal research on midlife, MIDUS or Midlife in the United States. The original survey consisted of over 7000 Americans aged 25 to 74 and is considered as groundbreaking, as the multidisciplinary research team covers the fields of psychology, sociology, epidemiology, demography, anthropology, medicine, and health care. Ages for three groups of adults are defined: young adulthood, aged 25–34; middle adulthood, aged 35–64; and older adulthood, aged 65–74. Most people by the age of 35 have established themselves in a career or job, and this delivers midlife status. The boundary around age 65 represents the common retirement age in the United States.[1] National follow-up research on midlife continues as MIDUS II (2002) and MIDUS Refresher (2011–12).[2]

Midlife is a particularly critical time. While many uplifting aspects of living occur during this long developmental stage, there are losses. Any loss can upend your future dreams and drop you into uncharted territory. A significant loss unsettles even the most positive people. Ignoring loss is not adaptive and may lead to feelings of bitterness and/or resentment. Midlife adults who acknowledge their losses and embrace a grieving process can germinate new goals to have the best chance of future health and happiness. When loss hits home in midlife, you need a *growth mind-set* in order to map your way forward. MIDUS II research found that setting a positive purpose in life helps midlifers recover from trauma.[3] Rediscovering purpose in life after loss includes meeting a handful of five basic needs – to regain daily energy, possess a sense of intentionality, and realize goal directedness to guide daily behavior. No one is required to experience a full-blown midlife crisis!

Normal grieving does not follow set rules; it resembles more of a zigzag maze where one day you breathe a bit easier, only to pivot into sadness another day. There are many detours in a grieving process. Your loss story is a trauma, but it also is a *turn*ing point, a time in which you experience a significant life change.[4] *The approach in this book recognizes trauma, a noun, but considers "turning points" where you focus on resilient actions you can take to turn your life in a positive direction.* Action is suggested by the verb, "to *turn*." You can move through a grieving process to *turn* corners after loss. You can cultivate new behaviors to rediscover a positive future.

- *Turn* (from Greek, *tornos, circular movement*) means to move around an axis or center...in order to achieve a result.[5] Synonyms for the word *turn* are: pivot, circle, swing, twist, about-face, shift, spin, curve, swerve, veer, detour, sidetrack, U-*turn*, zigzag, and diverge. These words twist their way through this book.

MAN [OR WOMAN] IN A MAZE

The Native American O'odham people represent life's journey as a man (or woman) in a maze. They recognize that everyone's life maze experience has twists and *turns*: "You go down and then you reach a place where you have to *turn* around. ... Maybe in your own life you fall. ... You are sad. ... You pick yourself up and you go on through the maze." [6] Each maze traveler recognizes a path of choices that encompasses both happiness and sadness. In moving through the midlife maze, an individual reaffirms his or her goals. Each one brings a gift to ensure a "safe return from the depths." Upon reaching the center of the maze, life travelers have a last *turn* to look back upon their particular path before death. In the meantime, each individual embraces *Himdag* values, or commandments to maintain strong family relationships and cultural rituals, as well as to celebrate nature. *Himdag* values convey a path for the O'odham people to search for physical, social, mental, and

spiritual balance, both individually and with others.[7] The wider U.S. culture is less clear about how to find a safe return from the "depths."[8]

Everyone's personality builds upon personal and tribal stories. And everyone has his or her own individual and communal commandments. But how can you make sense of losses? How can you create balance when your personal world appears tipped upside down? You can *turn* yourself around by creating a personality map to find the treasure you need to dig yourself out of the hole of loss. You can retool for creative choices after loss to make positive changes in your family/work life. You can answer the question: What are your gifts to find balance within your life after loss?

Writing is one of my gifts in discovering balance after loss. I wrote and published my first "gift-book" in midlife after my beloved husband died of a sudden heart attack. I dedicated the book to him and to our joint venture, our precious children. *It Takes a Child to Raise a Parent: Stories of Evolving Child and Parent Development* targets the unique development of each parent in growing up, learning about life both from one's children and from one's adult perspectives on his or her own childhood. *Midlife Maze* focuses on midlife development and recovery from losses that can flood adulthood. Whether you are parenting or not, midlife years often seem too busy. And then something unexpected may happen to stop you in your tracks.

Loss can trip you. Just when you were on your way to reach for those happy items on your bucket list, you suddenly drop your guard, or your usual personality functioning. When you pick up your bucket list again, you find holes, or distressing thoughts and emotions. Nothing is "the same" anymore. Your past bucket list of wonderful possibilities slips away. You feel lost in a maze of emotions. Now what? You have to change to process grief. You have to *turn* some corners in your mind and in your daily life. *Midlife Maze* offers an explanation of how creativity can help you cope with *turn*ing points.

Most individuals prefer a stable job, a stable relationship, stability in health, as well as stability in the environment, but multiple *turn*ing points in such stable conditions are all too common today. While many positive changes occur – perhaps finding a job where you feel competent, completing career training or advanced degrees, marriage, having babies, growing up with those babies as they *turn* into young adults, and making lifetime friendships – eventually, loss happens. Loss of stable ground shakes us to the core. While there is no emotional Richter scale, many of us feel as if we experienced a magnitude 6.0 (or higher) earthquake of raw emotion due to a significant loss. Energy for all pursuits may dribble away. Some take to their beds and pull the covers up over their heads when loss hits home. As poet Edna St. Vincent Millay wrote at age 40 after the death of her mother, "The presence of that absence is everywhere." Instead of feeling "whole," there is a distinct notion that there is a very large hole inside of your life.

LIFE'S AFTERNOON

Midlife tends to be the longest developmental period of life. Swiss psychologist Carl Jung wrote about the many changes in midlife as the afternoon of life: "Thoroughly unprepared we take the step into the afternoon of life; worse still, we take this step with the false presupposition that our truths and ideals will serve us as hitherto. But, we cannot live the afternoon of life according to the program of life's morning – for what was great in the morning will be little at evening, and what in the morning was true will at evening have become a lie."[9] Most midlifers plan to stay stable, even when stability turns out to be a lie.

I remember the day when I received news that my beloved grandmother died. She died just after *turn*ing 94; I was 40. In my busy midlife, I thought that I grasped the "afternoon of life" analogy. But Grandma's death brought introspection: How would I feel if I had to leave my family? My emotional pain was immense, as I could not fathom leaving my young children or my husband. Grandma had painful arthritis. I recalled her crying during our last visit. Her death became a catalyst for questions: Was she ready to die? Was she afraid to die? Did she ever say good-bye to anyone in the family? My questions about death outnumbered my answers. Suddenly I felt unprepared to acknowledge the setting sun time coming ahead. I did not know that it would be my *turn*, too soon, to experience the death of much younger family members and to feel lost in the afternoon of life.

After many tears that October afternoon when I heard about Grandma's death, I decided to plant tulip bulbs in my garden so they could resurrect in the spring and remind me of my many wonderful memories. Grandma's spring/summer/fall garden was magical for me. I spent many happy childhood times puttering and pretending there. Grandma tolerated me tiptoeing through the tulips. I made flower bouquets for her graceful arts and crafts–style vases.

I loved going to her china cupboard to find vases which now are a part of my household. Vera Vinette's vintage vases are one reminder of the treasure from my childhood years, the morning of my life. It is this morning of our lives that lays the groundwork for how we handle the inevitable losses in our midlife's afternoon of life.

Everyone has different experiences from his or her youth. Some are lucky and experience loving caretakers. Others do not receive their fair share of rootedness. *Turn*ing points prove especially challenging for those who dredge up memories from their childhood where significant loss stalked them early. Comedian and TV personality Rosie O'Donnell was 11 years old when her mother died from breast cancer. In midlife, Rosie quipped, "When you have the death of your parent as a child, everything feels like a speed bump." After unexpected loss, you may ask, "What if I had_____?" or "What if s/he had_____?" Some morning memories provide solace and smiles, while others require forgiveness of yourself and/or others. Regardless of what happened in your childhood, as an adult you are in training for some of the toughest challenges in life. The good news is that much brain growth occurs in middle adulthood. New learning does not stop at any particular age. It is possible to nurture a growth mind-set. The way you choose to exercise your brain and body matters.

PART I: "THERE'S A HOLE IN THE BUCKET ..."

Stories of people who feel lost in midlife reflect a common theme: they are caught off guard as if a strong wind blew them over. A process model of grieving loss developed by nurses, the *Pinwheel Model of Bereavement*, can help you recognize loss as a unique life experience, a going-back-and-forth process where you learn to weather loss over time. Grief is depicted as wind: wind changes directions, blows hard or soft, and, sometimes, even knocks you off your feet. One day you can cope after loss, and another day you feel as if you hold a bucket with a hole in it, watching future dreams slip beyond reach. You look for refuge – perhaps in staying too busy or in numbing your emotions with alcohol. Psychologist Tara Brach calls these ways to avoid emotional pain *false refuges.*[10] A "true refuge" takes inner discovery. You learn to live more in the present moment.

You may experience an emotional breakdown in everyday places – the grocery aisle, at the gas pump, or in any place where a remembered fragment of your loss may fill you with remorse, guilt, sadness, anger, and/or insecurity. These emotions are normal. Everything seems precarious. While physical presence of a job, good health, or a beloved person may no longer be in your life, your grief can *turn* out as an experience of connection rather than total severance. With time and tools of creative actions, it is possible to connect to affirming memories and parts of your history that helped to make you who you are today. You reassemble memories in your personality. You share precious stories. Your storytelling is one way you can acclimate to present life after loss.

Many tools for processing your grief story are presented in *Midlife Maze*. Internal Family Systems (IFS) [11] language defines the parts or roles in your personality that identify your thoughts and emotions as you struggle to clear a path of action. You realize that you cannot manage loss. You recognize that you cannot live in the past. You draw a personality map to find the resources to help you cope. You view nighttime dreams as another way to reset painful memories. While your dreams sometimes confuse you, simple explanations of how dreams work can help you make sense of your grieving. You use *Turn* Tips and Your *Turn* exercises to refocus your energy. Keeping a *Turn* Journal during your grieving process provides valuable feedback about what loss means to you. You set an intention to find one or two simple things every day to be grateful for. Just when you feel totally lost, you begin focusing upon what is beautiful, what is life affirming, and what is even a small *turn*ing point in your day. You feel competent to meet your basic needs. You focus more on present moments.

PART II: "... WITH WHAT SHALL I MEND IT?"

Everyone's daily drama includes the ways in which basic needs are either met or unmet. Everyone's personality becomes a tool chest for meeting needs, a challenging task after a significant loss. *Midlife Maze* answers how you can find the necessary self-awareness to enable you to retool after loss to meet your basic five needs of energy, discipline, creativity, belonging, and ability. Hopefully you start your day with a nutritious breakfast, an energy boost. Backing up, did you have a good night's sleep? When in your day do you make time to exercise? You can already see that you need discipline to meet basic energy needs. Do you start your job on time every day? What about creativity? Everyone has to solve problems during their day. Do you imagine creative solutions? When is the last time you made time for any creative ventures that excite you? Now consider your belonging needs. When can you spend any time with significant others today? Wait! Are you using your ability well today? What is your true potential?

When you live with other people and have *their* needs to consider along with your own, schedules become complicated. Some basic needs go unmet in a busy day. Needs recycle, appearing repeatedly throughout each day. You tend to handle these needs in habitual ways in your personality, whether your habits are healthy or not. Are you overwhelmed by your needs and the needs of those close to you? A visual map can assist you in locating the parts or roles in your personality that help or hinder you in meeting needs. You learn to make space between the bossy, critical roles in your personality and the grieving, overwhelmed parts that carry with them too many worries and too much stress. When you feel lost in the maze of mixed-up emotions after loss, a concrete map of your personality highlights where you might make the next *turn*. In the past, you likely rearranged your personality without being conscious of what you were doing. Or, perhaps you believed that you could not change your personality once you reached midlife.

Research shows that adult personalities are not cast in concrete! You can change how your personality works for you. Your personality map can help you acknowledge grieving roles instead of just feeling *lost*. Your map can guide you through the midlife maze to identify and cultivate self-awareness. Simple techniques of mindfulness will help you slow down stress reactions, make space for creative problem solving, and live more of your days in gratitude and joy. Mindfulness, being aware of one *turn* at a time, can guide you through the midlife maze after a significant loss.

PART III: BEFORE YOU "KICK THE BUCKET," GRAB YOUR BUCKET LIST AND ENJOY!

When you find yourself lost in an emotional maze, you realize that certain plans no longer work for you. You still can choose hope. You can *turn* yourself to move forward in a positive direction. You can utilize your own creativity to look both inward (at your REM sleep and dreaming) and outward (at fresh dreams/goals for your future). Something interesting happens when you develop a growth mind-set and gratitude for your own unique personality.

One story of inspiration is that of the actor of the *Superman* role, Christopher Reeve, who experienced a catastrophic accident at age 42. He was in a horseback riding accident that paralyzed him as a quadriplegic, confining him to a wheelchair and ventilator. And yet, Reeve chose to exercise his brain. He championed human embryonic stem cell research. He set up a foundation to help others with spinal-cord injuries. He continued to work, acting in TV films and directing two production films with health themes.[12] Reeve declared, "Once you choose hope, anything is possible."

When you create your personality map, you will answer the question, "Who am I since loss entered my life?" You can discover the creativity, hope, and treasure you need to:

- Rebound from grieving a significant loss,
- Retool to make positive changes in your family/work life,

- Regain energy to renew your bucket list, and
- Recoup a highly satisfied life due to mid-life choices you make during this crucial life phase.

Offering the tips of sages, the loss stories from a variety of families, and step-by-step exercises, *Midlife Maze* walks with readers through a grieving process. Grieving is not easy, but there is wisdom in the process that cannot be gained without acknowledging loss as a part of life, whether it is the death of a person, relationship, or a symbolic death of health/well-being. A creative spin to coping with loss can help you renew a sense of purpose while you grieve. You can learn to refocus on the treasure of everyday present moments. You can grow in unexpected ways.

> I have great faith in a seed. Convince me that you have a seed there, and I am prepared to expect wonders.
>
> – Henry David Thoreau, philosopher and naturalist, *Faith in a Seed*

***

Many names of individuals in this book are fictitious. Real names only appear when information comes from the public record or words are delivered in a public forum.

Part I

"THERE'S A HOLE IN THE BUCKET ..."

Harry Belafonte's recording, *There's a Hole in the Bucket*, comes from a German folk song. Pete Seeger made the song popular. Initially, grieving seems a lot like a broken bucket – nothing seems to fix the loss hole of hurt and suffering, but a witness helps.

There's no pain on earth that doesn't crave a benevolent witness.

– Sue Monk Kidd, writer, *The Invention of Wings*

Chapter 1

Maneuvering Midlife

A developmental task is a task which … when the timing is right, the ability to learn a particular task will be possible. This is … a "teachable moment." It is important to repeat important points whenever possible so that when a student's teachable moment occurs, he [or she] can benefit from the knowledge.

– Robert J. Havighurst, physicist and aging expert, *Human Development and Education*

Life is made up of moments, small pieces of glittering mica in a long stretch of gray cement. … We have to teach ourselves how to make room for them, to love them, and to live, really live.

– Anna Quindlen, writer, *A Short Guide to Happy Life*

Sometimes a picture is worth a thousand teachable moments. A picture of *Lebenstreppe*, Life Staircase, from the year 1660 portrays life's developmental steps. The popular and cheaply produced image was hung in the living room of many private homes. Many male or female versions map the decades of life. A few versions show female/male couples. All versions depict a staircase with five ascending and five descending steps. Age 50 captures the center top step. In these double staircases of life's timeline, the beginning and ending are clear. Birth is depicted on the left bottom. Each life student shows age progression until death at the bottom right:

10 years – a child
20 years – a young man (or woman)
30 years – a man (or woman)

40 years – well done
50 years – standing still
60 years – old age begins
70 years – a frail old person
80 years – no more wisdom
90 years – children's mockery
100 years – needs the mercy of God![1]

The anonymous *T'Vrouwe Leven* (Steps of Life) depicting women's development provides clues – hourglasses and skeletons – to suggest life's brevity. However, life's beginning and ending are accepted with *equal* weight.[2] Our culture tends to glorify birth, but deny death. Youth is idolized. Aging is unappreciated. Other cultures venerate the wisdom of elders. In poet and novelist Alice Walker's words, "Part of my ancestry is Cherokee. And in that tradition you become an adult when you're 52."

MIDLIFE: BLOSSOM TIME

You are not "over the hill," as greeting cards suggest at age 50! Ancient Greeks and Romans viewed midlife as the time of life "in blossom."[3] Brain decline with aging scares midlifers. However, some research shows brain growth. Younger brains tend to use only one side of the brain at a time in an experiment to learn word pairs. Midlifers use more of their brain – both sides – in bi-lateralization: "Faced with a challenge … [mid-lifers] tapped into whatever they had, to do what they needed to do."[4] We now know that crystallized intelligence, stored knowledge gained from experiences and education, increases as you age. Abilities to utilize math facts, expand vocabulary, and maintain general knowledge are examples of crystallized intelligence. Researcher James Flynn finds each new generation of IQ test takers scores higher than previous generations. Reasons for IQ increase point to better education, nutrition, and health.[5] As you mature in midlife you exhibit greater capacity to see patterns for creativity. You gain a broader world perspective. Sheryl Sandberg, Facebook COO, understands that creative individuals may not have the most expertise in a given area, but they look for the broadest perspectives.[6] As Alice Walker suggests, our nature is to *bloom gloriously.*[7] Midlife is blossom time.

The word *midlife* first appeared in 1837.[8] Professionals have differing ideas about start/end times of midlife. Carl Jung and German-American psychoanalyst Erik Erikson defined middle adulthood as between 40 and 65, but respected aging expert Robert Havighurst set the limits as 35–60. The midlife span in this book refers to ages 35–64, as defined by longitudinal research, midlife in the United States (MIDUS).[9] Many people skip age lines altogether and define middle age as the period beyond young adulthood, but before the onset of old age. Realistically, age is in the eye of the beholder and the rightness of various developmental tasks is in flux today.

Psychologist Margie Lachman believes that less is known about midlife than any other age period. Despite a recent increase, Lachman finds that much midlife research focuses on work and/or relationships to other developmental stages. For example, many midlife studies exist on parents raising children.[10] Who wants to touch the topics of loss in midlife? Most midlifers are not keen on thinking about grieving, and they certainly do not want to discuss it. Songwriter Sarah McQuaid captures our culture's reluctance to face grieving: "Since when did grief become an illness to be cured? We don't wear black any more, we don't mourn, we don't talk about it, that's for sure ... the power of our anguish has us terrified."[11]

Have you ever attended a wake or memorial service and found that most of the conversation is about topics other than death? Midlifers feel vulnerable around the d-word. As social work researcher Brene Brown explains, "When we spend our lives pushing away and protecting ourselves from feeling vulnerable or from being perceived as too emotional, we feel contempt when others are less capable or willing to mask feelings, suck it up, and soldier on. ... [However] vulnerability isn't good or bad. ... Vulnerability is the core of all emotions."[12] One client shared with me how she and two other women experienced uncontrollable giggles in the middle of a funeral. Several senior citizens shared how they could not stop laughing when a deceased neighbor's left eye popped open in his casket. Relief from grief is necessary. Yet, when is the timing right for accepting and discussing loss? We do not have the once popular Life Staircase framed and hanging on our living room walls.

ERIK AND JOAN ERIKSON

If you are a student of human behavior, you may have on your bookshelf, but not as a coffee-table book in the living room, the most prominent Western staging of developmental steps, Erik Erikson's *Childhood and Society*.[13] My copy is paperback, well worn from graduate school days. I took coursework in childhood, adolescence, and young adulthood at Boston University. There were no courses in my doctoral counseling psychology program on midlife or beyond. Gerontology was not a household word, and midlifers were supposed to take care of themselves.

Erik Erikson was a psychoanalyst who collaborated with his psychoanalyst wife, Joan, to create an eight-stage theory of psychosocial development. The Eriksons were influenced by Sigmund Freud's theories. However, Erikson stages deviate from Freudian theory in important ways. Erikson stages do not focus personality development primarily on sexuality, and they affirm that personality continues to develop throughout life. Furthermore, Erikson stages consider influences of the prevailing culture at the time you enter each life step. Fortunately, Erikson stages list both positive and negative adaptations, providing a nonpathological way of looking at human growth.

Perhaps an early career dedication to children explains why 5 of the Erikson stages deal with development up to age 18. Erik Erikson began his career painting portraits of children. He taught art to children in a progressive school started by Anna Freud, daughter of Sigmund. Erikson studied Maria Montessori's methods for teaching young children before undertaking psychoanalytic training in Vienna. The important takeaway message from the Erikson model is this: your experiences today can heal the problems you encountered earlier.

An overview details the Erikson "steps" of life. You can assess what you accomplished, or attempted to accomplish, prior to midlife. You may experience a different timing of your life steps. Some still struggle to feed themselves well. Most midlifers do not have issues with toileting, although illness, certain disabilities, and the aging process can make an unwelcome return to toileting issues. Middle-age adults often go back to school to create career changes. Many midlifers struggle with a sense of power, purpose, and competence when they (or a family member) experience a job loss, critical illness, divorce, or death in the family. Loss in midlife needs more emphasis in developmental psychology.

ERIKSON THEORY OF PSYCHOSOCIAL DEVELOPMENT

Infancy (Birth–8 Months)

Trust versus mistrust

- Key issue: feeding
- Outcome: children develop a sense of trust when caregivers provide reliability, care, and affection. A lack of caretaking can lead to mistrust.

Early Childhood (2–3 Years)

Autonomy versus shame and doubt

- Key issue: toilet training
- Outcome: children develop independence and a sense of personal control over physical skills. Success leads to autonomy, while challenges may result in shame and/or doubt.

Preschool (3–5 Years)

Initiative versus guilt

- Key issue: exploration
- Outcome: children begin to assert control/power over their environment. Success leads to a sense of purpose. Exerting too much power may bring disapproval and/or guilt.

School Age (6–11 Years)

Industry versus inferiority

- Key issue: school
- Outcome: children cope with social and academic demands. Success leads to competence, while challenges may result in inferiority.

Adolescence (12–18 Years)

Identity versus role confusion

- Key issue: social relationships
- Outcome: teens develop a sense of self and personal identity. Success leads to an ability to stay true to oneself, while challenges can lead to role confusion and a weak sense of self.

Young Adulthood (19–40 Years)

Intimacy versus isolation

- Key issue: relationships
- Outcome: young adults form intimate, loving relationships with other people. Success leads to strong relationships, while challenges may result in loneliness and isolation.

Middle Adulthood (40–65 Years)

Generativity versus stagnation

- Key issue: work and parenthood
- Outcome: adults create or nurture things that will outlast them, often by having children or creating a positive change that benefits other people.

Success leads to feelings of usefulness and accomplishment, while challenges can result in shallow involvement in the world.

Maturity (65–Death)

Ego integrity versus despair

- Key issue: reflection on life
- Outcome: adults look back on life and feel a sense of fulfillment. Success leads to feelings of wisdom, while challenges can result in regret, bitterness, and/or despair.[14]

While there is support for the Erikson stages of personality development 50 years after publication,[15] there is evidence to suggest that the stages overlap and are actually not separate from one another. For example, psychologist Dan McAdams sees identity as continuing well beyond adolescence. He believes that intimacy and generativity are best understood as identity concerns.[16] Joan Erikson recognized the overlapping of stages in assessing her own life through creating a weaving. Instead of focusing on the exterior, she used the underside of her yarn weaving to explain life: "The underpinnings show us where we got off the track. ... I look at all the knots I've tied and say to myself, this knot in early childhood got me into that knot in adolescence, and wow, look at how uneven the rows became until I worked through that problem or straightened out that course."[17] Notice the irregularities Joan Erikson found, and yet, she did not despair about them. Erikson used her missteps to learn more about life. She created a ninth stage for ages 80's and 90's and considered that elders may confront all eight previous stages.

Erikson listed the vulnerabilities of each stage first to emphasize challenges in later life.[18] Just like the male *Life Staircase* and female *Steps of Life*, art, birth and death come full circle in the Erikson model. Joan Erikson labeled her ninth stage of development *Old Age* as she lived to the ripe old age of 95, outliving Erik, who died at age 91. However, most midlifers do not want to face vulnerabilities or loss. Isn't that old-age stuff? Yes, life challenges increase for elders, but loss visits families at every life stage.

The Midlife Maze Within midlife, your identity and relationship issues – finding intimacy *versus* isolation and juggling generativity *versus* stagnation – can exist as both cause for celebration and suffering. As a midlifer you likely grapple with both intimacy and isolation. Similarly, you likely generate positive directions for younger people somewhere in life, but you also encounter stagnation times. An interesting detail to the Erikson stages is the word "versus":

- Versus (from Latin *vertere, to turn*) means the alternative to or in contrast with.[19]

Your goal is to find ways to *turn* your challenges into productive behaviors. But what happens when you cannot think of an alternative, when you feel completely lost in the midlife maze? Stan sums up his life in this way: "I have a beautiful wife, three great kids, a terrific job, and a lovely home. Why can't I be happy?" One answer is that there is an unresolved loss in Stan's life story.

When loss is pushed aside in your life, you may lose touch with intimacy and/or generativity. Feeling a vague sense of bad stuff piling up, a negative spin escalates and attaches to almost every topic. McAdams studies adult development and finds that some individuals focus most of their daily attention upon difficulties in their lives. They tell life stories filled with "bad ruins, spoils ... [that] contaminate the good [events] that precede it. ... Most midlife adults we interviewed included at least one explicit contamination sequence in their accounts."[20] Feeling lost in the maze of life describes a lot of adults between the ages of 35 and 64; it especially describes those who experience a significant loss. After my husband's sudden heart attack, I had a frustrating dream one night:

> I tried to pick up my new hybrid car, but I got lost in a huge car dealership. It was like a maze – so many different buildings – I tried to go back to my old car to get my bearings, but I could not find where my old car was parked. (The scene shifts.) Suddenly, I was with my husband, but then we separated while we were running errands. I called him on my cell phone to tell him where I was. He didn't answer, so I left a message for him.

When I woke up, I realized that the day before I used an analogy of a "rat in a maze" with one of my clients. After my dream, it was clear to me that I was lost in the midlife maze also. It was impossible to go back to my old-car life.

Loss knocks on the door of every family in one way or another. A job loss, or even a loss of desired career advancement, can be catastrophic. You may sense that your job no longer feels right, but what job seems right? How can you leave your coworkers? Loss of a family member, including the loss of children moving away from home, or loss of a romantic partner through divorce or death, can cause even more emotional upheaval. Loss of your dreams for a child through infertility, miscarriage, illness, or death unsettles the most positive people. Usual patterns of coping may not apply to your loss. Most are unprepared to handle sudden losses. Your stagnation appears as self-absorption. You cannot focus well. There is an overall inability to move forward in meeting goals. When you experience a significant loss, your initial grieving punctures a hole in your bucket list of future dreams.

There are holes of loss in everyday life as well. If you just started a career, you may feel isolated. You may find yourself at the beginning step of a job and discover an unsteady career ladder. Others are on the top step, at the height of a career, but winds of corporate change carry risk with increased job responsibilities. Perhaps no greater complaining takes place among friends than job complaints. Some jobs are careers, and other jobs are just jobs. Midlifers complain about both. Latrice complains about a stingy boss; she wants a pay raise, but never asks for one. She is angry because she works two jobs just to pay for the basics. Norm believes that he works harder than anyone else on his team. He says his boss does not notice his overtime hours. In fact, his boss routinely gives him more work than others.

MIDLIFE CRISIS IS NOT A REQUIREMENT

Midlife simultaneously covers being on top of one's game as well as juggling unbidden strife. The adage, "settle down," is applied to midlife. You either choose a life partner or perhaps reconcile that you will remain single. Midlifers may choose to raise children. Many raise careers. While these events can make life pleasure filled, there are inevitable losses. Enter the term, "midlife crisis." In a 1965 article, "Death and the Mid-life Crisis," Canadian psychologist Elliott Jaques joined the words midlife and crisis. He described the now-overused phrase as the timeframe when adults realize their own mortality: "When I say that the mid-life crisis occurs around the age of 35, I mean that it takes place in the middle-thirties, that the process of transition runs on for some years, and that the exact period will vary among individuals." [21] This sounds like a life sentence rather than blossom time.

SOS! You do not have to experience a midlife crisis. Those who do enter a full-blown crisis may have the triggering event of loss. However, psychologist Margie Lachman researches midlife individuals and finds that only one-third of midlife crises were triggered by events such as job loss, financial problems, or illness. She accurately points out that such events also occur at any time in adulthood. It is your particular *personality* that has influence upon your unique way of coping. For example, Lachman's research suggests that those who are more psychologically unstable are more likely to experience midlife crisis. [22] The myth of a necessary midlife crisis stems more from the movies than from reality.

Coping strategies are necessary for every age and stage, but the stakes are higher as personal responsibilities mount. Financial concerns topple the list of what keeps midlifers awake at night – credit card debt, escalating rent, taxes, mortgage payments, child care expenses, medical bills, home repairs, college tuition/loans, and nursing home bills for elderly parents. Even when stressors mount in midlife, you are not required to suffer in ongoing crisis mode. Cognitive neuroscientist Patricia Reuter-Lorenz sizes up midlife: "Instead of a crisis, middle age should be thought of as a time for a new form of self-investment. This time of life brings so many new opportunities to invest in your own cognitive and physical resources, so you can buffer against the effects of older age."[23] There is much diversity in midlife aging experiences.

Diversity relates to such factors as gender, sexual orientation, socioeconomic status, race, ethnicity, religion, culture, region of the country where you live, personality, marital status, parental status, employment status, and health status. Some midlifers have an easier time than others. Some individuals have stable careers with little mobility, while others experience multiple layoffs and/or unemployment. The economy affects almost everyone's job stability. Technological advances may exclude workers due to outdated skills. Some middle-aged adults experience age discrimination in employment. After losing a job, finding a new job in midlife is challenging because the income demands of older workers are higher than those of younger workers. When 52-year-old Tynice was laid off in an economic restructuring at her company, it took her 18 months to land a job. She reentered the workforce at a lesser position and salary. Most midlifers experience an aspect of their life in the loss column. It is up to each individual to find a coping path through the midlife maze.

GROW, GROW, GROW YOUR MIND-SET

Loss can have a dual effect: while you are caught off guard from accessing your usual personality functioning, you also can grow new perspectives to acclimate to your precious future. To traverse the midlife maze with a degree of success, you need a *growth mind-set*. Psychologist Carol Dweck identified two mind-sets:

- *Fixed mind-set* – You believe your qualities are set in plaster – you have a fixed IQ, a particular personality, and a certain moral character that defines you.
- *Growth mind-set* – You can cultivate new basic qualities through your efforts – your true potential is unknown. Dweck's research points out, "The view you adopt for yourself profoundly affects the way you lead your life. ... No matter what kind of person you are, you can always change substantially."[24] It is possible that you hold a fixed mind-set in some areas of your life, while you maintain a growth mind-set in other areas. Dweck found that she needed to change her own fixed mind-set. In midlife you have many choices. You will decide what areas of your life might benefit from change.

If you have avoided traumatic health issues in your family/friend tribe, you still face future health scrimmages, as well as the mundane changes of thinning and/or loss of hair, wrinkles, reading and/or bifocal eyeglasses, and beginning hearing loss. During midlife such conditions as high blood pressure, high cholesterol, and/or arthritic pain may appear. Some health issues relate to lifestyle choices. Smoking, drug use, unhealthy eating, alcohol abuse, and a lack of exercise carry a bodily toll. Menopause occurs for most women around ages 42–51. While some women have an easy time with menopause, others undergo a physical/mental roller coaster that is unsettling. Some aging changes require eyeglasses, hearing aids, medications, and/or dietary changes, but even normal changes bring up the issue of mortality. You may ask, "How can I have a growth mind-set about illness and/or death?" There are no easy answers, but sometimes a serious accident, loss, or illness in midlife serves as a wake-up call to change aspects of your life that need a new direction. A growth mind-set helps you cultivate healthy choices.

MENTAL HEALTH IN MIDLIFE

Your mental health is just as critical as your physical health. Research shows up to 51% of patients who suffered orthopedic (musculoskeletal) injuries went on to develop post-traumatic stress disorder, or PTSD. Individuals in car accidents, motorcycle accidents, and falls from heights (such as from a ladder or roof) are among those with PTSD symptoms such as nightmares, flashbacks, insomnia, emotional numbing, or hyper-arousal.[25] A growing number of soldiers returning to civilian life have PTSD from combat exposure. As Navy Seal Eric Greitens writes to a fellow veteran who battles PTSD, "As long as there has been war, warriors have found the journey home, the journey back to normal, as trying as battle itself. ... There's no training program at the end. ... No one can build your resilience for you ... [and] nobody's ever going to hand you a prize for resilience. There is no certificate. No T-shirt. And don't even think about a tattoo. ... You and I are not in search of an achievement, but a way of being."[26] Veterans experience a growth mind-set when they feel safe and find a compassionate witness to their suffering. As psychiatrist Bessel Van der Kolk underscores, "Being able to feel safe with other people is probably the single most important aspect of mental health."[27]

Forty-year-old Frank is a veteran. He was coached by older vets, "Suck it up and have another beer," when he shared that he did not feel safe at night and experienced ongoing insomnia. Frank was terrified by July fourth fireworks. Tragic memories flooded his awareness with every loud burst overhead. Abruptly, Frank left his family at the park where they enjoyed a picnic before fireworks. Frank's experience is not unusual. Today we have some effective therapies to treat returning soldiers and others who suffer from PTSD. For example, Internal Family Systems (IFS) therapy developed by marriage/family therapist Dick Schwartz uses nonpathologizing, everyday language to help individuals identify hidden aspects of their personality.[28] Eye Movement

Desensitization and Reprocessing (EMDR) developed by psychologist Francine Shapiro provides relief for trauma suffering when talk therapy has failed.[29]

Mental illness affects the entire family. The role of the caregiver is stretched to the limits in caring for a psychotic relative. Professor of pastoral theology at Princeton, Donald Capps, outlines how life changes with an onset of mental illness in a family member: "Family members may ... experience a sense of loss comparable to the process of bereavement. ... Their loved one is 'lost' to them."[30] Various surveys measuring depression from the U.S. Centers for Disease Control (CDC) report that the highest rate of depression, 12.3%, was found in midlife women aged 40–59. Sadly, only about a third of people with severe depressive symptoms reported having seen a mental health professional in the past year; less than 20% of all Americans with moderate depressive symptoms had a therapist. Significantly, the loss issues in poverty are an important factor in depression rates; poor individuals were more than twice as likely to have depression when compared to those living at, or above, the poverty level.[31] Anxiety disorders are the most common mental illness in the United States. Again, only about one-third of anxiety sufferers receive treatment.[32] Such mental health issues often include unresolved grief from the past.

There is a disturbing statistic about life in the midlife maze when a person cannot imagine having a growth mind-set. There is an increase in suicides among baby boomers from 1999 to 2010. The CDC shows the highest increases are among men in their 50s, whose rate skyrocketed by 50% (30 suicides per 100,000 men). Cultural factors seem important, as the highest number of suicides were among Native American and Alaskan men. The rate of suicides among women in their early 60s increased by 60% (7 suicides per 100,000 women).[33] Research from the National Institute for Occupational Safety and Health finds rates of workplace suicide have sharply increased from 2007 to 2010. Rates were highest for men who worked in law enforcement and as firefighters, private detectives, and security guards. Also at high risk were men in farming, fishing, and forestry work.[34] Sociologist Brad Wilcox sees a link between suicide and weak social/belonging connections. Men are more likely to kill themselves when they are disconnected from society's core institutions such as marriage, religion, and work.[35] Clearly, we need more focus on loss and grieving in the United States.

RESILIENCE LEADS TO GENERATIVITY

Midlife is not an easy time of life. It is the time when many have the most responsibility they will ever have. It is a time of reckoning. Loss in its many forms delivers the message of impermanence. It is crucial to grow a mind-set of growth and resilience. The task of the generativity stage is forward thinking. Helping future generations through parenting, teaching, coaching, supervising, and/or mentoring prevents isolation while providing meaning for life. Research showed that baby boomers had higher levels of generativity regarding concern for the next generation than either younger adults, born after 1964, or older adults born prior to 1946. Women's generativity scores were not a direct function of being a mother. Parenting was a distinguishing factor for men: fathers had a higher generativity score than men who had never been fathers.[36]

Highly generative and less-generative adults were asked to tell life stories. Both groups revealed similar stories in self-mastery, status, achievement, and empowerment. However, life stories of highly generative adults differed in their accounting of childhood years; they were significantly more likely to say that they were singled out in childhood with a special advantage. One man received a special family name. Another was a teacher's favorite student. Highly generative adults were "more sensitive to the suffering of others at an early age." For example, highly generative individuals commented on how they had observed discrimination and injustice on the playground when they were children. They *noticed* retarded individuals. Significantly, these highly generative adults told life narratives in which bad events and negative feelings were immediately followed by good events and positive feelings.

McAdams links such *redemption* stories to Erikson's stage of generativity. An example of a *turn*around or *redemption* story involves the loss of a family member in a traffic accident. The aftermath *redemptive/*generative story is that after the fatal accident the insurance money allowed another person in the family to pay for college.[37] Having a generative attitude serves you well in all kinds of tragic situations. Observing war-torn refugee camps, Navy Seal Greitens discovered that the people who were doing best in the camp shacks were parents/grandparents caring for young children. They had to cope and be strong for someone else.[38] They nurtured a growth mind-set.

FROM "MANAGING" MISFORTUNE TO BEING HERE NOW

Internal Family Systems (IFS)[39] language explains how generative midlifers can talk about the fears in loss as well as their *redemptive* personality roles. Dick Schwartz developed IFS language after listening to his clients' wording about opposite "parts" of their personalities. One client admitted to Schwartz, "Part of me wants to stay married and faithful, but another part wants to be free to get laid every night of the week with a different woman."[40] My client, Lucinda, agonized over her job: "Something in me hates my job, but I'm also worried that I'm not smart enough to get a promotion." Schwartz labels such worried personality parts as "managers," or "exiles" when they are not consciously acknowledged. Such personality parts take a protective role to patch any holes of emotional pain.

Everyone has vulnerable and fearful roles in their personalities. Most feel unsafe while struggling to clear a path of action after loss. You may hide or exile your true feelings after loss. How many times have you heard someone respond, "Fine," to the question, "How are you?" when you knew that the individual felt terrible? You may experience shameful or embarrassed roles of your personality when you are not "fine," but you cannot admit to yourself or others that you feel such vulnerability. What if your loss was an eviction? Millions of Americans are evicted every year; at least one in four pay rent that is over 70% of their income.[41] U.S. culture embraces the popular phrase, "pull yourself up by your bootstraps." No, there are times when you cannot even find your boots, with or without straps.

After my husband's death, some people admonished me to "keep a stiff upper lip" when my face looked too sad. It is OK to feel your sadness or loneliness without needing to hide it. Be prepared to hear from others that *their* protective personality roles are not ready to handle your vulnerability. Wanting to protect yourself from suffering is a normal reaction. However, in midlife you realize that you simply cannot manage a loss out of your life. One mistaken assumption many make is that during midlife individuals have control over their life. Your controlling role is another manager or protective part in your personality. You will learn more about personality roles in chapter 5, but start thinking about the roles in your personality that help you grow. Please know that as an active learner with a growth mind-set, you can change aspects of your personality to recover from loss and rediscover a vital purpose for living.

TURN TIP

I've been absolutely terrified every moment of my life and I've never let it keep me from doing a single thing that I wanted to do.

– Georgia O'Keeffe, artist

Each chapter offers two exercises for further exploration. Choose one or do both. To jumpstart your growth process, here are a few questions to *turn* over in your mind. One way to map your grieving process is to keep a *Turn* Journal either on your computer or in a notebook while you read this book. Psychologist James Pennebaker researched the value of writing. Writing about *turn*ing points improves both physical and mental health.[42] In journaling, Carl Jung said, "I should advise you to put it all down as beautifully as you can – in some beautifully bound book." Write in any way that seems comfortable – on loose-leaf paper to gather later in a folder, online in a saved folder, or in a *Turn* Journal of your choice. As you continue reading and growing, you will find answers to assist you in *turn*ing a few corners in the midlife maze.

You will keep good company if you keep a journal. Philosopher Ralph Waldo Emerson lost his father when he was eight years old. The family was thrown into poverty, but his father had been a distinguished minister and young Emerson was accepted at Harvard at age fourteen. He began writing his lifelong journal. Emerson lost both his brother and his young wife, Ellen, to tuberculosis. In a second marriage, his firstborn son, Waldo, died at age five. Emerson affectionately called his journal his "savings bank."[43] Japanese Zen writer Zeami Motokiyo affirmed the power of writing for cleansing the mind, enabling one to achieve serenity through purging "tangled emotions" onto the page.[44]

Detangle your emotions with these questions:

- Does your grieving a particular loss surface at certain times? What are these times?
- Do you ever find a *turn*ing point after intense sadness?
- What are the circumstances when you can *turn* a corner on sadness?
- See yourself through a friend's eyes. Does your self-compassion increase?
- What do you yearn for?
- What is your psychic miracle–gro, or your motivator for a positive change to blossom?
- Is there anything you want to get away from?

YOUR TURN

The sun is shining … that is the magic. The flowers are growing –
The roots are stirring. That is the magic. Being alive is the magic –
being strong is the magic. The magic is in me … it's in every one of
us.

– Frances Hodgson Burnett, English writer, *The Secret Garden*

Dig up some enthusiasm for your future. Emulate someone famous who serves as a positive role model for you. Then answer the following questions as if your role model provides the words. Choose an individual several decades later than your current age.

- I am 30 (40, 50, 60, 70, 80, 90) years old. It's the year:
- My job is:

- I live in:
- The things I like to do best are:
- At work, I'm really good at:
- At home, I'm really good at:
- Here's what I like most about my life:
- This is the kind of 30-year-old (40-, 50-, 60-, 70-, 80-, or 90-year-old) person I am:
- The most important thing I learned from my parents or caretaker was:
- The most important thing I learned from my grandparents or other elders was:
- The thing I like best about myself is: [45]

Now, answer the questions again in terms of yourself, without emulating another's responses. Make the age your present age. What do you notice about the two sets of answers?

Chapter 2

Acclimating to Loss

The midlife passage is an entranceway into the deepest layers of one's soul. The growth and transformation that can occur at this transition is nothing short of remarkable.

> – Kathleen A. Brehony, psychologist, *Awakening at Midlife*

What saves a man is to take a step. Then another step.

> – C. S. Lewis, Irish writer

Singer and civil rights activist Lena Horne captured the essence of holding onto stress and loss in life: "It's not the load that breaks you down, it's the way you carry it." Another way of viewing Horne's sage advice involves a plastic glass – a client gave me the glass with two visible bottoms. One bottom is at the halfway mark; it is a glass that is either *half-full* or *half-empty* depending upon your viewpoint. In my workshops I often take sips of water from the halfway glass, saying how I prefer to say my glass is *half-full*. Stress mounts inside your body, but it is not the heaviness of your *glass* of life, but how long you hold onto stress that matters. How much muscle pressure you exert to squeeze your glass makes a huge difference to your body/mind. It is not the particular loss load that you carry, but the attitudinal way in which you carry yourself. You may ask, but how can I view my glass as *half-full* when my loss feels so great? My answer is that you can make it happen – one interaction at a time or one *turn* at a time.

Let's back up this homey story about a *half-full* attitude with research. Health psychologist Kelly McGonigal had to revise her lectures at Stanford University on the effects of stress after finding research results on U.S. adults who were asked how much stress they had encountered in the past year, and if they believed that stress was harmful to their health. Eight years later, indeed, high levels of stress increased the risk of dying by 43% for these thirty thousand individuals. However, this increased risk applied *only* to people who also believed that stress had put their health on the line! "People who reported high levels of stress but who did not view their stress as harmful were not more likely to die. In fact, they had the lowest risk of death of anyone in the study, even lower than those who reported experiencing very little stress."[1] McGonigal advises, "As soon as you think about the positive things you care about – like going to an interesting work opportunity, why your work matters to you, why your family matters to you – you're already transforming your physiology and your attitude."[2] There is stress in experiencing a loss, but you have many choices in living the rest of your precious life.

A *half-empty* attitude may lead to a chronic stress condition: "Chronic stress is believed to be the most important causal factor in depression aside from a genetic predisposition to the disorder."[3] While you recognize that you are no longer as invincible as you felt in young adulthood, you can train your brain in many positive directions. According to Fred (Rusty) Gage, professor in a genetics laboratory, your adult brain is capable of growing new nerve cells throughout life. Physical exercise and cognitive enrichment increase your brain's ability to generate more neurons.[4] British poet David Whyte focuses on freeing up emotional turmoil: "You must learn one thing: the world was made to be free in. Give up all the other worlds except the one to which you belong. Sometimes it takes darkness and the sweet confinement of your aloneness to learn anything."[5]

TURNING POINTS

On a family vacation in Arizona, I learned a powerful Native American viewpoint in predawn darkness. In ceremonial robes to greet dawn on a mountaintop, a Havasupai medicine man wearing eagle feathers on his head slowly began drumming. I watched him *turn* to face each direction. He spoke with authority as he greeted the four directions: "It is a good day. ... It is a good day. ... It is a good day. ... It is a good day." Poet Maya Angelo also speaks of gratitude for each day: "This is a wonderful day. I've never seen this one before!"[6] While you may not have an actual mountain in your vistas, how might your days be different if you *turn* to greet your emotional mountain climbing each morning by saying, "It is a good day"?

What about when it is not a wonderful day? Just two days after my husband's sudden death, a person asked me, "What are you going to do?" What could I say? Tear my hair out? Wear mourning clothes all year? Fortunately, out of the blue, in one *turn* outside of time, words came out of my mouth from somewhere: "Make something good happen every day." This motto remains with me. I like it. It sustains me on days when "it" does not feel like "it" is going to be a good day. I remind myself that I have set an intention for such a day. On really difficult days, there are a few jumbled words: "Good grief! Make something happen! Every day. ... Make every day good. Did I really say, every day?" I stumble through these words at times. I take a deep breath or three. I reset myself. Yes, I remind myself; I can *turn* a corner and make something good happen today. My glass remains *half-full*.

In reacting to loss you may feel as if you are back at the original scene of calamity over and over. You may not realize that you can about-face or pivot to be mindful in the present moment. As a loss survivor, initially you may not recognize new opportunities. Survivors of significant loss often disconnect from their emotions. A protective part of your personality can allow you temporarily to feel as though you left your body, or have the sense that everything is unreal around you. While such reactions may scare you, they are short-term pathways you use to acclimate yourself to the new "normal." Remind yourself that you can learn something from these experiences. Instead of feeling lost in a maze, you swerve a corner or two, or perhaps you take detours around 22 corners, but eventually you sidetrack to evolve in meaningful ways. Many believe that a grieving individual should let go of the grief or relinquish emotional ties. Medical models of grieving often support this notion that a person needs to "eliminate" their grief.[7] Rather, you can better acclimate to sorrow by making *space* for a relationship with grieving that eventually can evoke creativity and new meaning in your life.

TAKE THREE DAYS OFF WORK ....

Some companies require a grieving employee to apply for the take-three-days-off-work "benefit" rather than have a supervisor offer it. This stance may say more about the culture valuing work over family than it does about a lack of sensitivity to grieving.[8] However, it is not popular in America to take much time for grieving. "Take your benefit," a boss says to Miriam who lost two beloved parents. Miriam's father died after an extended illness. Three months after grieving this death, her very sick mother also died. Time takes on different meanings for the grieving individual. Not only are there many memories to replant, but Miriam has to clean out her parents' home of 55 years. Each item that Miriam handles in her childhood home feels sacred. Which items can she relinquish? The amount of work that lands in her lap seems overwhelming at a time when Miriam feels immobilized with her grief.

Lucia receives three days off work, but she cannot shake her anger at her sister's physician. She was at her sister's side when the doctor in the hospital announced in a matter-of-fact tone, "Chemo is not working." Lung cancer had spread from her sister's initial diagnosis of breast cancer. Her sister bravely asked, "What will kill the cancer?" Lucia swipes at tears when she recalls the physician blithely respond: "Nothing." Her beloved younger sister died in her arms a week later. Realistically, when do doctors take time to grieve a patient's loss? Doctors seldom receive three days off duty.

Grieving occurs more often and for longer periods of time for individuals (including health care providers) than people usually admit. Death is not the only loss that midlifers grieve. Many midlifers suffer from chronic illness and/or pain which "may bring a feeling of losing oneself and experiencing a sense of discontinuity with the world. ... Any significant loss, regardless of its origin, has the potential for creating a similar pathway for grief recovery comparable to the experience of loss by death."[9] The loss of bodily functions, and perhaps the ensuing loss of the ability to hold a job, results in complicated grieving. Grieving slides a person's perspective into a different sense of the morning-noon-evening timeframe of the working world. After a death, most grieving adults do go back to work after their three-day allotment for tears and termination, but there is inner as well as outer work that remains unfinished. Three months may pass and the grieving person barely notices the passage. This time disconnect bothers friends and family of the grieving person: "Isn't it about time for him/her to let go?"

No, it is not about time. *There is no perfect amount of time that a grieving person needs for their process of grieving. However, all of us might help with another's grieving if we were more comfortable with the topic ourselves.* "It's a strange phenomenon what happens to people when they hear that a friend or loved one has cancer. Most people don't know what to say. They don't want to say the wrong thing, so they end up saying nothing. A cycle of avoidance and denial only deepens the loneliness and isolation the cancer patient feels."[10] Often, we Americans view grief as a taboo topic, certainly not one to discuss much. One misinformed etiquette and communications coach advises how detrimental the discussion of grief might be for polite dinner conversation: "I recommend that you do not talk about politics, religion, death, bereavement or anything that is too spicy." Unfortunately, this denial of exiled emotion is rampant. Life is spicy.

Tami lost her daughter. She came to the realization that the U.S. culture is grief illiterate. She desperately wanted to talk about her daughter, but found that people avoided her. "In other cultures there are rituals; you are allowed to cry and scream and wail. ... You might look fine, but you're not. People don't want to disturb that and think you might have forgotten for a few minutes, but a mother never forgets." Tami made up her own grieving ritual; when she wanted to hear her daughter's name out loud, she went to Starbucks. Tami gave her daughter's name instead of her own so that the barista would shout out, "Haley! Latte for Haley!"[11]

LOSS OF BABIES

Significant loss can happen in a healthy family's life. Often overlooked, loss frequently occurs in pregnancy and/or delivery. One in 160 pregnancies in the United States ends in stillbirth.[12] Miscarriage, or the spontaneous loss of a fetus before the 20th week of pregnancy, is much more common. Approximately one in four pregnancies ends in miscarriage. With about 4.4 million confirmed pregnancies in the United States on an annual basis, about one million result in a pregnancy loss. An estimated 19% of the adult population experiences the death of a child through miscarriage, stillborn babies, or the loss of older children.[13] Mark Zuckerberg, chief of Facebook, announced on his social networking site that he and his wife, Priscilla Chan, experienced three miscarriages. However, he did not release his personal message until a viable pregnancy was on the way. Zuckerberg disclosed, "You start making plans, and then they're gone. It's a lonely experience. Most people don't discuss miscarriages because you worry your problems will distance you or reflect upon you – as if you're defective or did something to cause this. ... So you struggle on your own."[14] In spite of how common it is to lose a child, it is rarely discussed in the United States.

Lila and her partner Rickie waited to have their first pregnancy. After starting her career and saving money for a child, Lila was thrilled about welcoming a baby into their cozy home. However, after three months of pregnancy she experienced terrible cramping. She faced a D&C (dilation and curettage to remove tissue from the lining of her uterus) rather than a healthy pregnancy. Wasn't it yesterday that she and her mother laughed heartily about her pregnancy? How can you feel positive one moment and in the next minute feel lost in a maze of unwelcome emotion? Lila marveled at the sheer coincidence of discussing her up-and-down emotions only 24 hours earlier. Could a conversation be some kind of preparation for the weird cramps she endured half the night? Lila believed there was some kind of emotional preparation for death, but pre-procedure she only harbored numbness. As she waited for her physician to enter the room, Lila steeled her eyes on the charts about birth control on the wall and vowed not to sob uncontrollably.

When it comes to birth, control is an oxymoron. Everyone knows that so-called birth control methods are not 100% effective, and pregnancy is not a 100% guarantee for a healthy baby. Yet, midlifers are caught off guard when a baby is lost. For a mother who miscarries, seeing a healthy baby in the grocery aisle can create a microburst of grieving. I recall leaving a grocery store quickly when this happened to me after I miscarried. You may have an expectation that there is a way for you to feel or behave, but what is it? You may hunt for the courage part of your personality to make some change, but what change is possible right after losing a baby? Even though you feel lost in a maze, your questions are part of the normal grieving process.

The Cuddle Cot, developed in England, has a cooling system to preserve stillbirth infants for several days; it provides an opportunity for parents' grieving rituals.[15] Miscarriage is a death, but there are few miscarriage rituals in the United States to help grieving parents. Shelly and Mariana created their own sacred rituals. Shelly was four months into her pregnancy when she miscarried. After her D&C she experienced nausea and vomiting from the anesthesia, a common side effect. Upon leaving the hospital she was given a towel to hold in case she had to vomit during the car ride home. Shelly still has that towel. She has asked family members to bury it with her when it is her time of final transition. Mariana's due date would have been the Valentine's Day. After her miscarriage, she honored her *intention* of having that child every Valentine's Day. She also honored how special it was for her and her husband to cocreate a healthy child after the miscarriage.

Christof Koch, chief scientific officer of the Allen Institute for Brain Science in Seattle, describes his "horrid experience" of sudden infant death syndrome when his twin daughter Elisabeth mysteriously died at eight weeks. Years later he visited her gravesite alone. A stranger had placed a small terracotta angel with broken wings on Elisabeth's tombstone. Koch was overcome with emotion: "What I learned that day is that a symbol, in the right context, can abruptly release long-dormant memories and emotions."[16] Yes, symbols trigger grieving undercurrents.

UNFORESEEN PARTS OR ROLES IN YOUR PERSONALITY

We know from spicy science that people have "mirror neurons." Discovered in the 1990s, mirror neurons can help you understand why you feel so much pain when you attend ceremonies to commemorate a death that is not among your immediate family/friend tribe. Mirror neurons in your brain respond with equal strength when you experience something firsthand, or when you watch someone else experiencing something, including a loss.[17] This emotional contagion explains why tears readily come to your eyes when you see someone crying on screen in a movie. The choked-up feeling in your throat is because of your mirror neurons; when the heroine or hero gasps in disbelief at a tragic outcome, you also gasp. In a sense, you enter the movie as a bystander actor, silently echoing the notion made famous by President Bill Clinton when he said, "I feel your pain," to an AIDS activist. Yes, you can feel another's pain. And it serves a purpose. A saying from China's lower Yangtze Valley further explains what happens in such present moments: "We use the occasions of other people's funerals to release personal sorrows."

What about times when you veer off your usual path, but the end result is an unforeseen loss with unrecognized personality roles placing a stranglehold on otherwise good days? Devon experienced a depressed role in his personality after his separation, even though he was the initiator of the breakup. He initially denied his sadness. "After all," Devon asked himself, "Wasn't a divorce what I wanted?" He was so busy locking onto anger and hurt roles in his personality that he had only one goal in mind – leave the relationship. His ex-partner met his angry challenges tit for tat. Both showed meanness to one another. One day Devon realized that he needed to have compassion for his ex. He still wanted a separation, but there were children's needs to consider above any petty bickering. After *turn*ing a corner, or shifting around a dozen corners, this couple learned to coparent their children successfully. *It is possible to honor the love of someone, past or present, instead of honoring the pain.*

Successful author Geneen Roth and her husband lost their life savings when their financial advisor, Bernie Madoff, lied about reported earnings. Along with thousands of investors, Roth was a victim of Madoff's fraudulent Ponzi scheme. Actually, money problems are Americans' top cause for stress according to an American Psychological Association survey.[18] While Roth's area of expertise is how people relate to food, she began to equate the issues of food and money. She discovered that many individuals have addictive and compulsive personality roles around both topics, as both involve wanting, giving, and receiving. The health conscious part of you that knows what to feed yourself and how to budget money says, "I'm going to be good. I'm going to pull myself up by my bootstraps, discipline myself, and be the person I think I should be." However, another role in your personality that binges and splurges may retort, "Did you say that I'm not allowed to eat bread or buy that hat? Ha! I'm now going to eat the ENTIRE LOAF and move on to the crackers, chips and tortillas. And if I am forced to limit what I eat, I am going to charge up a storm. No one gets to tell me what I can and can't eat or buy. Got that? No one."[19] With time, Roth *turn*ed around her glass *half-empty* thinking when she came to grips with focusing on what she did have, instead of lamenting about what she did not have.

Personal growth publisher Louise Hay and grief counselor David Kessler offer this advice: "Our thinking creates our experiences. ... The pain of grief is one thing. Our thoughts then add to the suffering."[20] Neuroscientist Andrew Newberg and communications expert Mark Waldman back up this notion with the science of neurochemicals. A single negative word or phrase is powerful; the more you focus on negative words, the more likely you "actually damage key structures that regulate your memory ... and emotions. You may disrupt your sleep, your appetite, and the way your brain regulates happiness, longevity, and health."[21] It turns out that feeling bad on an ongoing basis is bad for you!

WHAT TIME IS IT? TIME TO GRIEVE ....

You must give yourself permission to grieve, as denial takes your sadness role underground, or out-of-conscious awareness for a period of time. Express your grief to compassionate listeners. However, our culture often makes the process of grieving a loss feel shaming and out of touch with others. Hay and Kessler discuss "disenfranchised grief," or grief not acknowledged by others, that may exist for gay/lesbian relationships breaking up, drug addiction deaths, or suicides.[22] College professor Vicky Whipple outlines special issues of lesbian widows who grieve their partner's death. Legal and financial hassles are even more pronounced than usual for couples who do not have a legally recognized relationship. Families and/or colleagues may offer no support due to their rejection of a widow's sexual orientation. The LGBTQ community is a diverse group and includes individuals who hide their private lives from others. Invisible grieving is very lonesome.[23] If there is no support from the culture and/or family, loss can seem embarrassing. No loss deserves this fate.

When a crisis of loss occurs, family members may experience chaos; healthy functioning can shut down as "everyone blames everyone and seeks the source of the problem in the past or in the stars or in society."[24] Psychiatrist Frank Pittman believes that he was "raised to be a family therapist, as perhaps we all are." Whether you chose a psychotherapy profession or not, the aspect of Pittman's pithy phrase that rings true is that each person has decisions about relating with responsibility and caring within family/ friend tribes in times of significant loss. This is no small task. In Pittman's theory of family crisis, there are two persistent themes: responsibility and functioning.[25] Both themes take your time and attention – even in happy times. However, responsibilities feel especially challenging in times of grieving, and functioning falters.

Perhaps no one has given more thought to the responsibility and functioning of dying persons, their families, and their health care providers than Swiss-American psychiatrist Elisabeth Kubler-Ross. She has been unjustly criticized by researchers who attempt to categorize her overlapping stages of death and dying. Kubler-Ross' own statement 35 years after publishing her famous book, *On Death and Dying: What the Dying Have to Teach Doctors, Nurses, Clergy and Their Own Families*, suggests stepping back from thinking that there are specific stages of grieving: "People often think of the stages as lasting weeks or months. They forget that the stages are responses to feelings that can last for minutes or hours as we flip in and out of one and then another. We do not enter and leave each individual stage in a linear fashion. We may feel one, then another, and back again to the first one."[26] The original linear list of Kubler-Ross' stage theory follows, but does not consider, the stages as 1, 2, 3, 4, and 5. View the stages as circular or reoccurring. Follow Kubler-Ross' later advice: know that you may flip-flop in grieving stages. Grieving truly is a mazelike process. You cannot know what will happen around the next bend, or hour. You may or may not experience every stage. Also, Kubler-Ross believed that the stages apply to grieving a loss other than death.

KUBLER-ROSS' THEORY OF GRIEF[27]

Denial and Isolation

When presented with a terminal illness, most people told Kubler-Ross, "No, not me, it cannot be true." It did not matter whether they were given their diagnosis initially, or whether they figured out their prognosis on their own. Kubler-Ross saw denial in a healthy way, as few feel comfortable hearing that they do not have long to live. Denial of a loss may be either conscious or unconscious, and it is usually temporary. After his son was killed in a gang war, Marcel revealed, "Sometimes I close my eyes and imagine he's still alive." As with other kinds of deaths, this is a normal reaction.

Anger, Rage, and Envy

Kubler-Ross viewed anger as an important feeling state in grief: "When ... denial cannot be maintained any longer, it is replaced by feelings of anger, rage, envy, and resentment. ... (People ask) why me?" Anger is especially prevalent when a dying person has been in control all their life. A terminal diagnosis creates havoc with the managing roles of one's personality such as perfectionist or organizer parts. Also, Kubler-Ross found that those of her patients who were full of anger and resentment often held a reservoir of anger from childhood issues.

Bargaining

In Kubler-Ross' words, "Bargaining is ... equally helpful ... though only for brief periods of time." A terminal patient, or a family member of someone dying, may wish for an extension of life, or just desire a few days without pain/discomfort issues. Some bargains are religious in nature and are kept secret, as in promising to dedicate oneself to God if a person can be spared. An individual facing an unwanted divorce may try to bargain another way: "Can we still be friends?"

Depression

Reactive depression stems from the mounting issues that can include anything from financial burdens of an illness to the loss of making dreams on a bucket list come true. Preparatory depression is focused on impending losses. Often depression is a silent grieving process. Like other stages, Kubler-Ross saw it as necessary and beneficial. She advised that depression is best acknowledged by a touch of one's hand, or just silently sitting together.

Acceptance

This stage in the grieving process occurs when a person reaches some peace and acceptance. A dying person may experience almost a void of feelings. It is also a time when family members and friends may need more support than the person who is dying, as a dying patient may find acceptance a long time before the people they leave behind.

While Kubler-Ross' stages are widely quoted, it is important to consider that they are not the complete grief story. In fact, longitudinal research of 233 adults' grief process following a family member's death from natural causes (Yale Bereavement Study) found that acceptance, rather than denial or disbelief, was the most frequently endorsed state of adult grieving. Yearning, an unmentioned stage by Kubler-Ross, was the most prominent state from 1 to 24 months after loss, rather than anger or depression.[28] With so many different grief reactions and personalities, no set pattern of grieving exists for all.

PINWHEEL MODEL OF BEREAVEMENT

A developmental model of grieving loss, the *Pinwheel Model of Bereavement*, is based upon the nursing research of Susan Carter, as well as the clinical work of Ann Solari-Twadell and her colleagues at Loyola University, Chicago. Nurses collected narrative accounts of grieving adults who lost a loved one through death. The Pinwheel Model defines complexities in grieving and can help you recognize loss as a unique life experience, a back-and-forth kind of process. One day you face learning to live your life after loss; another day you feel as if you are lost in a storm of grief. While these changing emotional states are unsettling, you need to know that this is normal. This grief process model addresses both responsibility and functioning as life themes that are important in every family crisis: Who is the deceased in relationship to you? What was the relationship between the two of you? What were your shared hopes and dreams? The model considers important details as additions to the ideas of Kubler-Ross:

- *Grief's up-and-down nature* (waves of intense grieving can occur years after a death)
- A *"holding" of the significance* of someone after death
- *Expectations about how to grieve*, both socially and personally

Importance of your personal history prior to the current death[29]

There is no specific resolution, or one set of stages to master in your grief process, but more of an incorporation of the loss into living forward. You learn to live your life after loss by mulling over stories about your loss. You discover new meaning for yourself and about life itself.

Picture a toy pinwheel. The pinwheel is set into motion by an initiating wind of loss. The image of a frail pinwheel buffeted by strong gusts is poignant, as some people almost disintegrate in their calamity strike. While windblown by loss, most survive. However, to not only survive, but to thrive after loss, consider the very center or anchor of the pinwheel as your personal history. The *turn*ing and spinning of your pinwheel of grieving depends upon your core resilience as built up over your lifetime so far. When a loss blows into your life, swirling issues may billow quickly or slowly. The complex issues of grieving include the following:

- *Being stopped or interrupted* in your life following loss
- *Pain and hurting* emotions (not everyone experiences anger, but most feel sadness)
- A *missing or yearning* for all that has been lost (a wishing for the loved one's presence, feeling a "hole" in life)
- A *holding desire*, often holding onto what was good about the person
- A *seeking* of meaning, comfort, and support
- *Valuing* what matters most and provides meaning in life

For every time you revisit your loss, and this will occur for most people, the time spent in the grieving whirlwind usually is of a shorter duration with the cultivation of strengths. As time passes you consider grieving through the various roles of your personality. While a smell, a place, or a time of year may trigger fresh grieving, you also rediscover your *present* strengths. The steps include the following:

- *Surrender or a releasing* experience which can occur at any time; you *turn* more and more toward an openness to reality; your hope, trust, and confidence increase, and you *reach out* to belonging relationships, finding a new path of balance to rejoin life. You invest love and energy in new people and new situations.[30]

TURN TIP

You drown not by falling into a river but by staying submerged in it.

– Paul Coelho, Brazilian novelist

- Creative writing professor Louise DeSalvo views writing as a healing process that can stabilize an individual. She always closes her own healing writing with what she is grateful for. She finds that many famous writers have used writing to heal from a variety of losses – dislocation, violence, racism, homophobia, rape, incest, illness, as well as religious and/or political persecution.[31]

As journalist Judith Viorst aptly suggests, "Wherever I looked ... all of us – were struggling with issues of loss. ... We lose not only through death, but also by leaving and being left, by changing ... and moving on."[32] The grieving process of holding on to what was good about a person/situation, and later retooling your personality, means that you change your loss stories over time. Just as you clear out lifeless stalks in the garden after winter, you periodically clean up your stories that you tell yourself and others. You bring a new perspective to your grieving process when you retell a story about your life. The time to clear out aspects of a loss story varies with each person; there are no set times, just as there are no set regulations for gardeners. Most midlifers find that they change their life story gradually after going through tough times.

- Choose a time in your life when you experienced a loss. Take a second look at the story you tell yourself (and perhaps others) about that time. Choose a particular part of that story about your life that you find compelling or puzzling.
- Rewrite the story. Look for today's meaning. Does the story have McAdams' "contamination script," or tell of a good time suddenly going sour? Do life events seem "contaminated" thereafter?[33] An example of such a story could include the birth of a healthy child, only to discover later that the child has a serious disorder.
- Perhaps your chosen story has a "redemption" theme, where growth and progress flow as outcomes later on. A story might begin with a significant

loss in childhood, but later there is a positive twist. You discover a resilient outlook in adulthood.[34]

• Redemptive stories tend to energize you, while contamination stories result in stagnation. If you uncover a contamination story, can you locate any effects upon your personality today? What can you think of that could *turn* your story into one where you honor love instead of honoring pain?

IS YOUR GRIEF LIKE MY GRIEF?

Like Emily Dickinson in her poem, *I Measure Every Grief I Meet*, you may wonder how grief affects others: "I wonder if It weighs like mine—Or has an Easier size. I wonder if They bore it long—Or did it just begin. ... I wonder if it hurts to live." How often is your wondering about grief an inward exercise, not one you share with others? What if you aired and shared your wonderings with others? What if you asked others about their grieving *turn*ing points? What difference would this make with how you treat grieving individuals? And more importantly, how less lonely would a grieving person feel to have an opportunity to say out loud to you what is on his or her mind?

Something interesting occurs when a person is asked, "What is a *turn*ing point that you are dealing with in your life now?" Just asking the question allows openness to another's world. Some personal veering has more good stress, or eustress, attached than negative stress, or distress. Some events start out with eustress, but end up later in the distressful category. For example, a wedding is a positive *turn*ing point. But what happens when the couple divorces? Having a child is a positive *turn*ing point. What happens when that child has a serious illness or disability and/or dies? No one expects children to have serious mishaps or die before their parents, yet in early times it was commonplace that babies and children died. However life delivers a calamity, you can make U-*turns*, but this may take setting an intention to shift your behavior.

One powerful intention is to reset your focus upon what you are grateful for. Research on heart failure patients shows that an attitude of gratitude is related to better moods, higher-quality sleep, and less inflammation in the body. Spiritual well-being also is related to each of these health issues.[35] In a research on middle-aged adults, ages 35 to 54, participants had to jot down each night three things that went well for them that day and to give a brief explanation. Not only did the participants' degree of happiness rise over a three-month period of time, but their depression continued to decrease after they discontinued the practice.[36] They *turn*ed to a growth mind-set.

YOUR TURN

For those friends now gone, like gardens past that have been har-
vested, but who fed us in their times that we might have life thereafter.
For all these we give thanks.

> – Max Coots, minister and sculptor, *Garden Meditations*

One way to *turn* a corner on grieving is to keep a list of things that you are
thankful for in your *Turn* (to gratitude) Journal. I kept a gratitude journal for
two entire years during midlife – one year of journaling what I was grateful for was after the unexpected death of my husband at age 54; another
journaling year was after the expected death of my father at age 90. There
are different ways to keep such a journal. I chose a simple way. Every night
before going to sleep I wrote one or two things in my journal that I was grateful for that day. This exercise served a double purpose: since my intention
was to be grateful each night, during the next day I would prompt myself to
think of small *turn*ing points throughout the day. Then at nighttime, I not only
had something to write about, but I was able to put myself into a relaxing
place for sleep.

Here are sample entries, one from each of my year-long *Turn* (to gratitude)
Journals:

I am grateful for two wonderful children! The three of us went to the Tech
Museum of Innovation in San Jose. I watched my children at computer termi-
nals – my son investigating and my daughter sending email to college friends.
I thought what a fortunate mother I am to have such bright stars in my family!

I am grateful for the many cultural opportunities offered at Millennium Park.
Today I went to tango dance lessons on the main stage. Never mind that my
tango "partner" was a head shorter and at least 10 years older than me – we
were able to follow the teacher and laugh at ourselves, the guy counting out
loud every step of the way!

Chapter 3

Pursuing a Personality beyond Loss

It is a common experience that a problem difficult at night is resolved
in the morning after the committee of sleep has worked on it.

> – John Steinbeck, writer, *Sweet Thursday*

Through our dreams, sleep opens up a pathway to other dimensions,
other times, other parts of ourselves, and to deeper insights
that lie beyond the reach of our waking consciousness.

> – Ariana Huffington, *The Huffington Post* founder,
> *The Sleep Revolution*

Grief over a loss can embody an experience of connection rather than total
severance. It is possible to use your memories, dreams, and history that
made you who you are today to retool for creative changes in your life. You
assemble your personality story by story. You chunk together your stories
and dreams, sometimes with contamination or negative themes, and sometimes with redemptive or positive themes.[1] Middle-aged individuals often
feel stuck in their middle chapters. You may have to let go of the physical
presence of a person or the daily routine of a job. Especially after loss it is
a struggle to resume any particular direction for present actions. Conflicting
personal pathways characterize the midlife maze.

You may sense that overwhelming grief will never end. You may travel
to your personality edges, or insecurities, while grieving a loss. Forty-year-
old Lucinda had a disturbing dream after her father's violent death: "I was
in some institution. People thought that I was crazy. I had the word, 'die' on
my back." Actually, Lucinda had a violent desire: one part of her personality wished for her father's killer also to die violently; another part of her

knew that she would be jailed for life if she acted on her wish. And if she ever became institutionalized, a third role feared "going crazy." Long before dream research, William Shakespeare's Hamlet expressed great wisdom about dreaming: "A dream itself is but a shadow." The grief process contains a nighttime dream shadow, as grieving does not confine itself to daytime hours.

THE COMMITTEE OF SLEEP

Your brain never stops working. In fact, when you enter rapid eye movement (REM) dreamtimes during sleep, your brain activity is as high as when you are startled during waking. J. Allan Hobson, a psychiatrist and researcher of the neuroscience of sleep, explains an important difference in these equally active states: "The mode of processing during dreaming appears to be much less constrained by the external rules of space and time than is the case in waking; thoughts are less ordered by linear logic. … Dreaming is a more metaphorical mode of information processing."[2] While you dream for about two hours each night, you may have trouble remembering even five minutes of your dreamtime. And these dream fragments represent only 25% of the whole dream! Most of your nighttime dreaming shadow is not recalled at all. Hobson provides a scientific reason: during REM sleep, your brain cells that secrete chemicals necessary for memory to endure are shut down. This fact explains the dreamtime loss of self-reflective awareness, critical judgment, and linear logic.

Processing aspects of your grieving through dreaming is both fascinating and helpful. In addition to taking more of an interest in your dreams, you need to know how valuable dreaming is to your overall health and energy levels. Psychologist Rosalind Cartwright, called the Queen of Dreams, devoted 40 years to sleep research. She opened a sleep laboratory at Rush-Presbyterian-St. Luke's Medical Center in Chicago. Cartwright's sleep theory suggests that dreams are mood regulators. Dreams act as an "inner therapist" to aid you in playing out experiences and emotions: "If you go to bed worried, upset, anxious, you should wake up feeling better, if the dream process is doing what it should." Her research found that dream data could predict with 82% accuracy which people would more readily recover from their depression (after experiencing loss in divorcing) based upon their dream patterns.[3] The difference between the depressed individuals who improved and those who did not was related to the amount of dream complexity. These complex dreamers were "putting things together in new ways, changing their minds during sleep."[4] Even in your dreams, it pays to pivot or make a few *turns* in your thinking.

While you may not remember much from your dreamtime currently, you can increase your recall of dreams, and your night dreams can help you grieve a loss. After her mother's death, 56-year-old Donna dreamed about her mother, her sister, and a niece. All arrived smiling and together in an airport. Donna felt reassured and made this interpretation: "Mom is in a good place." Later, Donna dreamed about her father, who also had died: "Dad is standing at one end of a wooden gazebo and I am at the other end. Dad looks young, muscular, and healthy. He's OK now." Instead of viewing her parents as inflicted with their life-threatening diseases and suffering in declining health, Donna was able to free herself from her agony over both parents' suffering at the end of their lives. "Grief dreams allow us to reconnect with our deceased loved ones. ... [They] can serve as gentle reminders that our loved one is still part of our life."[5] When her dreams showed her parents as OK, Donna was able to relax her thoughts of them as invalids. She could stop worrying about whether she, too, might become an invalid. The poet Anne Sexton captured this wisdom in her poem, *Old*: "In a dream you are never eighty."

Psychologist Gayle Delaney focuses on the insights of connections that are gleaned from night dreams.[6] Your dreams at night may awaken you with their strange combinations of remembered scenes mixed up with surreal movie-like characters, animals, and various strange landscapes or settings. This is normal dream behavior! Your waking life experiences and past *turn*ing point events may trigger your dreams, but dream stories shift into mysterious material. Your dream rarely represents a real-life event in 100% accurate terms due to your visual recall becoming inactive during REM dreamtime. However, dream emotions feel real, as processing from the limbic system – where emotions are supported in the brain – is active during dreaming. Joy, anxiety, and anger are common in dreams. Threat perception and harm avoidance show up frequently.[7] Shareen was 41 when her mother died. She began to experience scary dreams of being chased. Later, her dreams *turn*ed from fear into joyful encounters with her mother. In dream territory, Shareen enjoyed family meal times and walks with her mother. Her mother was happily engaged with her grandchildren, appreciating their developmental growth in dreamtime. These dreams consoled Shareen in her grieving process.

To underscore the important *turn*ing points in dreams, many famous people claimed that when they were stuck in life, they discovered a path forward through a dream. The amazing story of inventor Elias Howe's discovery of the sewing machine needle having its hole in the sharp end of the needle, instead of the blunt end (as in a hand-held needle), came from a nightmare he had one night. Easier to believe, Mary Shelley wrote *Frankenstein* and Robert Louis Stevenson took inspiration for many of his stories, including *The Strange Case of Dr. Jekyll and Mr. Hyde*, from nighttime dreaming. Also, musicians based future music upon dreams: Mozart, Beethoven, Billy Joel, and Paul McCartney are examples. McCartney's entire melody for the hit song, *Yesterday*, is an example of this phenomenon. The German pharmacologist Otto Loewi found that a compelling dream helped him work on medical experiments that resulted in his shared Nobel Prize for the discovery of acetylcholine, a neurotransmitter that activates muscles; in an odd coincidence, acetylcholine is involved in dreaming![8]

Another Nobel Prize–winning scientist, Danish physicist Niels Bohr, worked on a quantum theory question involving the placement of atoms and electrons in his dream about horses in a race. When he awoke, he quickly sketched the theory that he received via dreamtime on the back of an envelope. And as unbelievable as it seems, in his later life the genius Albert Einstein told about discovering the theory of relativity from an adolescent dream of speeding down a hill on a sled! Einstein told the journalist Edwin Newman: "My entire scientific career has been a meditation on that dream."[9] Salvador Dali, Max Ernst, and Rene Magitte all benefited from dream images for their paintings.[10] Perhaps all dream fragments carry clever messages, but we frequently miss out because we have no recall. The Jewish Talmud advises: "A dream which is not interpreted is like a letter which is not read."

DREAM-WISE

I have not received any prizes or made any scientific discoveries from my own night dreams, but I do find many kernels of creativity and truth in them. My clinical as well as personal experience shows that dreams about a loved one who has died are one way to acclimate your personality beyond loss and find meaning for current living. Here is a dream that I had after my husband's sudden heart attack:

A Snapshot of Emotional Gravity (my title after reviewing this dream):

Our family's dentist was helping our family put together a photography collage. … We had a color picture that had my husband in it, but we cut out my husband's picture. There was a second photo, a black-and-white photo, picturing me alone with our children. We put the two photographs in some kind of clear liquid, some solution. Then we put the color cutout picture of my husband at the top (standing behind) our black-and-white photo. I remember asking in the dream, "Why is my husband in color when the three of us (in our family) are in black-and-white?" (The scene shifts.) My husband, our daughter (who appeared much younger than her actual age), and I were in the dentist office for dental exams. I went first. Our daughter was playing outside on the sidewalk with other children. When it was my husband's turn, he got in the chair and I went off to check on the kids playing. In a short time, my husband and the dentist came outside. My husband said he had changed his mind. He wasn't going to get his teeth fixed today. I said to myself (in the dream), "He's going to put it off because he knows he's only got two weeks to live." We went to some restaurant (where the dentist also went, but sat at a different table) to join some other people for a long lunch.

Upon waking, I realized immediately that the dentist and my daughter were in this dream together because my daughter had reminded me the day before that our family dentist had asked her to purchase her college logo coffee mug for his collection. Is the word *collage* a stand-in for "college?" Is the dentist going to a restaurant to drink coffee in a mug? Dreams have word games! Also, I recently had frustrating thoughts about my husband not finishing some extensive dental work; he had said that he wanted to avoid dental work "at all costs." However, these two dental themes took on a circuitous route dream-wise. Memory consolidation that takes place in REM sleep takes curious *turns*.

Dreams are mystery short stories. Every dream reader is hooked by certain details. I pondered how my husband, standing apart from his color photo, rejoins his family in a second photo. Upon waking, I sketched a picture of this cutout-reconfigured foursome because it was such a strong dream image. In one view, the dream seems to highlight the rugged individualist personality of my husband ("cut from his own cloth"). Then there is the poignant message about having only two weeks to live. Yes, death is inevitable. How many weeks do any of us have left? Sudden death in midlife is scary. More musings led me to ask questions: What can the black-and-white lives do without the colorful one who always had our backs, and served as a backbone for many of his employees? And where is the colorful one without his devoted tribe, his family trio?

My answers to myself are again musings, as dream interpretation is in the eye of the beholder. I thought about all of the backbone people in the world. Ancestors pave a way forward for children and grandchildren. Fortunately, my children had an active experience with their loving father, as so many children grow up today without a positive father role model. However, I wondered why the living people were in a monochrome photo and the one who died was in color. One part of me asked about an afterlife. Another part considered that color is a sign of a summer-to-autumn garden where plants grow and then die, while black-and-white is like a winter dormant garden where much growth is expected from the rooted plants in later seasons. Those of us who are alive can expect much growth from ourselves in later seasons.

I had more questions than answers, just like in most of my waking hours. Nothing seemed clear in the dream, especially that *clear* liquid. The meaning of "some solution" sometimes eludes me. What are the solutions to grieving a significant loss? The best solution that I have found is to live more in pres-ent moments, to focus my attention with clear intentions. Someone leaves, yet rejoins loved ones. On the whole, or "hole" from the cutaway picture, this dream appeared circular to me. This prompted more far-out questions: Why do planets and stars end up appearing as circles? Gravity holding them was my answer to myself. Then I mused on the notion that there is an invisible yet *clear* form of *emotional gravity* that holds people close. Perhaps this emotional gravitational pull is magnetic? Isn't this nature? Scottish-American environmentalist John Muir advised, "When we try to pick out anything by itself, we find it hitched to everything else in the universe."

I read about magnetic attraction and dying stars on the Internet. Magnetic force is complicated. Families are complicated. I found that a dying star is called a red giant – this is very colorful! It was reassuring to find that our Sun is considered a middle-aged star and probably will not die for another five billion years. Does the death of a person have any characteristics of a dying star? What happens to a family's emotional gravity after the death of a member? My next thoughts raced to review a recent therapy session from my private practice with a widow coping with the death of her husband. Fifty-year-old Collette experienced a feeling of dread *prior* to her husband's death; she had a recurrent dream that she and her husband were at the ocean and a tidal wave was coming. Her dream included her fear of what would happen to her children. Soon after this, her husband died and her children got into terrible fights. Some families pull together after a family member dies, but other families are ripped apart. Sometimes family members stop talking to one another. Magnetism "can either pull two objects together or push them apart."[11] This describes the nature of families.

SLEEPWALKING AND DISTURBING DREAMS

Psychologist Carl Jung's opinion of dreams is fascinating: "Personal opinions are more or less arbitrary judgments and may be all wrong; we are never sure of being right. Therefore we should seek the facts provided by dreams. Dreams are objective facts. They do not answer our expectations."[12] Try to tell these statements to an overtired family member of someone who is a poor sleeper! Many people have interrupted sleep/dream patterns. Most people dismiss their dreams even if they recall a fragment or two. Dreams are in the woo-woo camp for many individuals because they have not received any education about the necessity and value of dreaming. According to researcher Hobson, there are many myths about dreams. For example, sleepwalkers do not enact their dreams when they sleepwalk, and it is not dangerous to wake up a sleepwalker.[13] Anyone who has sleep disturbances can take part in a sleep study to learn the facts about their sleep patterns and what they might do to obtain a good night's rest. Most midlife adults are short on sleep because worry keeps them from falling asleep with ease, or they stay up too late. Family members affect sleeping patterns as well, as in having a snoring partner, or experiencing children and/or grandchildren who awaken too often in the night. Some individuals experience bad dreams or nightmares. There are a number of different causes of scary dreams. It is possible that a nightmare can be triggered by late-night eating which increases metabolism and sends a message to your brain to be more active. Also, nightmares can exist due to side effects of several medications. Withdrawal from alcohol can cause nightmares. Sleep deprivation, as well as sleep apnea and restless leg syndrome, may contribute to nightmares. Anxiety, stress, clinical depression, and posttraumatic stress disorder (PTSD) are other factors.[14] Surgeon and writer Atul Gawande experienced recurring nightmares as a young physician when his patients died; patient corpses seemed as if they were in his own bed. He felt responsible for their deaths. In dreamlife, he tried to haul bodies back to the hospital without anyone noticing, but he found it impossible to find their rooms. Someone would shout "Hey!" and start chasing him before he awakened feeling clammy.[15] Gawande admits that his medical training did not prepare him to handle patient losses.

Neurologist Oliver Sacks explained the origin of the word nightmare as relating to a mythological demon, the mare, who suffocated sleepers by lying upon their chests. Sacks pointed out that some cultures are so fearful of nightmares causing death that individuals have been known to die in their sleep when they had no apparent health issues. Sacks cited over 200 nighttime deaths in a group of Hmong refugees from Laos who immigrated to California and were unable to continue certain religious rituals during their relocation.[16] However, there are interventions for nightmares. One intervention, Imagery Rehearsal Therapy, uses a rescripting method to calm an individual after a nightmare. In a research study, chronic nightmare sufferers participated in four group training sessions. After eight hours of training, the participants were assessed in a three-month follow-up. Overall sleep quality improved in participants and the number of nightmares decreased. In this cognitive-imagery method, the dreamer tells or writes their nightmare. Then a new dream script is imagined, as in a structured daydream. With a positive twist to the previously scary dream, the person rehearses their new dream version.[17] Night terrors are different from nightmares. Night terrors are frightening episodes where an individual may experience intense crying and sweating, but not be fully awake. They occur about 90 minutes after going to sleep and are more frequent in children than adults.[18]

Whatever you experienced in the past about dreaming, take an interest in your current dreams and see what you might discover. Your dreams about loss, whether they refer to the death of a job, marriage, or person, may help you in your grieving process. There are several types of grief dreams.

Visitation dreams bring the deceased loved one into some contact with you, perhaps recalling a memory. Often these dreams bring a sense of comfort. *Message* dreams bring some kind of important information or even a warning, as in instructing you to take better care of your health. In *reassurance* dreams, you may sense that the deceased gives you an affirming message that they are OK and you are OK, like the dreams Donna had about her deceased parents.

Realistically, many dreams have reassurance about the deceased person being OK, but often it is the dreamer who has questions about being OK. Carl Jung had a dream about his deceased father six weeks after the death: "Suddenly he stood before me and said that he was coming back from his holiday. He had made a good recovery and was now coming home. I thought he would be annoyed with me for having moved into his room. But not a bit of it! Nevertheless, I felt ashamed because I had imagined he was dead." Two days later, Jung had the very same dream and he was puzzled: "I kept asking myself, 'What does it mean that my father returns in dreams and that he seems so real?'" Jung claimed that this dream prompted him to think about life after death for the first time.[19]

While it is less frequent, the *trauma* dream often follows tragic deaths (murders, suicides, and accidents),[20] as in Lucinda's disturbing dream after her father's violent death. Jungian therapist and dream-work trainer Jeremy Taylor believes, "No matter how it appears, death is always associated with the growth and development of [the dreamer's] personality and character."[21] He views death in dreams as symbolic of old attitudes dying so that there is a renewal into a richer and deeper life. When you can reach a sense of acceptance that change is an ongoing part of your life, you are open to new experiences.

Other cultures treat dreams as extremely important. In the Amazon rainforest of Ecuador, the Achuar people place so much meaning in their dreams that they rise each morning at 4:00 AM before sunrise to share their dreams with others. They review their dreams before making important decisions. Dreams are interpreted by either their community leader or a spiritual healer (shaman). Some of the Achuar dreams have been *message* dreams of imminent threat to their environment. For example, after dreaming about the demise of their homeland, neighboring tribes informed the Achuar community that oil companies were moving into the territory and were destroying the rainforest. To the Achuar, the rainforest is their hardware store, pharmacy, clothing store, food store, and home improvement store.[22] The Amazon indigenous people treasure dreamlife.

TURN TIP

"That's the effect of living backwards," the Queen said kindly. ...
"Living backwards!" Alice repeated in great astonishment. "I never

heard of such a thing! "But there's one great advantage in it, that one's memory works both ways." "I'm sure MINE only works one way," Alice remarked. "I can't remember things before they happen." "It's a poor sort of memory that only works backwards," the Queen remarked.

– Lewis Carroll, English writer, *Through the Looking Glass*

The first step to finding any treasure in night dreams is to remember them. Initially, this may not seem easy, as all of us tend to forget our dreams unless we are interested in pursuing dream wisdom, or if nightmares scare us into waking.

Here are tips for remembering dreams:

- Set an *intention* to recall your dreams. Since dream memory is a creative act, you will remember more dreams if you have curiosity about dreaming.
- Be open to record/explore dreams in visual, verbal, auditory, tactile, and kinesthetic senses. For example, drawing a sketch of one dream image upon waking increases your ability to remember/understand a dream. Your waking life experiences trigger your dreams, but details from the past slip and slide into dreams too.
- Prepare your method for retaining dream stories. Recording dreams is as simple as having pen and paper at your bedside. You may have more dream memory if you first review your dream *without moving* before sitting upright to write anything.
- Remind yourself as you go to sleep that you have set your *intention* to recall/comprehend a dream. Also, getting enough sleep is important in dream retention. Taylor suggests that mindful exercises such as prayer, meditation, contemplation, and yoga may help you focus on your *intention* to recall nighttime dreams.[23] Delaney suggests that you consider becoming a dream self-interviewer rather than an interpreter. She also suggests writing a short, focused question before you go to sleep if you want to resolve some issue in your life. She advises that repeating the brief question after getting into bed (and just before sleeping) can increase your opportunity for dream recall.[24]

LUCID DREAMING

It is possible for you to experience lucid dreaming where you become conscious that you are in a dream while the dream is happening. Again, setting an *intention* is an entry point. With practice you can increase your ability to awaken mid-dream and encounter this fascinating dream experience. In a nightmare, this lucid moment can take the form of questioning a hostile image: "What are you doing here in this dream? What do you want?" Instead of waking up with fear after a nightmare, you may stumble upon insights for your life.[25] As poet Elias Canetti suggests, your dreams can remind you to recall important details in life: "All the things one has forgotten scream for help in dreams." There are many benefits to lucid dreaming. You may receive inspiration or a solution to a vexing problem. You may relieve some anxiety or fear. In lucid dreaming, you find another way to connect with ignored parts of your personality that may be hidden from your awareness.

While the science of dreaming may be new, dreams have a long history. Nearly all major religions have believed that dreams contain omens or guidance. Ancient Greek myths held the notion that dreams contained visions given to them by the gods. The early Muslims believed dream interpretation was a part of their religious discipline.[26] Hindus and Buddhists treat lucid dreams as part of their spiritual practice. Some Buddhist sects view the mid-dream awakening experience as a path to enlightenment. One understanding of the term, enlightenment, is *habitual intuition*. Christian interpretations view nighttime dreaming as having spiritual messages also. Dream-work trainer Taylor points out that Eastern cultures, as well as the Plains Indians of North America, have embraced lucid dreaming for more than nine hundred years. A Native American understanding of dreaming connects dreams to death in this manner: "To die is to walk the path of the dream without returning." Whatever your particular beliefs are about religion, Taylor is correct that the experience of nighttime dreaming "holds the promise of changing one's relation to death itself." Some have referred to sleep as "a little death."[27] This French phrase, *le petit morte*, also is used to describe the physiology of an orgasm!

SLEEP'S "LITTLE DEATH" INTERPRETATIONS

There are many different theories about dream interpretation, but you are your own best guide in understanding your own cryptic dream images. As you can see by a variety of cultures and ethnic groups paying attention to dreaming, interpreting dreams is an ancient practice rather than a new-age practice. For example, there are 21 dreams recorded in the Bible; 11 of them appear in the book of Genesis and, of these, 6 of the dreamers are kings.[28] Like the Achuar people of Ecuador, Pharaoh has a dream of impending doom in the environment. When Pharaoh cannot interpret his troubling dream, he receives a helpful interpretation of survival from a common young man, Joseph, in Genesis 41:

> "In my dream I was standing on the banks of the Nile; and seven cows, fat and
> sleek, came up out of the Nile and fed in the reed grass; and seven other cows

came up after them, poor and very gaunt and thin, such as I have never seen in all the land of Egypt. And the thin and gaunt cows ate up the first seven fat cows, but when they had eaten them no one would have known that they had eaten them, for they were still as gaunt as at the beginning. Then I awoke. I also saw in my dream seven ears growing on one stalk, full and good; and seven ears, withered, thin and blighted by the east wind, sprouted after them, and the thin ears swallowed up the seven good ears. And I told it to the magicians, but there was no one who could explain it to me. ..." After asking many people, Pharaoh hears about Joseph who had interpreted others' dreams. Joseph was handsomely rewarded for interpreting Pharaoh's dream, as he was put in charge of stockpiling food in Egypt for his prediction of a coming seven year famine.[29]

Dream predictions for the future are not so uncanny once you consider how dreams lack time and space parameters. Remember all those famous dreamers who found discoveries in unlikely dream stories that were just what they needed to advance their work? Psychologist Delaney cites that many of her clients in the careers of law, business, mathematics, architecture, writing, and the arts have tapped their dream creativity for product development through the ideas generated in nighttime dreams. She finds that dreaming is not defensive like much daytime thinking, so a person is much freer to see problems and challenges objectively. Her findings support Jung's concept of the objectivity of your dreams. Delaney also emphasizes that you do not need a psychotherapist to interpret your dreams.[30] She encourages people to pretend that they are from another planet when they interview themselves about their own dreams!

Turn up the volume on your nighttime dreams and tune in more frequently to see what your brain distilled while you rested. Not only will you find creativity and surprises in *le petite morte*, but you may discover how nighttime dreams can help you to cope with loss. Yes, there really is a committee of sleep that works the night shift to resolve issues from the day shift.

YOUR TURN

Each of our sub-personalities tends to speak in a different and unique voice in the midst of sleep.

– Jeremy P. Taylor, Jungian dream-work trainer

Record dreams in a dream journal as soon after waking as possible. Use first person and present tense, and write your dream as if you are reexperiencing it. At a later time, you can return to the questions below. Give your dream a catchy title if you wish. The following outline is an adaptation of dream expert Robert Hoss' dream interview process.[31] Notice that there are no set symbols for dream objects. Your associations to your own dream are what matters. Do not feel compelled to answer each question. Consider your dreams as maps; use only the roads – aspects of the outline –that further your understanding.

1. **Look for metaphors in the dream story.**
   See if there are phrases that relate to any current situations in your life. Underline special phrases and descriptive words.
2. **Work on a dream image in layers.**
   Choose one or more dream images that seem important, curious, or emotionally significant. Let the image have a voice. You might speak from the point of view of the dream image. Ask the following questions and record your statements:
   • Who or what are you? Describe yourself and your feeling.
   • If the dream character is someone you know, then describe that person as the speaker.
   • In what ways are you like the dreamer? In what ways are you different?
   • What is your purpose or function?
   • What do you like about being that dream image?
   • What do you dislike about being that dream image?
   • What do you fear most as that dream element?
   • What do you desire most as that dream element?
3. **Relate your dream to a life situation.**
   Do the "I am" and "My purpose" statements sound like a role or part of your personality that you play in waking life? Do the "I like" versus "I dislike" statements sound like a conflict between personality roles? Do the "I fear" and "I desire" statements sound like waking life fears and desires?
   Or, if the dream character is a person you know, do one or more of his or her statements relate to current ways in which you approach a waking life situation? Alternatively, does this dream character have a personality role that you admire, or wish you had more of, in order to handle a waking life situation?
4. **Look for color in your dream.**
   What associations do any of the specific color images trigger for you? What new perspectives does color add?
5. **Consider a unifying or transformative message.**
   Relate the dream now as pertaining to your waking life story. Write a brief summary in your *Turn* Journal to help you grasp the dream's message.

Taylor believes, "Dreams always … reveal new information and promote health and wholeness through further development." He wonders about people only using self-interpretation, as they may not search for insights beyond what they already know. On the other hand, a dream group's interpretations have the pitfall of others' projections of their own personalities onto your dream. While it is useful to hear another's point of view, you want them to begin any of their dream observations with the phrase, "If it were my dream … ."[32] The value of mapping your own dreams is that you know your prior experiences and what is on your mind currently. As poet Adrienne Rich describes in her poem, *Diving into the Wreck*, "I have to learn alone to *turn* my body without force in the deep element. … The words are maps." With practice, you can find treasure embedded within your dream maps. After all, who would have been capable of telling young Albert Einstein about the theory of relativity from his sledding dream map?

Part II

"... WITH WHAT SHALL I FIX IT?"

"Fixing" your life after loss can feel as though you are lost in a maze. Which direction will take you to recovery? Perhaps your personality roles do not agree on how to fix the loss hole in your bucket. Drop a fixed mind-set. Create a growth mind-set.

A good solution solves more than one problem,
and it does not make new problems.

— Wendell Berry, novelist and environmental activist,
Solving for Pattern

Chapter 4

Celebrating Needs

I like living. I have sometimes been wildly, despairingly,
  acutely miserable, racked with sorrow, but through it all
I still know quite certainly that just to be alive is a grand thing.

> – Agatha Christie, English crime novelist

Gather yourselves. Banish the word struggle from your attitude
  and vocabulary.
All that we do now must be done in a sacred manner and in
  celebration. For we are the ones we have been waiting for.

> – Elders of the Hopi Nation

Middle-age adults handle their basic needs in habitual ways, whether these habits are healthy or not. The old saying about "creatures of habit" is true. Equally true is the idea that you take your everyday habits for granted. Often, you are not very aware of your habits. As British writer Samuel Johnson pointed out, "The chains of habit are too weak to be felt until they are too strong to be broken." For example, Lamar described having a hole in his gut whenever he thought about his father. Lamar harbored painful memories from his childhood. His father drank too much and showed erratic behaviors when he came home late from a bar. Lamar stuffed himself with sweets from an early age, as if he could fill up the empty attachment hole he felt in his stomach. When his overeating caused stomachaches in terms of weight gain and teasing from classmates, Lamar substituted one habit for another. He began overdrinking as he moved into adulthood. By the time Lamar reached midlife, his father had died of a heart attack and his own alcoholism cost him his job.

A big question in relieving grief in your life is, "How can I heal myself?" Another way of asking this question is, "Where is *wholeness* to be found when it feels like there is a hole inside of me?" No one expects loss in midlife, but there are losses that hurdle their way into your life like unexpected asteroids barreling down into craters or holes on earth. The hole created by your loss can interfere with your capacity to meet your basic needs. Your personality is a tool chest for "fixing" yourself, but you may not feel as though your tools are effective in dealing with a crater of loss. Some resist grieving because they find many feelings too disturbing. Psychotherapist Alexandra Kennedy explains that the grieving process may seem abnormal, or perhaps you fear that you will make your friends uncomfortable with your grieving behavior: "Since we live in a culture that expects quick fixes and avoids pain, there is a tendency to pull oneself out of grief prematurely."[1]

EMOTIONS AS ENERGY PERCEPTIONS

When loss hits home, you may not feel capable of finding any space for self-reflection as you muddle through such common questions as, "What just happened? Why did this have to happen?" You may feel sick to your stomach like Lamar, or experience some other somatic complaint. Emotional roles pop up when you least expect them, and often in a physical sense. Science backs up the idea of emotional bodies. In fact, neuroscientist Antonio Damasio explains how your emotions, as complex thoughts or energy perceptions, are key to your survival by signaling your body to respond in certain ways. Your body talks all the time! For example, you do not hyperventilate because you are fearful – you feel scared because of the hyperventilating sensations that circulate through your body.[2] Self-awareness is necessary to meet your ongoing and recycling need transitions daily. If you lack enough self-awareness, your day-to-day actions/reactions can seem random or haphazard, as if you have no idea of what to expect from yourself. While you keep replaying some of the same thoughts over and over in your mind, you probably have one or more basic needs that remain unmet.

Sheila was 51 when her younger brother died. She did not know of any illness he may have had; the death seemed surreal to her. For days she tried to convince herself that the news was untrue. Then, the unhappy details in her own life surfaced like rising floodwaters, washing over her already-raw emotions. Every loss that she had experienced previously begged for some kind of acknowledgment. There was the rape when she was a teenager, the loss of a much-loved pet, and a too-soon marriage that ended in divorce. She finally sought psychotherapy when she realized that her current marriage was at a breaking point. Her husband was absent a lot. Later, she found out that he was having an affair. Sheila admitted to me, "It took me two years to accept the fact that my brother was gone." Her energy level was tied to a standstill post. Most of her basic needs had remained unmet for years.

Unmet needs can result in your day filling up with apathy, the "blues" or depression, conformity, disorder, and even a sense of ennui or listlessness.[3] Not only is there little space for self-reflection in such confusion and disorganization, but you do not have much energy for the tasks of daily living. Imagine the everyday occurrence where you meet one basic need, only to find that the next need follows immediately. Think of a waterfall. I watched in wonder as I witnessed one waterfall after another from a train window in beautiful Norway. There seemingly was no end to those tiny water droplets. They just kept coming. In fact, everyone's basic needs seem like a gushing waterfall that just keeps cascading, spilling one need after another, especially when you live with other people and have *their* needs to consider along with your own. Basic needs do not disappear when you are grieving, but they may appear as different from your preloss functioning. For example, your appetite may shrivel, your discipline for basic exercise may wither, and your creativity may wilt. You still need to eat nutritious food, exercise your body, and latch onto creativity somewhere in your life. In fact, it is more important than ever before that you meet your basic needs now. Your health is on the line.

FIVE BASIC NEEDS

The ideal situation is where midlifers develop generative skills to meet not only their own basic needs, but also are in a position to assist family members, clients, and/or coworkers in meeting basic needs as well. *Everyone has certain basic or survival needs – energy, discipline, creativity, belonging, and ability needs.* When you are conscious in daytime, your energy needs (food, sleep, exercise, and sexual needs) and discipline needs (a few positive habits to organize your day) mingle in your mind – or perhaps not. If you are a parent, child needs may bombard you first. You may not have the luxury of meeting some of your own energy needs if a crying baby's (or grandbaby's) energy needs reach your ears before a clock arouses you. For the caregiver who gains energy by early morning jogging, a baby's exercising lungs demand a detour from the first-I-run scenario. A you-better-feed-me message is the alarm clock in many families and calls for a caretaker's discipline to know (and have in the house) what to feed a child for nutrition at a particular age. Meeting energy and discipline needs calls for adults who can organize the first tasks of helping family members eat a nutritious breakfast and move on to school, work, home, and/or community commitments. Actually, your basic energy and discipline needs require a good night's sleep the night before to ensure that the next morning's needs have a reasonable chance of being met.

Moving onward, you have more basic needs for your day to run in a productive path with creativity and ability needs, and for you to feel connected – through belonging needs – with others. Midlife adults constantly contend with basic needs; their own, family members', friends', and coworkers' needs all clamor for attention. The waterfall of needs just keeps cascading. Adults encounter needs all day long. Rather than seeing needs as a burden, the generative adult employs creative problem solving to find ever-new ways to meet needs skillfully. You must set aside times to engage in creativity, belonging, and ability activities of your choosing. However, acknowledging your creativity needs often takes last place even in good times. We will address creativity in chapter 8, but start thinking now about ways that you can meet this need today. What is your most joyful creative play experience from childhood? What is your most joyful creative play experience from midlife? Do not miss out on one of the most joyful experiences you might have in a given day. Creativity knows no bounds. Each person defines creativity in unique ways.

Midlife adults experience trouble meeting their belonging and ability needs also. Successful writer Sarah Ban Breathnach wrote a *New York Times* best seller, *Simple Abundance*, and became a multimillionaire almost immediately. However, when bad business investments, a bad economy, and a divorce hit home, her good fortune dried up as quickly as it had arrived on her doorstep. At the age of 61, Ban Breathnach lost her home and had to move in with her sister. It was then that she focused upon meeting her basic needs. She wrote a new book and put her attention onto everyday choices. Ban Breathnach discovered how the meaning of the word "thrift" meant the condition of one who thrives.[4] Her renewal advice applies to all: "It doesn't matter whom you love or where you move from or to, you always take yourself with you. If you don't know who you are, or if you've forgotten or misplaced her, then you'll always feel as if you don't belong. Anywhere."[5] After a significant loss, your main task is to discover for yourself the particular conditions that allow *you* to thrive and meet not only basic needs, but to have some energy left over to make a new bucket list.

It takes thoughtful and creative planning to fulfill your ability potential along the trail of needs. While all of us possess the same basic needs, we approach them in very different ways. Young children frequently require adult help to meet needs. Your ongoing task as a parent, teacher, or coach requires that you model how youth can learn to meet their own needs successfully as they grow. This modeling role challenges even the best caretakers and those who do not experience any significant loss in midlife. Realistically, most adults desire some amount of modeling and companionship in meeting their own basic needs. In healthy families, the members keep learning positive and interactive ways to meet family members' needs every day. Children help parents and grandparents meet basic needs by reminding them that everyone requires daily exercise. "Grandma, can you do a cartwheel?" asks 10-year-old Nisha. In all of her 59 years, Grandma Joycie has never performed a cartwheel, but that fact does not interfere with her creative response: "Honey, when I was your age, I pushed many carts with wheels in the garden!" Both Nisha and Joycie learn something from their banter! Joycie later chuckles about her humor with her granddaughter, but she admits that she does not even push a lawnmower these days. She decides to start walking for daily exercise.

There are complex interactions among family members along the trail of needs. When loss enters your home, it can become a huge challenge to meet any basic needs. Jeff was 39 when his wife announced that she had met someone new; she said she was "sleeping with someone." This revelation sent Jeff into such a tailspin that he did not believe that he would ever recover. He considered suicide. He barely ate food, and when he did eat, he stuffed himself with so much junk food that he felt sick to his stomach. Sleep eluded him unless he took sleeping pills. He tried prescription medications, self-medicating with 12-packs of beer every weekend, and marijuana whenever he could make the purchase. The result was only more anger and depression. His buddies talked roughly about his spouse, but Jeff could not shake the fact that he still loved her. The reality is that your heart may not split up along with the breakup. When you care deeply about someone, there is a death of a dream that you once held, but your love can still feel attached.

You know the common phrase, "Time heals all wounds." Rose Kennedy, mother of two assassinated sons – President Kennedy and Bobby Kennedy – also lost her eldest son to war. Who can imagine losing three sons? In addition, Rose Kennedy endured the marital unfaithfulness of her husband and having a mentally disabled daughter. Her version of the old adage may be closer to your thoughts: "It has been said, 'time heals all wounds.' I do not agree. The wounds remain. In time, the mind, protecting its sanity, covers them with scar tissue and the pain lessens. But it is never gone."[6] Yes, you will retain memories of the losses in your life, but it is possible to change how you think about loss. In fact, changing your thoughts is a type of brain training. As your brain communicates with the rest of your body, actual changes in what you believe can affect how your DNA is expressed. "Studies have even shown that environmental factors can override certain genetic mutations. ... These altered genes can then be passed down to offspring, allowing the offspring to express healthier characteristics, even though they still carry the genetic mutation."[7] My version of the old adage is this one: time helps in healing when you have a growth mind-set.

THE EMOTIONAL MULTITUDE

Every individual has times of having a fixed mind-set, but, hopefully, every-one also has the awareness to engage life with growth mind-set roles in his or her personality. In Walt Whitman's *Song of Myself*, the poetic truth of your varying emotional roles is captured: "Do I contradict myself? Very well then I contradict myself. I am large, I contain multitudes." It is possible to retool your personality and *turn* your life toward a positive direction after loss. My experience of how this happens is to make the conscious choice to become more self-aware. Allow your sadness. Allow anger and fearful roles. But also realize that you can embrace happiness. You are allowed to be *present* to meeting your own basic needs.

Sometimes people merge so completely with a spouse that they no longer view themselves as a separate functioning individual. Nine months after his marital separation, Jeff told me that he was surprised to find that he could be happy: "It's strange, but in a way I almost feel like I stopped really living when I got married. ... I'm starting to feel more alive than ever. ... I can just be me. I don't have to prove anything to anybody about who I am spiritually ... a sensitive, caring person. I can let people know who I am. I don't have to apolo-gize for being me. I'm O.K." When you feel OK about yourself, you have a bet-ter chance of meeting all five basic needs along the trails of the midlife maze.

You can easily remember the five needs as E, D, C, B, A, or the ABCDEs in reverse order. While the needs are listed in a linear fashion to help you remember them, energy, discipline, creativity, belonging, and ability needs sidetrack and revolve in varying ways for each midlifer. All five needs relate to your most basic of needs, your instinctual need for survival. Each survival need intersects with other needs, both within a person and among family members. For example, obtaining enough nutrition and sleep energy affects how well you use your ability each day. A child's energy levels intertwine with a caretaker's energy levels; a partner's energy collapse or ennui affects everyone around her or him. Your colleagues can either energize you or drain you on a given day. As you become better able to notice and name the mul-titude of feeling states that may zigzag in your environment, you can make conscious choices about which ones you will meet next.

You likely handle some of your energy needs in ways that are reminiscent of your family of origin. Consider 50-year-old Terrance's youth; mealtimes were hectic and most food in his home had a high fat content. A mixture of anxiety and poor nutrition continued to follow him like a stalker, as if his daily habits had underground roots. While he tried a variety of diets, each time he gave up after a brief trial. "I just don't like the taste of foods that are not salty or sweet," he complained. Terrance was fearful that he was about to be fired from his job. His car passed a donut shop on the way to work each weekday. He arrived at work early, stuffing negative emotions and several iced donuts under his belt before the boss arrived.

APPROACH DISCIPLINE VERSUS AVOIDANCE DISORDER

The strategies you use to cope with loss, or even your perception of a coming loss, are covered under two umbrellas – avoidance practices versus approach practices.[8] Avoidance tactics initially may prove useful to you, as they give you an opportunity for recovery and adaptation after a loss. You can reflect upon what your loss has changed in your life and what this may mean for your future. This rest period can be a necessary step while you gather energy for making something new come into your life. The down side of avoidance is that unresolved grieving may take you into ennui or listlessness, disorder, conformity, and even a sense of the "blues" and total apathy. Does this sound like where you see yourself now? When you are unable to meet five basic needs (energy, discipline, creativity, belonging, and ability), you may plunge yourself into despair and find it difficult to drag yourself out of bed every morning. The discipline to set your alarm and get up at a reasonable morning time may elude you temporarily.

Your shift to approach strategies signifies that you have some positive energy; you are making a disciplined attempt to meet your basic needs (and helping with the basic needs of children if they are a part of your life). Approach actions involve flexibility and a growth mind-set. You may initiate new skills, meet new people, or connect to others with a deeper sense of belonging. You review what has happened to you and find meaning wherever possible. Perhaps you become interested in religious or spiritual traditions. You learn how meditation can alter your stress level. Perhaps you engage in psychotherapy, join a support group, or on your own, focus upon talking to yourself with resilience. Change just keeps rolling, along with the rotating seasons, so a sense of resilience will put you in a good place for future losses. Did I just put loss and future in the same sentence? Yes, I did. You want to focus on approaching life, not avoiding what life brings. In the afternoon of midlife, you know that other losses are coming.

You may ask, "How can I be resilient and have an approach-life-just-the-way-it-is philosophy when my loss is so tragic?" This is a very good question. One answer comes from the American Psychological Association (APA). The horror of September 11, 2001, had just occurred in New York City. People were reeling, including even those who did not have a personal acquaintance with someone who lost their life in the Twin Towers' disaster. APA staff formed focus groups in Los Angeles, Indianapolis, and Baltimore and found that many people in the groups reported having chronic levels of stress that predated 9/11. After that infamous date, these individuals were determined to find personal strength after their initial emotional impact. They did not seek only to cope with grieving, but they wanted to be resilient in life. This is the attitude of an "approach" skillset. Notice how an approach vision of life is the essence of a growth mind-set. APA gathered research to augment their focus group data and produced a brochure on resilience, as well as a documentary for TV: *Aftermath: The Road to Resilience.*[9]

- Resilient (from Latin *resilire, to leap back*) means to be able to recover readily, as from misfortune.[10]

   Sculptor Christopher Saucedo lost his younger brother, a firefighter who was a first responder for the north tower of the World Trade Center. It is hard to believe, but Saucedo faced later losses when his New Orleans home was flooded to the attic level during the levee breach in Hurricane Katrina. He then moved his family to New York City, seven feet above sea level, but the onslaught of Superstorm Sandy filled his Queens home with five feet of water. Saucedo *turn*ed to art to find resilience from his three incredible losses. He created memorials to 9/11 and Katrina victims with his creativity. Saucedo shifted from his usual sculpting materials of metal and wood. He created the ethereal *World Trade Center as a Cloud* papier-mâché art with a brilliant blue background, a remembrance of the beautiful blue sky on 9/11 before disaster struck. Saucedo's efforts are transformative and an inspiration to those who view his work.[11] As art therapist Pat Allen points out, "When we respond to 'great' art it is because the artist was able to express something we feel as a deep truth."[12] The ritual of art making can help you *turn* a corner in your grieving process, as well as help those who witness the art at a later time and with a different loss.

   Some grieving midlifers express their grieving by talking with others who have experienced loss. They find solace and understanding through the accepting conversations at Death Cafés. Participants meet with other adults who are willing to discuss death topics. A British web designer, Jon Underwood, calls himself a death entrepreneur. He wanted to have a forum for open conversations about death. Underwood patterned his nonprofit Death Café after an idea by a Swiss sociologist, Bernard Crettaz, who established pop-up *café mortels*. Underwood initially wanted to offer his meet-ups in London cafés, but he did not find a positive reception from restaurant owners. Instead, he began his death discussions in his own home and was assisted by his mother, Sue Barsky Reid, a psychotherapist. They served tea and cake in his basement while adults discussed death. After Underwood launched a website, Death Cafés were set up in many parts of the world.[13] Each café is led by a hospice worker, social worker, or another professional who has some experience with death topics. Caring witnesses help you move forward with your life after loss.

TURN TIP

My experience is what I agree to attend to. Only those items which I *notice* shape my mind.

– William James, psychologist, *The Principles of Psychology*

Finding a path of resilience will look different for you than it will for another person. What may work for another person in your family may not help you. For a short time you may need avoidance strategies. As Mary Oliver's sunflower poem indicates, *turn*ing your life into a celebration is not easy. Like Carl Jung, I found that working in my garden was part of my recovery from grieving losses. I studied to become a master gardener. I volunteer in many different settings to teach both children and adults about amazing plants and how they enrich our lives. You will find your own paths of resilience.

Here are some questions adapted from the APA brochure on resilience.[14] Write your answers in your *Turn* Journal and/or discuss them with a friend:

- What kinds of events in your life have been most challenging?
- How have those events typically affected you?
- Have you found it helpful to think of important people in your life when you are distressed?
- To whom have you reached out for support in working through a *turn*ing point?
- What have you learned about yourself and your interactions with others during difficult times?
- Has it been helpful for you to assist someone else going through a similar experience?
- Have you been able to *leap back* after encountering obstacles, and if so, how?
- What helped to make you feel more hopeful about the future?[15]

Your grieving process can *turn* into a source of self-knowledge.

IS THERE A HIERARCHY OF NEEDS?

Psychologist Abraham Maslow created a hierarchy of needs that he termed "basic" or "biological." Maslow likened these needs to the human need for salt or vitamin D: "Safety is a more ... pressing, more vital need than love. ...

And the need for food is usually stronger than either." You do not see safety listed as one of the present list of five basic needs, as *all* of these needs are about your protection or your sense of everyday health and safety. Survival is a concept important to all creatures, not just people. Maslow coined a concept he termed *self-actualization*: "Furthermore, all these basic needs may be considered to be simply steps along the path to general self-actualization, under which all basic needs can be subsumed." Maslow sought to solve "many value problems that philosophers ... struggled with ... for centuries," as he considered that his model of meeting needs encompassed "self-realization, integration, psychological health, individuation [a Jungian term meaning the process of becoming your own person, different from others] ... autonomy, creativity, and productivity ... [to become] fully human. ... But it is also true that the person himself does not know this."[16]

My list of five basic needs is a user-friendly version of what Maslow discussed in the 1960s with a few differences. Maslow viewed needs as a hierarchical list for you to meet *before* you achieve self-esteem (liking and respecting yourself) and, finally, self-actualization. Maslow's hierarchy includes the following: physiological needs (for food, water, rest, and sexual expression), safety needs (for security and freedom from fear), and belongingness/love needs (for affiliation.) Upon meeting these basic needs, Maslow believed you might next reach an esteem need (a sense of worth and respect.) The final pinnacles of personality development in Maslow's hierarchy are self-actualization, as well as an aesthetic need for beauty and creative expression.[17]

My experience, both as a psychologist and a lifetime observer of people, suggests that your basic needs intertwine in a variety of ways rather than follow a hierarchy. While it is helpful to have a way to remember the five basic needs by their E, D, C, B, and A labels, they actually do not follow a hierarchy. Rather, the needs intermingle all day. Each person meets his or her needs in unique timeframes and in various ways. For example, creativity does not deserve an endpoint on some hierarchy. Many individuals who are incredibly creative have not mastered Maslow's steps of safety, belongingness/love, and/or esteem. Also, my view of self-territory is different from Maslow's self-theory. I believe that it is the birthright of every person, not just a pinnacle reached only by some individuals.

Maslow's self-actualization concept is not very inclusive, since his list of self-actualized people presents a short list of famous individuals: Albert Einstein, Eleanor Roosevelt, Jane Addams, William James, Albert Schweitzer, Aldous Huxley, Benedict de Spinoza, Abraham Lincoln (in his last years!), and Thomas Jefferson. Maslow considered a second list of contemporaries for "partial cases," although their names were not given.[18] While the above-mentioned individuals were accomplished in various ways, there are many more people who have made amazing contributions, both locally as well as in a global sense. Actually, all midlifers have important lives. When "self-actualizers" are presented as a select group, Maslow made it clear that few could climb his hierarchy to the top rung. Notice how Maslow pictured only a few women as capable of the climb. His list is devoid of much diversity. My opinion is that we need psychological models that are inclusive, not exclusive.

YOUR TURN

There was only one thing that had an absolute value for each individual and it was just that original impulse, that internal heat, that feeling of one's self in one's own breast.

– Willa Cather, writer, *Alexander's Bridge*

To facilitate remembering five basic needs, trace your handprint on a piece of paper or in your *Turn* Journal. Native American tribes often painted a handprint on the side of a warrior's face or horse to symbolize human life; the handprint symbol was believed to channel energy to the wearer.[19] There are many petroglyphs or pictures carved into stone in the Southwest that show handprints. This ancient art goes back at least to 30,000 years ago in the Chauvet Cave in France (chapter 7).

- Label your thumbprint as *energy*. Your thumb is so important to your hand, and energy is so important to your entire life. As primates, thumbs that are opposable to the other fingers allow for grasping, holding, carrying, and throwing actions. Similarly, cultivating energy allows you to perform many important actions.
- Label your handprint index finger as *discipline*. Have you ever waved your pointer finger at anyone to signal them to stop doing something? Perhaps you received discipline from a caretaker's wagging index finger. An upward pointing index finger also stands for victory, or rating as number one, as in a sports competition. Make your meaning for discipline a positive one with an upward pointing index finger signaling a fine point or a positive way forward.
- An upraised middle finger in Western culture is sometimes called "flipping the bird," and sends an obscenity message to another person. When someone thinks you are not handling your car well enough on the road, he or she may "give you the finger!" Give the middle finger a makeover – label this finger as *creativity*. After all, it is your middle finger in collaboration with your energetic thumb that enables you to make music by finger snapping!

- It will not surprise you to label your ring finger as *belonging.* An ancient myth about the ring finger is that a vein, *vena amoris* (Latin for "vein of love"), runs from the heart to the ring finger! In the beginning of the eleventh century, Western culture endorsed the ring finger as the proper finger for wearing a wedding ring. When you wear a friendship, engagement, or wedding ring, you acknowledge your sense of belongingness.
- Last, but certainly not least, label your little finger as *ability.* This finger may be the smallest one, but your need to meet your ability potential is not a small matter. The pinky finger is the finger you use on your keyboard to hit the letter A. While it is not necessary to receive all A's in academic work in order to make use of your ability potential at a later time, it does signify that you had aptitude for certain academic work, studied hard, or perhaps had a special belonging relationship with your teacher.
- Now, *turn* your paper over. In the area of the palm of your handprint, label the palm as *self.* On your real hand you can curl all of your fingers inward; they touch the center of your symbolic self-territory. This exercise will help you remember E, D, C, B, A needs, as well as a centered self (chapter 11 further discusses self-territory).

Chapter 5

Rearranging Personality Roles

I welcome that first mistake. Because then I can shrug it off and keep smiling. Then I can get on with the performance and turn off that part of the mind that judges everything.

– Yo Yo Ma, violinst

Do one thing every day that scares you.

– Eleanor Roosevelt, First Lady

What starts out as a few nonverbal poses from your infant personality develops later into your personality tool chest of both verbalized roles and nonverbal poses. Preschool and kindergarten children gather powerful images that underlie their later sense of "who I am." My five-year-old client, Monice, grappled with her fear of the dark as she told me a pretend story about a puppy puppet. Monice danced the floppy puppet on her arm as she explained in her tiny voice how the brave puppy learned how to fall asleep and not be afraid: "Pretend like I'm making light coming out of her, 'cause she's going to disappear magically. ... She's going to form a different way. ... I have a really good feeling. ... She's already changing. ... We change all the time!" We sometimes learn our best lessons from paying attention to what comes out of the mouths of babes. Every person from school age to mature age can benefit from rearranging their personality roles when they discover that negative thoughts hold them hostage.

Business consultant William Bridges suggests that the transition or change times in your life can trip you. He defines transitions as predominately psychological. Many transitions involve grieving a loss. Bridges readily admits that transitions of job loss or demotion are notorious for catching people off guard, and organizations "lack a language for talking about it." To survive transitions and thrive, you have to let go of previous routines and perhaps part of your identity. This identity weeding process is not easy. Before reseeding a new beginning, there is often a lost-in-the-maze phase. Bridges calls this the *neutral zone*, a time when critical psychological rearrangements take place.[1] Especially when previous losses have not been addressed, the latest loss can leave you with a fear for your own safety. At the tender age of five, little Monice did not have a stockpile of losses. Change for adults is more complicated, as loss affects various roles of your personality in different ways. You may feel sadness, but anger takes over to protect you. It takes a while to realize Monice's perspective: "We change all the time!"

PERSONALITIES HAVE PLASTICITY

The "Big Five" traits of personality – conscientiousness, agreeableness, neuroticism, openness, and extraversion (CANOE) – are one definition of personality; they have linkages with your genetic heritage. The interaction of genetic and environmental input is a continuing debate.[2] There is evidence that these personality traits cross cultures.[3] At one time, it was believed that personality was set like plaster at the age of 30, but research findings show that some traits of personality have more plasticity than plaster in adulthood: "People changed less in Conscientiousness after age 30 than before age 30, but they clearly did not stop changing. … Agreeableness accelerated in the late 20's and continued to increase rapidly through the 30's before slowing down in the 40's." With advancing age, there is a slight decline in openness. Also, research results find differences for women and men in some traits. Women declined substantially in neuroticism (a pessimistic attitude characterized by anger, anxiety, and/or depression) throughout adulthood, while men declined to a lesser extent. Men increased slightly in extraversion with age, while women decreased slightly.[4] Change in personality is both ongoing and uneven.

The Pixar movie *Inside Out* is a delightful exploration of five emotional roles of personality – sadness, joy, anger, disgust, and fear/surprise. The clever story reaches both child and adult audiences. Memories are stored on "memory shelves" in "Headquarters." The most powerful memories power the "Islands of Personality." Cartoon emotions operate a brain control panel that is challenged by an ongoing stream of memories, thoughts, and emotions that often are at odds. The movie shows *all* emotional roles as normal and equal in value. The important message is that sadness and joy can learn to work together in healthy personality functioning.

Both the researchers and moviemakers suggest that personality traits/roles are influenced by your particular environment. As psychologist

Dan McAdams points out, it is your ongoing life stories where you " keep a particular narrative going" that influences your behavior.[5] Perhaps the plaster theory of personality held up more often when people worked at the same company for 50 years and collected a gold watch or set of matched luggage for loyalty. Today's academic and work role changes are more fluid. One university reports that their graduate school students often are over age 40.[6] Careers and education have plasticity today. For our purposes, personality includes the big five traits, but most midlifers use other wording to describe the variety of emotional roles they play out daily. And much of your personality functioning happens as you move in and out of opposite emotional roles without much *conscious* awareness. This may cause you to ask yourself, "Who was I yesterday when I made that comment?"

By naming roles, you calm your emotional circuitry in your brain. As psychiatrist Daniel Siegel recommends, "Name it to tame it!"[7] You become conscious of your behavior and understand your ever-moving emotional roles. One definition of the word "emotion" suggests consciousness, while a different dictionary implies that your emotions can arise without consciousness. Both definitions are useful as you may recognize certain emotions with consciousness, while other roles erupt without any conscious awareness:

- Emotion (from Latin *emovere; move out*) means an affective state of consciousness in which joy, sorrow, fear, hate, or the like is experienced[8] – a mental state that arises spontaneously rather than through conscious effort and is often accompanied by physiological changes.[9]
- Role (from Old French *rolle; roll of parchment, on which an actor's part was written*) means the part played by a person in a particular social setting, influenced by his or her expectation of what is appropriate.[10]

When you grasp the complexity of your own personality functioning, you are better able to cut yourself some slack when you say or do something that later seems out of character. Of course, this also applies to how you look at others' bodily actions and accompanying mental states too. Is there anyone you know who deserves a bit of slack from you?

Now you have a better understanding of plasticity in emotional roles. Consider the layers of loss endured by some individuals. For some, personality roles flow like water rushing through newly created rapids in a flooded river. We are composites of diverse personality roles constantly flowing – one moment we fill with joy. In the next moment despair or anger roles may flood our bodies. Consider the dual personality roles of Big Bird and Oscar the Grouch. The voice behind both Big Bird and Oscar for the past 45 years is that of 80-year-old Carroll Spinney. When he began his puppet work, Spinney did not make enough salary to pay for apartment rent. He slept on the couches of friends. Perhaps he did not sleep well and this gave him grouchy material! In any case, Spinney's easy *turn* from the irascible, negative Oscar to the lovable, sensitive Big Bird is just one example of how all of us have opposite roles in our personalities. Everyone has a version of Oscar and Big Bird roles. The question to ask yourself is, how large is the role you allow your Grouch versus your Lovebird? Which one guides your day-to-day functioning more of the time?

Naming parts or roles in your personality has a healing effect. When you can label that lost-in-the-maze part of you, you allow into consciousness a truth about yourself. You learn to hold the loss-related sad and depressed roles in yourself with compassion, knowing that they are only part of your personality, not all of you. Think about all of the times you have heard someone say, or perhaps you said to yourself, "I am depressed." A more accurate way of addressing yourself is to say, "The depressed role of me took over today." You have much more than sadness in your personality. It is easy to forget about having any joy in the storm of grieving. Austrian monk David Steindl-Rast reminds, "Joy is the happiness that doesn't depend on what happens. ... You can be unhappy, and yet joyful. We don't think of that. But there is a deep inner peace and joy in the midst of sadness." Label this inner joy as your birthright, a "real" self, or self-territory.

A "REAL" SELF

A major focus in your understanding of personality is to become aware of an inner self-territory that undergirds traits, roles, parts, subpersonalities, or whatever words are meaningful to you in describing the various aspects of your day-to-day personality functioning. Psychologist Abraham Maslow identified this inner aspect of personhood in this manner: "A real self: a firm identity; autonomy; uniqueness ... transcendence of self ... recovery of creativeness."[11] Like Monice's ever-ready imagination, adults also need creativity. Maslow was concerned about people misunderstanding the real self, as many seemed to confuse the word "self" with being "selfish." Nothing could be further from the truth. Also, a real self is not the same as having self-esteem. The esteem role in your personality is more of a rating scale: "It taps the extent to which a person is generally satisfied with his or her life, considers himself or herself worthy ... or alternatively, feels useless, desires more respect."[12] Your real self does not have ratings. It simply is present there for you without judgment.

In recalling significant stories about your past, perhaps you can identify with inner self-territory. Or, you may not have been aware that inside of you there exists a holder of wisdom, an inner source of well-being that does not leave when the going seems so tough. Everyone experiences times of feeling lost in mazelike uncertainty times. However, the holder or keeper of your stories is much like rooted ground that holds and sustains plants. Self-territory holds onto the experiencing of both affirming and challenging roles within your personality without judging them. Through balancing opposite roles in your personality, such as sadness and joy, you can realize a sense of personal balance as you trudge through muddy times. This is not being selfish. Another description of self-territory is all-encompassing compassion – having compassion not only for all emotional roles in your own personality, but having compassion for all the roles in others' personalities too. Like the territory of an underground root system streaming in several different directions, self-territory inside of you connects you to the self-territory of others.

A real self provides roots for your personality. There are many ways to describe self-territory, but dictionary definitions uncover the root definitions:

- Self (from Old English, *zelf*) means the uniting principle, as a soul, underlying all subjective experience and ... that which knows, remembers ... as contrasted with that known, remembered.

Some refer to this uniting self as soul:

- Soul (from Old English, *sawl; related to sea, fancied habitation of the soul*) means the spiritual part of man regarded in its moral aspect.[13]

    Perhaps our special linkage with water reflects our earliest lives in the sea territory of our mother's womb. All of us survive on a planet of water and land or territory. With the word territory, we initially conjure up images of land, turf, and borders or boundaries. A dictionary definition provides underlying root words:
- Territory (from Middle English, *terra; land*) means a field or sphere of action, thought; domain.[14]

A definition for self-territory therefore encompasses many layers: a uniting foundation underlying all your personal experience, a spiritual/moral aspect, and a keeper of memories. The sphere of self includes both action and thought, or territory.[15] "There are all kinds of evidence supporting the idea that insights, self-awareness, and self-knowledge may be interesting but they don't necessarily lead to constructive action. ... Change is really about action rather than reflection."[16] The word territory conveys both thought and action. Your focus on *turn*ing a corner takes both reflection and action.

Marriage/family therapist Dick Schwartz defines *self* as becoming aware of "a state of calm well-being and lightheartedness." His definition of the real self can answer the question, "Who is the reporter that witnesses the various parts or roles in your personality?" This aware and witnessing state is similar to what people describe when they meditate. Information about meditation techniques will follow in chapter 8, but taking a few deep breaths is an entry point for both self-territory and meditation. Schwartz' use of imagery with his clients uncovers self-leadership that can help them shift into self-compassion with their suffering. Schwartz further explains how a core or real self is both a compassionate witness and an expansive state of mind: "Quantum physics has demonstrated that light is both a particle and a wave. ... Likewise, the Self can at one time be in its expansive state when a person is meditating (fully differentiated from his or her parts) and then shift to being an individual with boundaries (a particle) when that person is trying to help the [personality] parts or deal with other people. It is the same Self but in different states."[17] Self-territory is both expansive as well as grounding.

Perhaps definitions of self-territory are better understood by a variety of words and visual images. Here are some of my definitions for self-territory, but feel free to add your own wording:

Fountain or source of wisdom
Place of solidarity
Vital essence
Anchor
Roots
Calm harbor
Peace of mind
Inner resilience
Sanctuary for solace
Experience of spaciousness
Lighthouse for the body/mind
Origin of possibility and potentiality
Sense of being awake in and aware of *this* moment
Aspect of listening to every one of your thoughts ever thought[18]

Taking several long, deep breaths may slow down your thinking enough to enter a calm state where you feel your heart pacing at a comfortable rate. Creating a drawing of a symbol for self-territory may help you realize that you can slow down your racing thoughts. Consider how AAA maps might show a star or circle to denote the state capital. You understand that the symbol serves as a marker, rather than an elaboration on the nature of the city. Any kind of art is a representation and open to interpretation.

PERSONALITY ROLE LINE UP

In addition to recognizing self-territory, your focus in moving forward in life must take your personality roles to heart. You can change your personality when you become conscious of how your various personality roles express your emotions, values, and personal stories. Schwartz suggests that your multidimensional personality parts act internally in sequences that are similar to or opposite of relationship patterns in your family.[19] You may copy a parent's or caretaker's personality roles without really thinking much about it. However, you also copy certain personality roles from caring partners, friends, and/or mentors. Or, perhaps you consciously avoid responding in a similar way to perceived problematic roles of a caretaker or partner. However you assemble your personality, these emotional roles help and/or hinder you in meeting your basic needs every day.

Sometimes called subpersonalities, your various personality roles assist you in daily living: "Whenever these 'subpersonalities' are actively playing their different roles, each of them may have some control over different sets of goals and skills – so that each has a somewhat different Way to Think."[20] Each day brings new opportunities for you to find out more about your personality role line up and how certain roles perform. These personality roles represent "whole mental states. ... Any brief description of it can capture just a few aspects of it."[21] For example, your socializing can take the opposite roles of confident or shy in different situations. Perhaps you *turn* down the shy dial at work, but it surfaces at the weekend neighborhood barbeque. Of course, the reverse could be true for another person.

You create personal maps daily to meet your basic needs without realizing it. This book makes personality mapping a conscious act. Drawing a personality map can aid you in understanding your current growth pains. A map offers concrete directions for change by providing a simple mirror of who you are at one *turn*ing point. Adults discover new thoughts when they train their brain to be aware of *present* moments in their lives. Perhaps you are so busy meeting your basic needs (and those of children, partners, and work colleagues) that some days you scarcely notice your collection of physiological patterns and accompanying personality roles. Seemingly blind to much of your own personality functioning, you innocently may criticize others' conduct while engaging in the same roles yourself! In fact, psychologists Hal and Sidra Stone predict that you struggle most with people during your lifetime who frequently act out roles of your own personality that you do not like; they also assert that adults often marry people with such disowned qualities.[22] Certain family postures and personality functioning become predictable over time, and yet, you may be unaware of your part in these revolving patterns. When you do realize how you play into another's communication and behavior patterns, you can diverge and take yourself out of a conflict.

TURN TIP

I would use negative feelings and painful pricks of conscience to spot-light areas ripe for change.

– Gretchen Rubin's *Happier at Home*

A *Turn* Journal exercise that may appeal to those of you who find writing as a good release – and a surprising way to know yourself better – is the recommendation by writer Julia Cameron:

• Write morning pages, or three pages of longhand writing about whatever comes to your mind the first thing in the morning.[23] While this may sound daunting, especially if you are not accustomed to writing, you might amaze yourself with what finds its way onto the page. You might write about how you want to change a particular role. I began writing my first book in this manner.

A PERSONALITY MAP

One way of becoming more aware of your own personality is to draw a personality map. People are often surprised at how their personality roles relate to one another on a hand-drawn map. Ancient cartographers wrote, "Here be dragons," on the unknown parts on their maps to suggest dangers lurking in the unknown.[24] Many feel surprise to see their vulnerable roles pictured. Another surprise is how a simple creative drawing can help make the midlife maze seem less confusing. You may wonder whether you can draw. You may think that you do not have much personality. The common phrase, "So-and-so has no personality," has no truth at all. Everyone has a rather complex personality, or inner landscape of emotional roles, values, sensations, and personal stories.

To understand how a personality map illustrates both growing pains and blossoming in daily functioning, consider the initial mapping experiences of four women from four different decades; each experienced loss from the death of a family member, but each grieving process was unique.

In her 30s, Rachel's guided personality map began with a self-symbol followed by three roles of her personality that she expressed frequently:

• Self: "Prudential Rock … Brown, basic … also pinks and red. … Because it is feminine-strong. … I've put off therapy because I'm strong … my calmest moment I'm a rock. … But the absolute core is the heart, love."
• Anxiety: "Black marks. … Maybe it would be white? It comes and goes, sometimes it lasts 5 minutes … wind or waves … as encompassing as wind or water" (Rachel's anxiety lines took up much of the space on her map).

- Loyal: "A blue shield. ... I give a lot of people the benefit of a doubt. ... I used to say, 'She's a bitch,' but now I see people as having burdens. ... We don't always know [about them]."
- Compassionate: "A green smile. ... I always smile at children. ... Green is renewal, life-giving, spring. ... I've always loved green ... fertile ground."

A mother in her 40s, Athena's grieving took place amidst concerns in raising her family and her career. The roles from the center of her personality map illustrate her main issues at a glance:

- Self: "Pink heart with [outward] rays. ... I'm a loving spirit. ... I value relationships and reaching out."
- Guilty: "Black, jagged. ... It cuts through that sense of peace."
- Caring: "Blue heart. ... I'm doing my positive part."
- Grief/sadness: "Purple teardrop."

In her 50s, Emilia had recently retired and had time to address lingering issues from her grieving experiences of losing three members of her childhood family:

- Self: "Blue cloud with an ampersand [sign meaning "and"] of spirituality. ... [At one time] I disconnected from my spiritual part."
- Strong/resilient: "Pink cape and tiara ... Superwoman part."
- Empathy: "Green curving arrow. ... More often than not I try to understand why other people do what they do. ... I spend more time thinking about others than myself."
- Artistic: "Yellow house. ... The colors come so easily. ... When I was a very little girl I used to write floor plans."

Retired and in her 60s, Loretta was ready to address unresolved grief in her life story:

- Self: "Two blue flowers: Flowers mean a lot to me. ... But lately I go to TV. It puts me in another world. I just want to escape."
- Frustrated: "Black ... like a lightning bolt with a question mark. ... It always goes back to me. It's my fault."
- Anger: "Red jagged flames ... fire. I don't show it. I hold it in. Sometimes I get sarcastic. Then I feel bad."
- Determination: "Turquoise star: Part that tries not to think about things when I get angry."

As these initial personality maps show, there is much passion and angst mixed together when an individual begins to unravel their stories of grieving a significant loss. As you continue to grow and change your personality, you may rearrange certain memory details along the way as you make plans for your future: Every person incorporates "the reconstructed past and the imagined future into a more or less coherent narrative."[25] Your past personal stories have an impact upon your daily functioning today. When you become conscious at midlife of various childhood stories, you are in a better position to discover their meaning and purpose for your current life. You begin to understand how your various personality roles can work together or war at odds. Remember the saying, "You are your own worst enemy?" It is important to remember that all of your personality roles desire something positive for you. Yet, some personality roles can swerve you into behavior that makes a difficult situation worse. By understanding these roles, you will find plasticity, or ways in which you can change your behavior.

In order to shift into a forward direction, consider becoming more conscious of how your personality works. As William Shakespeare's Hamlet realized, "There is nothing either good or bad, but thinking makes it so." While all of us share some similarities in personality roles, our various roles play out nonverbal poses and verbalized expressions in unique patterns. And most of us have some personality roles that lie dormant for periods of time. For example, some aspects of your personality await rediscovery. Some of your current emotional roles are not your favorite ones. You may want to uproot them and give them a different space. It is important to begin observing your roles with compassion and curiosity, especially any ones you question. If you want to create a new habit or way of responding to certain situations, begin with conscious steps.

Instead of weeding out a role, try focusing upon how the role has protected you in some way. Even your anger can shift in emphasis with understanding. Meditation teacher Stephen Levine had wise words on welcoming anger: "'Take tea. Make yourself comfortable. Warm yourself by the fire.' Then anger can begin to float. And instead of 10,001 more times of anger there may be 9,999. Each moment that it is responded to mindfully instead of reacted to compulsively lightens the load and lessens the momentum of old mind. Each time we relate to anger, instead of from it, it demagnetizes."[26] Adjust the expression of your roles with compassion for yourself.

DISCOVERING MORE PERSONALITY ROLES

You may not want to relive every detail of your loss. Actually, recent research indicates that it is not a necessary step in order to work through single traumatic events.[27] It is always up to each person to decide what or how much to disclose about any given issue. For many people coping with loss, psychotherapy can be an enormous help. Some evidence-based therapies, such as Internal Family Systems (IFS) therapy and Eye Movement Desensitization and Reprocessing (EMDR) therapy, do not require that you relive every detail of your loss.

With or without a therapist, if you are a person who wants to grieve at your own pace and in your own time frame, drawing a personality map can help you. Artificial intelligence expert Marvin Minsky explains the importance of mapping: "A map is more useful to us than seeing the entire landscape that it depicts. ... Consider how messy our minds would become if we filled them up with descriptions of things whose details had too little significance. So instead, we spend large parts of our lives at trying to tidy up our minds – selecting the portions we want to keep, suppressing others we'd like to forget, and refining the ones we're dissatisfied with."[28] You may choose to share your map with a trusted friend or just keep it for your own use.

Each personality map is special. You can repeat this exercise by redrawing another map at a later time. You may add roles that you rediscover when your grieving does not carry so much intensity. However, it is not necessary for you to draw every single aspect of your personality or become obsessive about your drawing. Everyone uses a variety of roles in their daily functioning, but all of us have our main roles. It is important that you draw some roles that you may not be fond of, but you discover that you use them frequently. The mapping exercise organizes your current personality functioning into a concrete picture during one point in time. You can see where you might *turn* in a different direction. These rediscovered parts were additions in later maps:

- Intuition: "Red, heart in your brain ... smart love ... [also] purple. ... Make it really strong ... a crucial part of my family life."
- Steward: "Steward for children ... purple. ... It will catch, hug, but not carry. ... Children are getting older. ... I'm surprised that my oldest is so mature in directing her future. ... I'm enjoying every stage."
- Spirituality: "Yellow ... around everything, but also beyond."
- Problem-solver: "Green. ... It connects to empathy. ... It is related to my scientific part. ... It is a microscope."
- Flexible: "Purple ... a purple pretzel!"
- Strength: "Purple ... a weight-lifting dumbbell ... [now] there is a point where I can stand up for myself and be assertive."

YOUR TURN

One of the first things an explorer does when learning about a new territory is to map the locations that have been 'discovered.'

– Z. A. Bradley, writer, *Canyon de Chelly*

You create personal maps daily to meet your basic needs without realizing it. Drawing an actual map makes meeting your needs a conscious act. You learn to differentiate your core self from your personality parts or roles. An introduction to personality mapping begins with acceptance: You cannot make a mistake. Do not despair if drawing is not your passion. Art in your drawing is in the eye of the beholder. Everyone creates his or her own unique manner of mapping. You draw a map of your personality roles that seems right for today. Remember the plasticity of personalities. A later map can change from the one you draw today.

Find a piece of typing paper, 8.5 × 11 inches, or make your map in your *Turn* Journal. You begin your personality map with first drawing a self-representation. Select markers, crayons, or colored pencils to draw a symbol representing self-territory. You may choose a particular color, or you may find you want several colors.

- Somewhere near the center of the page, draw a design or shape that stands for your internal compass, the core self. It is a symbolic self-representation. Perhaps you recognize when you are in the space of self-territory because you are not troubled by anything. You feel calm, at peace, and perhaps reflective or intuitive.

    While an inner presence of self-awareness occurs quite naturally, a significant loss can disrupt such an inner sense of openness. You may not experience this state of grace in the midst of grieving a significant loss, as thoughts may tumble out at a rapid pace. Grieving can take up a lot of your energy and not leave much space for sensing a calm inner presence. Just take a couple of deep breaths. Allow a self-symbol to come to mind and paper. Everyone draws something unique and creative for self-territory. Continue your map.

- Add designs for your personality roles, one at a time, around your centered self-symbol. Just draw whatever comes to mind. Visualize your roles without judgment. Remember, a picture can express a thousand words. Sketch a role of your personality that seems to describe you during much of your day. Choose a role that you experience every day, several times a day. How do you envision the size of this part? How do you imagine its placement on your map in relationship to your self-symbol? Label each role as you draw it.

- Draw a second role in your day-to-day personal story. It may be quite different from the first. How do you envision the size of this personality role in relation to your self-symbol? How do you imagine its placement on your map in relationship to what you have drawn already? What color(s) do you associate with this role?

- Draw a third role of your personality. By this time, most adults draw three roles of their personality that describe either the ways they like to see themselves or, in some instances, one or two symbols representing challenging roles in their personality. This is because your brain tracks scary pathways just like a road map rates certain roadways as safe for travel. Both brain maps and road maps require updating from time to time.
- After drawing several roles and picturing the usual work-a-day personality line up, look for any parts that may not have favored status. Can you identify an opposite role to any you have drawn so far? Maybe there are roles in your personality that you do not show others. Maybe there are roles that you do not want to acknowledge very often. Where do these roles fit on your map? How do you envision their sizes? How do you imagine placement on your map in relationship to the self-symbol? What color(s) do you associate with these roles?[29]

A variety of personality roles may command you to repair the past; another group of parts seemingly demand that you fix the future so that you can avoid more loss. You may not know how frequently you drift into fantasies about your past or future. When you do not focus any time in self-territory, you may miss present moments altogether. True living does not happen by constantly rehashing the past. You want to learn lessons from your past, but then decide how to apply gained wisdom to move forward with a growth mind-set.

Chapter 6

Embracing Energy

If we could give every individual the right amount of nourishment and exercise, not too little and not too much, we would have found the safest way to health.

– Hippocrates, Greek father of medicine

Sometimes he believed he had become more memory than present. He replayed scenes from his life, like a spectator trapped on the outside. Seeing the mistakes, the inconsistencies, the choices that shouldn't have been made, and yet unable to do anything about them.

– Rachel Joyce, novelist, *The Unlikely Pilgrimage of Harold Fry*

British statesman Lord Stanley pronounced, "Those who think they have not time for bodily exercise will sooner or later have to find time for illness." Physician David Katz, founding director of Yale University's Prevention Research Center, also views health choices as critical to well-being: "Lifestyle is the most potent medicine we have." His short list of health factors is easy to memorize: "Feet, forks, fingers, sleep, stress, and love." Katz refers to the three Fs of feet, forks, and fingers as the "master levers" of medical destiny. "Decades of research implicate lack of exercise (feet), overeating and less than optimal food choices (forks), and tobacco use (fingers) as leading causes of premature death and chronic disease."[1] When your loss experience is linked to one of these Fs, you may become more sensitized to health risks, but is it enough to embrace wise choices for your health? Who wants the reminder that alcohol heightens or prolongs stress and anxiety levels?

Finding sufficient energy after experiencing loss is critical to your recovery. The most basic aspects of energy – good nutrition, a good night's sleep, and an ongoing exercise program – may break down when loss occurs. Your good intentions wither. Your enthusiasm dries up. Taking care of yourself seems too weighty. Furthermore, loss triggers the memory of earlier losses, of other times when you lost energy. As neurologist Robert Scaer suggests, the traumatic nature of your experiences is determined by the meaning that you attribute to them. Meaning is strongly influenced by "the cumulative burden of a myriad of prior negative life events, especially those experienced in the vulnerable period of early childhood. ... [A new loss can] resurrect old emotions and physical sensations related to a trauma that has been locked in unconscious memory."[2] Outlined in the Pinwheel Model of Bereavement (chapter 2), your history of coping with earlier *turn*ing points is key in how you process your current loss.

When a helpless personality role takes over, your energy level plummets. In extreme listlessness, a sense of ennui, or utter weariness and discontent, permeates your day. Psychologist Martin Seligman studied helplessness and coined the term, "learned helplessness." Experiments on dogs who received inescapable shocks learned that nothing they did mattered to stop the shocks. Not only did the dogs become passive and exhibit symptoms of depression, they died prematurely. By contrast, other animals and people receiving the same shocks, with the exception that they could *turn* off the shocks, had entirely different results. By taking action, their affect was positive and they experienced enhanced health.[3] The takeaway message is that actions matter! You can retool after loss. You can map a path for yourself where you make healthy choices for your health and ongoing energy.

Journalist Robert Wright adds humor to the topic of positive actions; he talks about "grim inspiration." Wright views history overall as a net positive with moral progress over time.[4] Yes, even after experiencing significant loss, you can fix your bucket loss hole with grim inspiration. I like the word inspiration, as it includes both energy and creativity. However grim your humor, your animating thoughts can lead to positive actions.

• Inspiration (from Latin, *in* + *spirare; to breathe upon or into*) means a person or thing that moves the intellect or emotions, or prompts action or invention.[5]

INSPIRING SLEEP

In order to recover inspiration, one of the first things you must do is to get a good night's sleep. Not only can you harvest dreams to help with grieving, but simply getting enough sleep will help you thrive. You function at your best if you spend about 33% of your time sleeping. The average adult requires seven to eight hours each night. Catching up on sleep on weekends is not a long-term solution for the sleep deprived. Also, putting yourself to sleep is more complicated than Russian-American composer Irving Berlin's song, "Count Your Blessings Instead of Sheep." It is a good idea to count blessings, or keep a gratitude journal, but a healthy night's sleep includes dream time (chapter 3). Interrupted sleep and/or insomnia interferes with dreaming. The Center for Disease Control and Prevention labels insufficient sleep as a public health epidemic. Romantic partners list insufficient sleep with even more dire terms: 61% of consumers crave sleep more than sex. Adults with lower marital satisfaction are more likely to report having problems sleeping.[6] Furthermore, the quality of wives' sleep was a more powerful predictor of happy interactions than a hard day at work or any other stressor.[7]

Sleep regulates how much you eat, your metabolism, whether you fight off infections, how creative and insightful you are, how you handle stress, how quickly you learn something new, and how you organize and store memories. Do not believe in shortcuts to getting enough sleep. If you lose as little as one and one-half hours of sleep on a given night, you may have daytime alertness reduced by a third. Sleep inspires your pituitary gland to release a growth hormone that affects every cell in your body, including resetting your immune system for optimal functioning. Going to bed at a regular time is best and is even more important than the number of hours of sleep. While you may sleep in on weekends, it is actually better when you have an occasional late night to get up at your usual time. Alcohol consumption is an important factor in your sleep ability. Even a glass or two of wine within hours of your bedtime can affect sleep quality.

Many midlifers turn to sleeping pills for a solution to sleep problems. Pills do not allow individuals to reach the deepest levels of sleep and may result in a hungover feeling the next day.[8] Furthermore, "By 2010, about 1 in every 4 adults in the U.S. had a prescription sleeping pill in their medicine cabinets. ... [But] a number of studies have shown that drugs ... offer no significant improvement in the quality of sleep that a person gets. They give only a tiny bit more in the quantity department, too." After many scary behaviors reported by people who experience short-term memory loss while taking sleeping pills, the Food and Drug Administration set up new rules requiring pharmacists to explain risks such as sleepwalking or sleep driving with certain sleep medications.[9]

Instead of pills and falling asleep on your job, consider taking a nap when your work life allows this. Other cultures are more accepting of this practice than North American culture. Research on daytime napping suggests that you can reset yourself with a 15- to 20-minute nap to regain a burst of energy. If you have time for a 30- to 60-minute nap, you can enhance your creativity and problem-solving skills.[10] The prolific artist, Henri Matisse, took a nap every day after eating lunch.[11] Founder of the *Huffington Post*, Ariana Huffington, broke her cheekbone when she collapsed in her office from sleep deprivation. Huffington reports that sleep problems began in college. Today she unplugs from technology 30 minutes before bed. She does not allow anything that requires a charger into her bedroom. Now she sleeps eight hours a night. Huffington provides nap rooms for employees in her Manhattan office space.[12] If naps do not refresh you, what about painting during a break from your routine?

British writer and philosopher Aldous Huxley suggested, "That we are not much sicker and much madder than we are is due exclusively to that most blessed and blessing of all natural graces, sleep." Yes, sleep is healing, but many shortchange sleep. Perhaps you experienced sleep issues even before a loss occurred. If your sleep disturbances are ongoing, a sleep study may prove beneficial. For example, some midlifers do not know that they have sleep apnea, a condition where breathing stops for ten seconds or more during sleep. A partner or sleep study may help you discover this dangerous condition. The cost of a study is prohibitive for individuals without an insurance plan that covers it; prices range from $2000 to $4000 per sleep study.[13] However, daily well-being is priceless.

Psychologist Peter Levine also has a doctorate in medical biophysics. He explains suffering of a traumatic event as having a "hole in the boundary of the body."[14] Levine advises how to fix the hole by paying attention to your body: "Your body ... is a ready tool to resolve various physical, emotional and psychological symptoms. ... It is a descent into the parts of ourselves that are alien, that we might prefer not to deal with."[15] If your denial role is well entrenched in your personality, it will sabotage efforts to meet basic needs. To put yourself to sleep naturally, try some simple calming tools. You can touch and train your own body to self-soothe and calm racing thoughts. Try three calming tools from Japanese Jin Shin Jyutsu, brought to the United States by Mary Burmeister. Put your right hand under your left armpit, next to your heart, and your left had on your opposite shoulder. This holding for two to ten minutes provides a settling as the body is a container of all of your emotions. Your shoulders are an important aspect of your body boundaries. A second holding is to put one hand on your heart and the other hand on your forehead. Just feel what goes on in between your two hands. Then replace your hands again: place one hand on your stomach and the other hand on your heart.[16] You may fall asleep easier.

A largely unknown detail about sleep is that in premodern times people experienced segmented sleep every night. They did not have TV/computer screens tossing artificial light into their eyes half the night; rather, people went to sleep when it was dark outside and slept until around midnight. Then they stayed awake for about an hour, using the time to good advantage: "praying, reading, contemplating dreams, urinating, or having sex ... perhaps the most popular." After some inspirational time, the second half of the night of sleep was enjoyed. This two-part nocturnal sleep pattern is found to have validity today when research participants are blocked from artificial light for several weeks. Not only do participants feel better rested, but they experience a chemical change during the hour spent awake in the middle of the night. They are as relaxed as if they spent a day at a spa or meditated! Their brains show a high level of prolactin, a stress-reducing hormone that is present after an orgasm.[17] Perhaps now you understand how sleeping pills are overrated.

Grieving a loss disrupts sleep, but without enough sleep even your grieving process suffers. After her mother died from dementia, 62-year-old Gloria could not sleep. She started grieving five years earlier when her mother was diagnosed with cancer. Gloria lamented, "She was always there for us." Not only did Gloria find it difficult to cope with her disoriented elderly father, she felt ill-equipped to cope herself. When she awakened in the middle of the night, she reached for a cigarette. However, nicotine is a stimulant. One of nicotine's side effects is insomnia. Smokers tend to be light sleepers and spend less time in deep sleep than nonsmokers.[18]

Alex, 63, also suffered from a lack of sleep. He had a habit of waking up around 2:00 AM and then not falling asleep again. He had retired after surgery for a heart valve replacement, although he did not want to retire so early. Alex enjoyed work. He recalled whistling on his way to work each day. His health and job losses were compounded by earlier losses of both parents. His father's death was due to alcoholism and his mother died from pancreatic cancer. Alex kept his emotions to himself, but his sleep difficulties started then. He was given a prescription of sleeping pills, but the pills were not helpful.

One healthy method to fight insomnia and improve sleep is mindfulness meditation. Research involving adults with moderate sleep problems in the age group of 55 and older put participants into two groups: one group completed a six-week sleep education class to learn ways to improve sleep habits and the second group learned mindful awareness practices. The participants who engaged in mindful meditation showed significant improvement relative to the sleep education participants.[19] This short-term approach suggests how powerful meditation is to your brain and your daily habits (chapter 8).

FEEDING YOUR MIND/BODY

Nutrition is a loaded topic these days. From school lunches to changes in McDonald's menu items to include fruits and vegetables, just about everyone has an opinion about a better healthful diet. Researchers at Columbia University Medical Center in New York found that a diet high in refined carbohydrates can lead to an increased risk for depression in postmenopausal women. Refined foods such as white bread, white rice, pastries, pasta, and sweetened beverages rapidly break down into simple sugars that cause a rise in insulin levels. The more highly refined the carbohydrate, the higher its score will appear on the glycemic index, a rating scale (0–100) for the amount of sugar found in your blood after eating. Seventy thousand women were studied in the National Institutes of Health's Women's Health Initiative Observational Study. The more sugars and refined grains the women ate, the higher their risk of depression. The study found a lower risk of depression among women who reported eating more fiber in whole grains, vegetables and nonjuice fruits.[20] What you put into your mouth matters – greatly or gravely.

You have your own ideas about what constitutes reasonable consumption levels and an optimal nutritious meal. Whatever diet you adopt as healthful, you still have many daily choices about how you take in food and other substances. You likely indulge more in unhealthy foods and substances when you are stressed. Many adults use food to alter their moods. For example, those who are sleep deprived experience an uncontrollable craving for carbohydrates. Serotonin, a major mood neurotransmitter, is largely found in specialized cells in your gut, not your brain. When serotonin levels are low, you likely feel depressed. When serotonin levels are high, you feel happier. Foods high in serotonin are walnuts, bananas, kiwis, pineapples, plums, and tomatoes. You may crave carbohydrates which can boost serotonin synthesis. You may grab foods such as meats, nuts, or cheese.[21] Who can think about the proper food in a bad moment? As the Roman poet Ovid (43 BC–17AD) reminded, "The mind ill at ease, the body suffers also." Are you an evereater? Are you an overdrinker? Do you smoke?

Forty-five-year-old Shawn began an overeating habit years ago. It was only when he caught himself yelling at his daughter one day, and saw a look of horror on her face, that he realized how he was repeating old stories. He was lost in a midlife maze of emotion. He followed parental patterns as if he carried their shadows upon his back. Shawn's parents divorced when he was a child. He does not know exactly what the reasons were, but he suspects that his mother was never happy in the marriage. She was expected to supply his father with a six-pack of cold beer every evening after work. When she did not comply, a disastrous evening was in store for the entire family. Yelling filled the entire house. After hearing this sad story, I commented to Shawn that it must have seemed like he could hardly breathe in the midst of such family chaos. Shawn's response was telling: "That's funny that you say that because I had asthma as a child." When Shawn was sick with an asthma attack, he felt like that was the only time that he was able to receive positive attention from his mother.

Fast forward to adulthood, Shawn's own marriage ended in divorce. When he talked about the role of fear in his life postdivorce, he said, "I see it as something that does not control me, but it is always there in everything I do. ... I could never please my parents enough. ... I was never safe or OK. ... I tried to be what I thought they wanted." In addition to this fearful role, Shawn identified a lethargy role in his personality that he said kept taking over the rest of his roles. When he focused attention on how this role grew so large a presence in his personality, he pictured himself as an eight-year-old boy who felt like a bad boy caught in a bad family drama. His midlife lethargy role manifested itself through him sitting on the sofa, munching junk food, and watching TV that he did not enjoy. While you may think, "Heh, just get up off the sofa and do something you *do* enjoy," you have to understand that this lethargy legacy from Shawn's family chaos had temporarily drained his energy. Shawn's craving for carbohydrates was a vicious cycle involving depression and overeating.

Actually, your mind knows what to feed your body. You can learn to shift or *turn* a corner on food and substance choices. Instead of sabotaging your health, you can retool by looking at your personality map. What part of you wants candy or ice cream? Are you truly hungry and needing food energy, or are you feeling lonely? Does a guilty role pop up? It makes a difference to know what exactly you may feel at the time you put some substance into your mouth. If you discover that you attempt to handle stress through excess food, try using a salad plate instead of a dinner plate to limit yourself to smaller portions. Make fresh vegetables and fruit a priority. Make your plate look as attractive and healthy as possible. If your appetite is low, eat several small, nutritious meals rather than three larger ones. Drink healthy liquids.

FEEDINGS AND FEELINGS

Feedings and feelings have a delicate relationship. As actor and director Woody Allen says, "Life is full of misery, loneliness, and suffering – and it's all over much too soon!" Even if you believe that your life is full of stress and loneliness, your suffering may not receive notice by others. It is likely that others harbor their own versions of suffering. Everyone works hard to keep up appearances that he or she is OK. However, hidden emotions consume a lot of energy. As artificial intelligence expert Marvin Minsky points out, feeling hurt emotionally can resemble physical pain. For example, "When you suffer the loss of a long-time friend, you feel that you've lost a part of yourself. ... And now, alas, the signals that those brain parts transmit will never again receive replies. This is just like losing a hand or an eye – and that could be why it takes so much time to come to terms with being deprived of resources that you could rely on before that loss."[22] When someone experiences a loss, we frequently give them a gift of food.

Eating disorder expert Geneen Roth runs retreats for compulsive eaters and recommends *intuitive eating* rather than conventional weight loss diets. For Roth, "Our relationship to food is an exact microcosm of our relationship to life itself. ... Everything we believe about love, fear, transformation ... is revealed in how, when and what we eat." She believes this is true because since adolescence she has gained and lost more than one thousand pounds! Roth experienced yo-yo dieting to such an extreme that she swung from anorexia (weighing 80 for two years) to being 80 pounds overweight. In her retreats, Roth teaches a form of mindful eating: "Take some time and notice what you put on your plate. ...Notice if you were hungry when you chose the food. If you weren't physically hungry, was there another kind of hunger present?" Roth guides her retreat-from-overeating participants in a gentle manner: "And looking at your plates, decide what you want to eat first and take a few bites. Notice how the food feels in your mouth. ... If it does what you thought it would do." She explains her belief that when you confront your behavior around food with acceptance, you come to know yourself on a very intimate level: "Our personality and its defenses, one of which is our emotionally charged relationship to food, are a direct link to our spirituality. They are the bread crumbs leading us home. ... Viscerally [you discover] that you are bigger than your pain."[23]

It is possible to recognize that life was treacherous at age eight, but you do not have to embody your childhood persona today. Perhaps you revisit age eight memories, but now you have the abstraction capability to see a larger picture. Realize that your parents were caught in their own midlife maze – only they were not reading this book to find ways to retool or *turn* a corner on the losses that they encountered. Your family of origin stumbled on the rocky pathways of life, and likely carried a few legacy shadows upon their backs. However, you do not have to repeat these behavioral patterns. Just recognizing the legacy roles in your family, and accepting that the roles played out old family dramas, will help you become more conscious of the energy messages that you pass along to the next generation. Past painful memories can evolve into powerful lessons for today if you are conscious of your personality roles.

TURN TIP

The greatest discovery ... is that human beings can alter their lives by altering their attitudes of mind. As you think, so shall you become.

– William James, philosopher and psychologist

Your hunger may not be for food. Psychologist Susan Albers specializes in eating issues. She focuses on mindful eating to conquer overeating, undereating, and yo-yo dieting: "If you are a mindful eater, you accept the hard reality of that urge to eat cheesecake and chocolate chip cookies. You just respond to that urge in a different way." Instead of living according to the old saying, "Eat, drink, and be merry," Albers advises that you adopt a healthier motto: "Say 'Eat, drink, and be mindful,' to yourself. Call this phrase to mind whenever you are struggling with a food choice or need to get back on track."[24] Learning how to slow down thoughts about food or harmful substances can happen with a growth mind-set and answering such questions as the following:

• How are you feeling right now?
• Is there anything troubling you right now?
• How does your body feel?
• Are you present in this moment?
• Is there anything on your mind that is causing you to worry?
• Are you smiling?
• Are your muscles tense?

MOVE, BABY BOOMER, MOVE

As Danish philosopher Soren Kierkegaard wisely said, "Life can only be understood backwards; but it must be lived forwards." You do not let go or forget about loss. Instead, you spend some time "walking backwards" in your mind to better understand your past. In China and Japan, literal backward walking is an ancient practice that is viewed as a way to correct mistakes of the past. The exercise develops different leg muscles than those involved in walking forward. Taking one hundred steps of backward walking is supposed to be the equivalent to one thousand steps of regular walking! You might try this in a safe environment. There are mind/body benefits. Your senses are sharpened. Walking backward increases cardiovascular endurance quickly. You burn more calories than in forward walking the same duration. Some runners add running backward to their training space, as improved balance and flexibility are side benefits.[25] *Turn*ing and trying out different directions with your physical body is a reminder that your mind also is capable of multiple perspectives.

We do not have to tell babies to move; they do it naturally. Why do we have to tell baby boomers to move more? With fewer jobs requiring physical labor in the new millennium, "We in the West are the first generation in human history in which the mass of the population has to deliberately exercise to be healthy."[26] Exercise for most midlifers is a choice. Popular intentions on January 1 often involve such habits as exercising more. Why wait for New Year's to make a resolution about healthy energy habits? You can make resolutions at any time of the year. I suggest that people consider making resolutions for positive changes on their birthday, although every day is a good day to begin a healthy habit.

Researchers have irrefutable evidence that exercise reduces the risk of almost every serious illness in middle adulthood – heart disease, diabetes, cancer, hypertension, obesity, depression, and osteoporosis. Great improvement in health status is possible when midlifers who are least fit become physically active. Exercise can slow down primary aging changes.[27] Primary aging refers to such characteristics as the need for reading and bifocal eyeglasses, beginning hearing loss, gray and thinning hair, and wrinkles. These changes are termed "primary," as they occur in everyone regardless of race, ethnicity, culture, or socioeconomic class. Secondary aging, on the other hand, is linked to unhealthy habits, such as smoking, drug use, unhealthy eating, alcohol abuse, obesity, and lack of exercise.

The benefits of exercise are cumulative, so short exercise bouts throughout your day are just as effective as one longer workout period. Some research suggests that interval training has more benefits. You can adapt working hard for a short period, back off for a few minutes, and then resume a higher level of intensity to any type of exercise. One way this action is useful is that it may keep you from sluggish sitting for long periods of your day. Researchers in a longitudinal study have made the bold statement that sitting down for extended periods can pose a health risk as insidious as smoking or overexposure to the sun. It is easy to break up your sitting time. You can walk around with a free weight to do a few biceps curls; this activity alone can lower your risk of disease and premature death. The minimum goal is to raise your heart rate by 50% for at least 15 minutes daily.[28] You may think of exercise as only being good for your body, but exercise is just as important to your brain and actually can create new brain cells.

One of the pitfalls of too much stress in your life is that it can drain your working memory. Exercise counteracts this brain drain, along with elevating your mood. "Short bouts of exercise specifically benefit the functioning of a network of brain regions ... which support thinking and reasoning and especially working memory. You can think of working memory as a kind of mental scratch pad that allows you to work with whatever information is in your consciousness. ... Working memory is one of the major building blocks of IQ."[29] Researchers found that exercise has a positive effect upon your mental health through brain-derived neurotropic factor (BDNF), termed a "brain fertilizer," which increases after a short bout of exercise. "Maintaining brain health and plasticity throughout life is an important public health goal ... [and] particularly crucial from middle age onwards, when the brain faces a series of challenges that can include ... neurodegenerative diseases like Alzheimer's disease."[30]

EXERCISED BRAINS AND BODIES

You stand to lose brain functioning if you do not move much. Psychologist Arthur Kramer directs the Beckman Institute for Advanced Science and Technology at the University of Illinois and is an expert on the role of physical fitness on cognition. Kramer is concerned that adults in the industrialized world are becoming increasingly sedentary. If this describes you in your midlife, an aerobic exercise prescription is in your best interests. Kramer's research shows that regular aerobic exercise, such as walking three times per week, strengthens your heart and muscles along with increasing the size of critical brain structures. Adults over 60 spent about an hour walking around a gym at a pace of 3 miles an hour. Results were significant in terms of brain volume for the aerobic trainers, but not for adults who participated in a stretching and toning control group.[31] You have heard the term, "Use it or lose it."

You may say, "But I don't feel like exercising," or "I have no appetite," after experiencing a significant loss. Meeting basic needs for energy is challenging after a loss, but trust me on how important it is to establish some discipline for maintaining a routine of getting enough sleep, eating a nutritious diet, and keeping an exercise program during your grieving process. I recall how I received a comment from a person in my exercise class about a month after my husband had died. A woman said, "My, you have lost weight!" I wasn't sure if she approved or disapproved, but when I said that my husband had died, she had a horrified look on her face and she retreated from me as quickly as possible. I took in her feedback – I kept exercising, but I started to feed myself better.

While grieving a loss can feel exhausting; exercise is the best prescription to reduce your fatigue. Perhaps you start riding your bike or simply go for regular walks. Other cost-effective activities are jumping rope, lifting free weights, and using resistance bands for strength training to build muscle. If you have not identified your preferred way of exercising your body, now is a good time to develop a plan of action. You can *turn* a corner on a sedentary lifestyle in your grieving process. Blame it on needing a distraction from intruding negative thought loops! Or, just view walking the dog on a really invigorating hike someplace new as necessary to change up your dog's brain neurons along with your own!

Do you have some problem that is tough to solve? Take a walk outside. Nature has a powerful influence on your thinking. Walking away from your

computer or worksite brings new possibilities and eliminates deadhead thinking. It's only when Gary takes a break from his computer coding problem,
and walks through a park on his way home, that a coding solution presents
itself. Have you ever considered taking up juggling? When people practiced
juggling for several hours a week, they had changes in their brains which
related to better communication among brain cells![32]

And if these ideas do not make your head spin in an exercise direction,
consider the research on exercise and the reduction of skin aging. Researchers at McMaster University in Ontario, Canada, studied a group of sedentary
volunteers ages 65 and older who had normal skin for their age. Physician
Mark Tarnopolsky, professor of neuromuscular and neurometabolic disorders, headed the study that biopsied skin samples from the participants' but-
tocks, as the research examined skin that was not frequently exposed to the
sun. Then, the participants began a three-month endurance training routine
of working out twice a week by jogging or cycling at a moderately strenuous pace for 30 minutes each session. When these new exercisers had their
buttock skin biopsied a second time, both their outer and inner layers of their
skin now appeared very similar to those of 20- to 30-year-olds! Regular exercise not only affects skin, but it can extend a person's lifespan by up to five
years.[33] Are you now convinced that you are ready for an about-face regarding
an exercise routine?

YOUR TURN

A stitch in time saves nine.

– English proverb

Finding a supportive role model to emulate can make a huge difference in
boosting your energy levels. Some individuals are aided by joining a support
group such as Weight Watchers for evereating/overeating issues, or Alcohol
Anonymous for overdrinking. Others do not want such a public forum and
find that the individual support of a psychotherapist suits them best. While
much progress has occurred in the new millennium and in the public eye
for valuing psychotherapy, there still are jokes and movies that belittle the
therapy process. Making fun of physician visits for a broken arm does not
receive jokes. The notion that a suffering mind is somehow different from a
suffering body is nonsense. In fact, it is the brain that registers both physical
and psychic pain.

Perhaps it is the more secretive and disturbing nature of psychic pain
that causes such a stir. Unless a person's body language conveys his or her

extreme sadness, strangers in the grocery store cannot see a grieving person suffering like they can see a cast holding a broken arm in place. Being conscious of another's psychic grieving makes many people feel uncomfortable, so jokes relating to mental health move the topic to everyday humor. However, finding the right psychotherapist who not only serves as a compassionate witness to your grief, but will help you in your search for new beginnings, can elevate your consciousness for all kinds of new behaviors. Ask a trusted friend or professional for a recommendation if you are looking for a therapist.

Less-structured support is often effective too. Friends, neighbors, and family members are key players in the lifestyle and grieving changes that midlifers face. Too often, grieving adults try to distance themselves from their emotional pain rather than focus on what they might learn about themselves through their grief process. As Geneen Roth points out, "Obsession gives you something to do besides having your heart shattered by heart-shattering events. Like watching your children get sick, like living while your spouse dies. Like being with your parents as they get old, wear diapers, forget their own names. ... There is madness in obsession, yes, but its value is that it drowns out the madness in life."[34]

- Rather than shut yourself off from others by diving into a solitary obsession, choose at least three other people to confide in and share what is on your mind.

Chapter 7

Achieving New Discipline Habits

A garden is a grand teacher. It teaches patience and careful watchfulness; it teaches industry and thrift; above all it teaches entire trust.

– Gertrude Jekyll, British garden designer

Don't ever take a fence down until you know why it was put up.

– Robert Frost, poet

The idea of discipline has a bad rap for many midlifers. Isn't discipline what kids need? Yes, but as adults we also have discipline needs to meet every day. Instead of viewing discipline as a protective form of guidance, many think of discipline as a negative, as in "don't do that." There are reasons why discipline has such a scolding voice in your ears. Perhaps you experienced a parent, caretaker, teacher, and/or boss who planted negative-based discipline in your mind. A second and even more compelling reason for your frequent focus on a negative definition for discipline is brain based. People and animals are hardwired for survival. Your brain is hardwired to maintain vigilance for possible threats.

All basic needs relate to survival. From cave days onward, people scanned their environment to ensure their survival in dangerous situations. It is likely that the discipline of early ancestors contained certain rituals for protection from harm. Remnants of some early rituals are found in caves. In remote tunnels of underground caves, the local minerals were used to produce vibrant paintings that likely communicated survival messages, but no one knows their exact meaning. The great value of such artwork is the same value attached to all art: there are universal qualities that evoke emotion from the artist, as well as viewers. The discipline of cave painters creates a legacy linking early ancestors to people today. Strong connections exist in stirred-up emotions.

The incredible Paleolithic art on walls and ceilings of ancient caves may depict a discipline of hunting prowess since most ancient cave art is centered on animals. In France's Chauvet Cave, fossilized animal bones were found on cave floors, along with both human and animal footprints in the clay. There are hundreds of animal paintings of horses, cattle, mammoths, lions, panthers, bears, hyenas, and rhinoceroses on cave walls. The calcite overlaying handprints on Chauvet walls is dated to about thirty thousand to thirty-two thousand years ago.[1] Perhaps the haunting cave scenes commemorate great hunters who lost their lives during a hunt. One cave painting shows a thin human who is lying next to a large, standing, and injured bison with a spear into his hindquarters. Beside the outstretched male figure is a second spearlike stick.[2] It is hard to imagine how frightening the mammoths and other animals would have appeared to cave people who possessed only crude weapons. Film, TV, and literary agent Julian Friedmann views early cave art as the first movies! He suggests that cave audiences looked at the art to rehearse their fears before having to kill animals.[3] We know for certain that cave dwellers had to use their hands skillfully in order to thrive, leaving their handprints on ancient cave walls as a tribute to their survival.

The tribal art of Central India carries on the survival ritual of painted handprints. In the Kol tribal village (Rewa District), handprints are displayed above doors and on both sides of doors. The protective goal of the handprints relates to health and prosperity for the household. The handprint ritual extends to their animals. The local people print hands on a newborn calf to protect it, as well as to protect its mother. Signs of having prosperity, such as owning a new calf, are thought to attract negativity. It is believed that negativity is something to ward off.[4] Today many U.S. adults use a different ritual: they arm themselves with guns for protection.

YOUR BRAIN'S NEGATIVITY BIAS

According to psychologist Rick Hanson, your brain has a negativity bias. Your body reacts more intensely to negative stimuli than to equally strong positive stimuli. It seems normal to first define negatives in almost any endeavor. The brain's nervous system has evolved for six hundred million years, given what we now know, but evolution just means that we have upgrades to an ancient system that is in place to warn us of possible danger. Your alert system is the amygdala – two small almond-shaped groups of nuclei – and it uses two-thirds of its neurons to detect negative information. When sensing any bad stuff, your brain immediately stores the negativity in memory for safekeeping. You also store positive experiences, but you might not store this material in your long-term memory unless you linger in your thoughts for a longer period of time – 12 seconds or more.[5] The good news about brain wiring is that you are programmed for survival.

However, the bad news regarding your brain's negativity bias is that you are prone to overestimate threats and underestimate opportunities. One way your brain overestimates a threat is how it handles physical pain. Psychiatrist and brain researcher Norman Doidge explains that it is your brain – not your body – that experiences pain. Yes, it seems unreasonable, because you say that your back is where you feel a backache. Perhaps we need to shift words: "brain pain" is more accurate in describing aches and pain. Doidge further explains how repeated trauma may cause your brain to overestimate or experience more pain than is justified, a condition known as chronic pain. When neurons in your brain maps are damaged, they can send false alarms. "Long after the body has healed, the pain system is still firing. The acute pain has developed an afterlife: it becomes chronic pain. ... One of the core laws of neuroplasticity is that neurons that fire together wire together. ... The brain maps for pain begin to fire so easily that the person ends up in excruciating, unremitting pain ... all in response to the smallest stimulation of a nerve."[6] Just being aware of this brain mapping around a negativity bias may help you refocus your attention to savor many more positive situations for longer periods of time.

TURN TIP

When people restrain themselves out of fear, their lives are by necessity diminished. Only through freely chosen discipline can life be enjoyed and still kept within the bounds of reason.

– Mihaly Csikszentmihalyi, psychologist, *Flow: The Psychology of Optimal Experience*

There are many ways to *turn* a corner on the negative roles in your personality's inner debate. Sara White, professor and leadership coach for the medical community, suggests keeping tabs on negative things you say to yourself in a creative way. This adapted approach takes discipline, as initially you may not feel very accepting of your negative thoughts, even though they creep into everyday use.

• Visualize your mind as your mental apartment or the place where you live with all of your thoughts. Your thought apartment is furnished with every thought that you think about yourself and about those around you.

- Many of your furnishings or thoughts are hand-me-downs, or thoughts that you picked up from other people. Some thoughts may appear negative and/ or harmful to you as you envision them now.
- Imagine that these negative furnishings or thoughts appear tired and worn.
- Acknowledge any self-limiting roles. When you can look for "the gift and opportunity in every obstacle you meet," you may be able to focus on accomplishments instead of setbacks.[7]

You may diverge from this imagery exercise and put your thoughts into writing. Writing is a powerful discipline to cope with grieving.

WRITING DISCIPLINE AS HEALING

Research psychologist James Pennebaker asked people to discipline themselves to write about the emotionally charged events in their life for 15 minutes per day for four consecutive days. The topics that poured onto pages included grieving about divorce, rape, physical abuse, and suicide attempts. When people left the research room, many were in tears. Pennebaker compared such an emotional reaction to seeing a sad movie – you may feel sadder initially, but you also feel wiser. At the end of four days, most participants told Pennebaker that the task was of profound importance to them. In a follow-up study, those in the expressive writing group made 43% fewer doctor visits for illness than the control group who wrote about superficial topics.[8] Emotional writing opened up space for both grieving and recovery.

Another of Pennebaker's writing studies targeted a particular group suffering loss – middle-aged men who experienced unexpected layoffs from high-tech jobs after working for the same company for over 15 years. Participants were asked to write about their deepest emotions about their job loss. A control group had a writing assignment to tell about how they used their time every day. Results showed that after eight months of writing, 52% of the expressive writing group had new jobs compared with only 20% of the control group. All of the men experienced the same number of job interviews. Emotional writing helped midlife men have a place to express their personality roles of humiliation, anger, and fear. When they went on interviews, they could express a positive attitude. Pennebaker found that the midlifers who benefited most from the expressive writing exercises were those who included others' views of the events of their trauma along with their own notions.[9] Grieving can connect people.

The discipline of writing is healing for many individuals. Veteran journalist Joan Didion wrote *The Year of Magical Thinking* after her husband died from a sudden heart attack. Adding to the gravity of her loss, her only child had experienced septic shock (after a diagnosis of pneumonia) and was comatose in a nearby hospital. Didion and her husband returned to their home after visiting their daughter in the ICU. Joan was preparing dinner. Then calamity struck. Didion's poignant words capture the haunting questions of many who experience a significant loss: "Would I need to relive every mistake? ... What would I give to be able to discuss this with John? ... What would I give to be able to say one small thing that made him happy? ... If I had said it in time would it have worked? ... Did I feel anger at John for leaving me? Was it possible to feel anger and simultaneously to feel responsible?"[10] As with any art, a writer's expression of mourning turmoil through words is therapeutic for both the author and for later readers who identify with expressions of raw emotion. While Didion's daughter recovered from pneumonia, calamity hit home once again; her daughter died at age 31 from acute pancreatitis the following year.

Chilean-American writer Isabel Allende expressed the importance of her grief writing in this way: "I couldn't afford therapy at the time I needed it the most, so I started writing."[11] Allende experienced multiple losses in her life. Her father disappeared when she was three years old. At age eight, she was sexually abused by a fisherman who was found dead the next morning. As an adult, Allende was forced to move out of her country after receiving death threats during a Chilean military coup that resulted in the assassination of her relative, Salvador Allende, president of Chile. A former journalist in Chile, Allende did not intend to publish books. She began writing a series of unmailed letters when her 99-year-old grandfather was dying. Her intent was to keep her memories of her family and country alive, as she could not return to Chile to visit her grandfather at the end of his life. Her letters *turn*ed into a five hundred-page manuscript (*The House of Spirits*) that zigzags personal and political themes. Allende later stated that this writing discipline saved her life.

Once she began, Allende kept writing. Her stirring memoir of her daughter's death, *Paula*, also started out as a letter. As Allende sat by her comatose daughter's bedside, she poured out her troubled family history onto pages. Paula died at age 28 from a hospital mishap causing irreversible brain damage.[12] Allende wrote *Maya's Notebook* to continue her family storytelling, but this time she wrote for the benefit of her grandchildren. A sobbing character does not want to accept that her pet dog has died. Allende writes about a wise grandfather character to give her grandchildren (and herself) this advice: "That affection is inside you, Maya, not in Daisy [the dog]. You can give it to other animals, and what's left over you can give to me."[13] If writing is not a role in your personality toolbox, pick some other kind of artistic, craft, social engagement, or computer creativity to *turn* a corner or two today.

DISCIPLINE AS DELIGHT

Actually, when you want to accomplish anything – from decreasing pain to learning to draw – it takes discipline. Let's say that you want to attract more positives for your day-to-day functioning. *Turn* your attention to look carefully at the word "attract." The last three letters spell the word "act." You must swing into action to attract positives. You first seed an intention. You plant a growth goal. What happens if you plant a little delight in your discipline garden? Most people daydream about goals that they can envision. Remember your growth mind-set? You imagine some details of what might transpire in making a particular goal come true. Then you begin planting your goal. As in gardening, you have to water frequently or keep your goal alive. This step often dies on the vine. Meeting a new goal can take you out of your comfort zone. You may need to transform such habitual personality roles as procrastination and worry in order to change day-to-day habits.

Loss can upend your previous discipline routines. It takes giving yourself permission to grieve your loss. At the same time you need a few discipline rules to get through bouts of sadness and other challenging emotions. Planning times to exercise may sound impossible, but this one discipline activity can lift your mood immensely. Trying some new habits, perhaps outside of your comfort zone, can establish new neural pathways in your brain. When my beloved spouse died, I joined a weekly belly dancing class as one way to lift my spirits. Not only did the jiggling feel good to my physical body, but my brain jiggled in a positive direction as well. I cannot claim that I mastered all of the intricate gyrations, but I did reap many benefits. It was delightful to swirl a huge silk scarf overhead and be in step (and hip) with a group of women of all ages. I learned that the belly dance form is most often performed as a folk dance with family and friends of all ages in the Middle East to commemorate special occasions, such as the birth of a child. Some dance moves exaggerate actual movements to ease childbirth. Initially, belly dancing was a religious dance. This is a very different connotation from the Western restaurant and nightclub performer who expects tips to slip her way.

It takes some discipline to swing into action for *any* new endeavor. It takes commitment. Intentions are great, but it takes discipline to carry through your plan. As Pulitzer Prize–winning poet Mary Oliver suggests, discipline is key for creativity to take place. Oliver always has a notebook in hand when she takes a walk. She listens to the world and scribbles snippets of her keen observations of nature in her notebook which she later *turns* into poetry: "Discipline is very important. I think we are creative all day long. We have to have an appointment to have that work out on the page … that meeting with that part of oneself, because there are other parts."[14] You may have other time frames than 5:00–9:00 AM for your disciplined time to accomplish something, but

Oliver found that she needed to give her best time to her poetry early in the day when she was employed in the traditional work world. Discipline is your ally in making a difference in your life. You literally engage in brain training with discipline and action. You diverge from the way in which popular culture views discipline. Discipline is positive for your life. Too often, discipline is an unmet need because adults never find delight in discipline.

DIGITAL DISCIPLINE

It is your choice to view any discipline as delightful or not. However, a bit of discipline is necessary to carry out the most basic human functions. As blogger Kris Carr views everydayness, "Delight reminds us to devote ourselves to people and projects that inspire rather than tire. It asks us to sit in the sunshine and eat a healthy meal on our lunch break, rather than wolfing down crap at our desks. Or ... . Delight reminds us to get up to pee when we need to – rather than holding it for a more convenient moment. ... And yet, why do I blow off my bladder in favor of just one more email?"[15] The email habit of constantly checking and rechecking for the latest message can hold you hostage. What email message is more important than attending to your basic needs? Who has enough discipline to set limits on gadgets?

Midori could not believe her eyes when she received a breakup by email. She read the two sentences over and over. What just happened? Why? When was the change of heart triggered? A digital breakup raises more questions than it answers. Often, the message is bland and brief. Grieving the loss of a romantic breakup is one of life's tough challenges. When the message is delivered remotely, it is particularly disorienting. Ironically, Noah found out that his romance had ended via Facebook; apparently, his partner could not "face" him. The awkward public breakup felt like a violation to Noah. Pop singer Britney Spears broke up with her husband, Kevin Federline, by a text message. Websites such as Breakup Butler have canned breakup messages so that the rejecting partner does not have to bother with any personal wording. BreakUpEmail provides a list of loser categories to help "generate a breakup email letter." Typical lines include, "It's not you, it's me. ... You're more like a sibling to me. ... We just aren't meant for each other. ... I've seen rocks that are more interesting than you." A dump truck sign on the site conveys the real message.[16] Nonverbal communication trumps verbal communication, but such messages often are misinterpreted. Do midlifers who want to break up recognize that a true split-up involves one or more roles in their personality wanting the separation, but there may be other roles that want a reunion on different terms?

It takes discipline to *turn* off cell phones and computers so that you openly communicate in the present moment. Captive to gadgets, you may find that a whole day slips by and your intended change for that day never happens. Words attributed to Siddhartha Buddha suggest, "Change is never painful. Only resistance to change is painful." Resistance and procrastination are well-watered weeds for many middle-aged adults, but acknowledge such roles. A growth mind-set helps to train your brain. As Doidge points out, "Every thought, especially when used systematically, is a potent way to stimulate neurons. When we think particular thoughts, certain networks in the brain are '*turn*ed on,' while others are 'switched off.'"[17] You can reset your brain to *turn* your focus to a positive definition for discipline. Many people confuse the notion of discipline solely with a form of limiting behavior. While having certain limits for behavior is helpful, discipline also takes into account that most daily conflicts stem from wavering attempts to satisfy basic needs. Even in good times, you can fall short of meeting your needs. Midlifers are busy not only with gadgets, but with the chores and work of life. However, there are consequences when you do not meet daily needs.

CHANGE HAPPENS BEST WITH DISCIPLINE

If you do not give yourself proper nutrition and sleep, you suffer in meeting the rest of your basic needs. By eating and sleeping well on one day, you have a better chance of meeting that day's needs. The next day requires more of the same attention to energy needs. Similarly, you require discipline to become proficient in meeting other needs. Loss adds confusion to meeting your recycling needs. Clouds of sadness can result in foglike thinking. William Stafford's poem, *Widow*, eloquently captures such ennui states: "She wandered the house – the forgiving table, the surprised-looking bed. Dishes in the rack needed putting away, and she helped them. But afterward she regretted – maybe nothing should move."[18] Even simple organization in your life may seem challenging today, and again tomorrow, after a significant loss. Activating discipline is such a practical approach, but loss can interfere with goal setting.

Focusing your thoughts matters in large and small ways. For Native American poet and environmentalist Linda Hogan, a focus on healing is important: "Some people see scars, and it is wounding they remember. To me they are proof of the fact that there is healing." However, it may take time to reach this healing view. Aurora sees open wounds in her family. Both of her parents have dementia. A sister endured two surgeries for cancer. When the whole family's health situation appeared fragile, Aurora faced doubts about her genes and her own health. As first one parent, then the other, lost ground, Aurora vacillated between being stoic and grieving for the happy family life she remembered. Her father's dementia took the difficult form of paranoia.

Aurora tired out her patient role. She took out her frustration on family members and friends.

Just as heated arguments mounted in the family, Aurora's father died. There were complicated emotional wounds for many individuals. The ancient adage by Publilius Syrus, Latin writer of moral maxims, seems true: "There is no fruit which is not bitter before it is ripe." Aurora vowed to replace her bitterness with something healthy, as she noticed that her joints felt stiff. She took up her favorite exercise of jogging again. She found that it cleared her head. She felt joy when the wind blew through her hair. As yoga instructor Antonio Sausys reminds, "Grief happens in the body,"[19] but bodily signs of grieving are ignored in our culture as much as mental anguish.

Progress in grieving often is a slow process. One of the leading scientists in artificial intelligence, Marvin Minsky, describes the suffering in loss: "The frustration that comes with the loss of your options; it is as though most of your mind has been stolen from you, and your awareness of this only makes things seem worse."[20] The emotional roles in your personality may feel as slippery as though you are choosing where next to step on an icy sidewalk. There is a paradox in change and exercising next steps. When you are living your life with few changes, you may not even consider options. You live most days by just keeping your keeping-on mode. It is only when a loss stops you in your tracks that you are likely to make changes. As business consultant William Bridges reminds, "When everything is going smoothly, it's often hard to change things. ... People who are sure they have the answers stop asking questions."[21] However, it is through the discipline of questioning that a person embraces a change process. If you have lots of questions about what's next, this is a good sign. You are in the process of rediscovering your priorities.

Perhaps you can find others who are in a similar *turn*ing point. Ask them what questions they have for future steps. Perhaps you find common ground with another midlifer. Here is where delight can enter. Have you ever met with a friend who was experiencing some snafu, similar in some ways but different in other ways from your own? Did the two of you end up laughing as you exchanged stories? Your stories undoubtedly had sad elements, but the way in which each of you characterized certain dilemmas in your storytelling provoked a knowing laugh or two. Humans benefit from talking about their losses with a good listener. Of course, you want to choose whom you talk with carefully. Some individuals are not good listeners, as listening also takes discipline.

Others hide their own secret losses and do not want to hear about another's loss. Some cannot engage any joyful or humor roles because it seems irreverent in times of loss. However, opposite personality roles are present in most of life's situations. When you find a true friend with whom to exchange loss stories, you already are changing. Change incorporates both exchanging and transforming:

• Change (from Latin *cambiare; to exchange or barter*) means to give a completely different form or appearance to: to transform.[22]

Consider poet and environmental activist Wendell Berry's wise words: "Ask the questions that have no answers. Invest in the millennium. Plant sequoias. ... Put your faith in the two inches of humus that will build under the trees every thousand years. ... Laugh. Laughter is immeasurable. Be joyful though you have considered all the facts." When you feel as though you are muddling through a maze, take heart in knowing that this is normal after a significant loss. There is a period of time between the shock of a loss and the next steps to reset your personality to face a hopeful future. Even when you feel a bit lost in an emotional maze, take some moments to be joyful even though you feel as if you have lost your way. Some of the first steps you might take are the ones to meet the five basic needs. You know the importance of getting enough sleep and enough exercise. What about your eating habits?

SILENT KITCHENS

Prior to the nineteenth century, we did not have our food focus upon restaurants and recipes. Multiethnic cookbooks did not exist. It was predominantly men who ate at restaurants.[23] Modern eating entails restaurants and fast-food enterprises. The average American spends around $1,200 each year on fast food, but 70% of Americans eat fast food up to three times a week and 7% consume fast food on a daily basis. Many fast-food choices contain more salt, fat, and sugar than a person should receive in one meal. The American fast-food diet has an annual food intake of 85.5 pounds of fats and oils, 53 gallons of soda, 23 pounds of pizza, and 29 pounds of French fries. The total amount of money spent in one year on fast food in the United States reaches nearly $384 billion.[24] Now you can understand why you see so many fast-food franchises. Fast food equals fast money.

Among many midlife adults, there is a fascination with specialty foods. Now you can find recipes and/or restaurants reviewed on your cell phone and computer. Many delightful recipes *turn* up on your computer if you want to feed yourself and your family more nutritious meals. There are adaptations for every kind of diet online, so no one has to feel excluded in recipe choices that are not vegetarian, vegan, or special in a particular way. However, discipline for cooking homemade meals has taken a nosedive in recent years.

Happily, more fathers today are sharing in cooking the weeknight evening meal. As one hassled working mother reports, "My husband and I both work full-time jobs and we both take care of our toddler son, but my husband gets home from work a couple of hours earlier than I do. This means that if we're going to eat a home-cooked meal, he will be the one slaving over the hot stove. As it *turns* out my husband is part of a growing group of men who are doing the cooking. Some of them are so into it, they're called gastrosexuals."[25] Men do not need a special name for their culinary skills, but if it helps to have one, call them gastrosexuals!

A curious finding is that male chefs dominate restaurants and hotels, but relatively few men cook at home regularly. Also, there is an overall decline in the amount of time that women spend cooking at home. A paradox exists as many people have interest in cooking shows, but they leave their own kitchens idle while they eat more prepared and packaged food or visit their favorite restaurants. According to market research, less than 60% of suppers that are served at home are cooked in the home. Regardless of socioeconomic status, all Americans are cooking less than in the 1960s. According to the Organization for Economic Cooperation and Development, not only do Americans spend less time cooking each day than in any other developed nation, they also spend less time eating than people elsewhere in the world.[26] When you size up the effects of the silent home kitchen, your health is at stake.

Journalist and author Michael Pollan wants to improve the health of families. He argues that Americans view cooking as drudgery. Realistically, this is how people may view all activities that require some discipline. What is forgotten is how it takes discipline to accomplish anything creative. Cooking is very creative, and the rewards of creating exciting meals are many. Pollan views the home cooking slump in this way: "The day is still only 24 hours long. The point is, we always find time for the things we value – and we've come to devalue cooking. ... When you realize all that not-cooking is costing us and our families, you'll be apt to carve out a little more time for it. And when you realize how pleasurable it can be, approached in the right spirit, you might just begin to devote some of your leisure to it."[27] People generally enjoy cooking with others. We need more cooking parties in the new millennium.

Pollan argues that when you allow prepared food to take over your steady diet, you eat sugary foods as your everyday diet and put yourself in danger of becoming diabetic. He calls our current eating habits a public health crisis. As a simple example, he notes how grocery stores market cereals. The sugary, less healthy choices are at eye level, while the boxes of oatmeal are on the bottom shelf. As an oatmeal breakfast fan, I have experienced this not-so-subtle marketing. Oatmeal is on the bottom shelf! One solution in choosing healthy food is to ask yourself whether your grandmother and great-grandmother called something food.[28] My 90s-something mother eats oatmeal every morning for breakfast. She tops it with walnuts, ground flaxseed, and banana slices. Her mother also had an oatmeal habit.

FOOD FOR THOUGHT

Just as important as the food you take in are the thoughts you take in – your food for thought. One activity that may help you in your grieving process is to allow time for both your imagination and insight to roam in a positive direction. Yes, you have relationships, work, and chores on your mind, but most of all, you have YOU to take care of in everyday ways. Make time for solitary imagination and insight. Albert Einstein believed that imagination is more important than knowledge: "Logic will get you from A to Z; imagination will get you everywhere. … Imagination is everything. It is the preview of life's coming attractions." Insight has similarities to imagination in terms of picturing ideas, but there are differences too. Make time and space for both:

- Imagination (from Latin *imaginari; picture to oneself*) means the ability to form mental images of things that are not present to the senses or not considered to be real.[29]
- Insight (from Swedish *insikt; inner sight or mental vision)* means the ability to discern the true nature of a situation, especially by intuition.[30]

Psychologist Gary Klein suggests that insight is "an unexpected shift to a better story."[31] Often, your imagination does this for you as well. The stories you tell yourself matter. Sometimes it is difficult to find positive thoughts after a significant loss, but having the discipline to allow time for resourceful thinking – both imaginative and insightful – can boost your energy level. Klein outlines insights appearing through making connections, experiencing coincidences, entertaining curiosities, finding contradictions, or simply realizing that you are in a state of creative desperation. In order to increase your chances for connections, coincidences, and curiosities, be open to unfamiliar possibilities. For contradiction insight, consider that some things work totally in a different way than you might predict. Giving up assumptions of "right" answers helps both contradiction and creative desperation insights.[32] As you know now, there is no prescribed discipline for grieving; you create your own grieving process.

Belgium-American writer May Sarton viewed discipline in this way: "The discipline of work provides an exercise bar, so that the wild, irrational motions of the soul become formal and creative. It literally keeps one from falling on one's face." While work and routine are important for grieving midlifers, so are relaxation and a balance of family/friend time versus solitude. One of the ten tips from the American Psychological Association brochure, "Road to Resilience," reads as follows: "Take care of yourself.

Pay attention to your own needs and feelings. Engage in activities that you enjoy and find relaxing. Exercise regularly. Taking care of yourself helps to keep your mind and body primed to deal with situations that require resilience."[33] Actually, this advice pertains to every midlifer every day, but it is particularly helpful when you feel lost in the midlife maze.

YOUR TURN

For a web begun, God sends thread.

– European proverb

Much of your discipline consists of rearranging roles in your personality into new configurations. Some changes seem implausible at first glance. Inventor Thomas Edison fiddled with a piece of putty while he attempted to make a carbon filament for a lightbulb. As he *turn*ed and twisted the putty in his fingers, a light literally went off in his brain. He suddenly discovered an answer to his problem. Edison realized that he could twist the carbon filament like he twisted putty into a rope.[34] Notice how he had the discipline to persist in his discovery process; he did not give up. Irish philosopher John O'Donohue suggested that adults often have difficulty understanding new meanings when they are overly familiar with habitual thoughts.[35] Approach changes in your life as if you are helping a part of yourself with whom you are just becoming acquainted.

* Rearrange how you view your life today to gain a new perspective. Start by choosing one situation in your life that puzzles you in some ways.
* Now view yourself for a little while as a stranger to your own deepest thoughts about this situation. Imagine looking at your memories by relating to the situation as an objective person who is reviewing an anonymous person's interesting life history.
* Jot down certain memories that appear to you. What perceptions occur to you as you preview these memories?
* What personality roles can you rearrange now that you have a different way of seeing what has taken place?
* Plan how you can use what you have learned from your visit. Write your brief messages and/or draw the roles you wish to adopt with your new focus.

The more you use positive emotions in your writing after a traumatic event in life, the more you can benefit from the experience. The degree to which you use such words as love, caring, funny, joy, beautiful, and warmth in your writing can predict improvements in your health.[36] As Holocaust survivor Viktor Frankl said, "In some way, suffering ceases to be suffering at the moment it finds a meaning."

Frankl wrote a book that helps millions. Perhaps you, too, have a book in you. Louise DeSalvo suggests that you can write the draft of a short book in a year if you have the discipline of writing five revised pages a week.[37] Writing can awaken you to the present moment.

Chapter 8

Tapping into Creativity

While we are asleep – in our beds or in our mother's bellies – our brain-minds are creating a fictive universe. This creativity makes us agents in understanding our worlds from a very early time in our developmental life. And we return to this fictive world for considerable amounts of time throughout our lives.

    – J. Alan Hobson, dream researcher, *13 Dreams Freud Never Had*

Experience has taught me that you cannot value dreams according to the odds of their coming true. Their real value is in stirring within us the will to aspire. ... An ordinary person, with strengths and weaknesses like anyone else ... [can] manage an extraordinary journey.

    – Sonia Sotomayor, Supreme Court Justice, *My Beloved World*

Treasuring creativity is at the heart of coping with loss. You cannot know how to grieve until it suddenly becomes your *turn*. Your grieving process will not duplicate another's person's process. So, do not worry about getting it wrong! You create your own path as you traipse through an emotional maze. Abraham Maslow spoke of the power of a recovery of creativity.[1] Look at your personality map again. Did you include a creative role yet? Your personality is your tool chest. I saw a snake charmer in Morocco. As the charmer opened his battered tool chest, a gyrating cobra wound its way upward into graceful dancing. Who would guess that such creative movements could rise from a dubious container? Open up your personality tool chest, no matter how battered it feels. What creative roles in your personality are untapped at this juncture in your life? Is there some change you desire? Unleash some gyrating creativity into your life.

If you need a little encouragement to engage in some artistic endeavor or social activity, consider this research. Rosebud Roberts works in the Division of Epidemiology at Mayo Clinic in Minneapolis. Her team studied adults ages 85 or above over a four-year period. The research focus was to identify risk factors for mild cognitive impairment and/or dementia. Nearly half of 256 participants developed mild dementia during that time. However, those individuals who engaged in artistic activities throughout *midlife* and later life were 73% less likely to develop mild dementia! Also, individuals who spent time in craft activities (such as ceramics, sewing, and woodworking) or social activities (as in book club participation, concert attendance, and traveling), both in midlife and later life, were about half as likely to develop mild dementia. Those who began using a computer in later life also had a reduced risk of cognitive impairment.[2] If you cannot imagine why you would begin some creative pursuit in midlife, consider how it could postpone cognitive decline later.

Whether these superagers who valued creative endeavors had a hardier neurology from birth onward is unknown, but the importance of how you spend time in midlife seems inescapable. You may say that you are not very creative. My guess is that you were a creative child, as the many children that I have been privileged to work with over a span of 40 years in clinical practice have taught me about incredible childhood creativity. As the diverse artist Pablo Picasso said, "Every child is an artist. The problem is how to remain an artist once he [or she] grows up." Perhaps our school boards have too many midlifers who forgot about their own creative childhoods, as there are cuts in school programming in art and music in too many states. We must treasure play our whole lives. As psychologist Keith Sawyer reminds, playfulness is one step in the creativity process: "Ideas come in unexpected zigs and zags. … They're not delivered on demand."[3] Look inward into nighttime dreams and daydreams for zigzagging gems.

CULTIVATING CREATIVITY

Dream researcher Hobson has a creativity focus: "My dreaming mind is seduced by its own creativity. … [Dreaming] can consolidate and integrate emotionally salient content effectively and efficiently … [making] dream meaning strikingly evident … via an emotionally driven shorthand."[4] Judge Sonia Sotomayer experienced a difficult childhood, including family problems and childhood diabetes, but she credits her childhood daydreams of becoming a lawyer with her eventual job-of-a-lifetime climb to the Supreme Court. She daydreamed that she was a defense attorney like TV's Perry Mason! Sotomayer is a role model of positive values and creativity: "People who live in difficult circumstances need to know that happy endings are possible."[5] Yes, joyful roles are possible after loss. When did you last use a happy role? What role(s) keep you from exercising joy? What would you rediscover if you recall your childhood play? Psychiatrist and play researcher Stuart Brown reviewed over six thousand life histories in his study of play. He found that killers have something in common – a severe deprivation of play characterized their childhood. Furthermore, Brown viewed adults who lose track of play in their lives as experiencing social, emotional, and cognitive narrowing which results in less ability to handle stress. Such narrowing is accompanied by depression. Successful adults experience a rich play life.[6] When you experienced a significant loss, you likely cut out play times. "How can I play at my age?" you may ask. Play is creative! Body play, as in dancing, qualifies as exercise as well as play. Likewise, athletic play reaps double kudos – you engage in exercise and socialization at the same time. Some families enjoy rough and tumble play, spectator play, social play (the game Twister is fun for every age), and ritual play, as in special holiday outings where the same activity is enjoyed every year. Imaginative solo play (pretending, daydreaming, drawing, writing poetry/stories) also counts. According to Brown, "Nothing lights up the brain like play." He views work and play as mutually supportive.

Thinking creatively happens whenever you reach for alternatives to usual behavior. However, as creativity consultant Michael Michalko describes typical thinking, you may rely upon thinking *reproductively*. It seems easier to copy habits you already know. Conforming to past practice may explain why you repeat the same mistakes. Creative midlifers value freedom of thought. Instead of relying on what worked before, try a new spin in your thinking. Creative people think *productively*, looking for as many different solutions as possible.[7] Architect Frank Lloyd Wright wanted to break the box, or design novel projects, rather than reproduce the prevalent Victorian architecture with square-box spaces. All problem solving receives a boost when you consider alternatives.

What if you cannot see options? You may view everything as "fixed" when you feel stuck in life. To rediscover creativity, psychotherapist Bill O'Hanlon suggests that you imagine teaching someone else to "do" your problem. For example, if Meryl Streep represented you in a movie, how would you coach her to act your situation?[8] Improv also unleashes creativity. Instead of finding fault with your life, consider substituting "yes *and*" for your "yes *but*" excuses for not trying something new.[9] Treasuring creativity truly is at the heart of retooling your personality. Add creative roles to your personality map whenever you diverge from your usual habits. Albert Einstein said, "Creativity is intelligence having fun." Where is your fun/funny role?

ASK QUESTIONS

Actor and director Ethan Hawke sums up midlife: "One of the things I've found incredibly difficult about middle age is the difference between meeting your responsibilities, and idealism, and where they intersect, and where creativity fits into that whole scheme. ... Life is a slog. It's more difficult than you think. And it's more subtle than I thought when I was a kid. ... There aren't these lines you cross and all of a sudden, you're done. Life keeps presenting new challenges." Yes, challenging times blow into your life like a sudden hailstorm. Just when you think that you have overcome one cloudburst, the next one appears. Your questions mount, but initially you have few creative answers. Which way should you *turn*?

The great innovators asked themselves a lot of questions. Then they answered themselves. Einstein asked himself, "What would happen if I rode a beam of light?" Walt Disney asked, "How can I create the happiest place on Earth?" Chemist Stephanie Kwolek, inventor of synthetic fibers five times stronger than steel (Kevlar), almost threw away her invention. Because of her continuous questions, she tested her strange solution again. It *turns* out that Kevlar supports bicycle tires, racing sails, body armor, musical instruments, and building construction to name a few uses. Computer scientist Grace Hopper took apart alarm clocks as a seven-year-old child because she questioned how they worked. In midlife, she invented the first compiler to translate written language into computer code. Hopper coined the words "bug" and "debugging" because she had to remove moths from her five-ton room-sized computer at Harvard![10]

Apple computer whiz Steve Jobs asked, "If today were the last day of my life, would I want to do what I am about to do today?" Jobs was so good at creating products that when he died of pancreatic cancer at age 56, he had 241 patents either individually or as a coinventor. However, Jobs was fired from a prestigious job. Afterward, he made a conscious decision to veer into new territory. Jobs told Stanford University graduates in 2005, "I didn't see it then, but it *turn*ed out that getting fired from Apple was the best thing that could have ever happened to me. The heaviness of being successful was replaced by the lightness of being a beginner again, less sure about everything. It freed me to enter one of the most creative periods of my life."[11] Jobs *turn*ed a corner after job loss: "Sometimes life hits you in the head with a brick. Don't lose faith. I'm convinced the only thing that kept me going was that I loved what I did. You've got to find what you love." Uncertainty in beginning anew did not stop Jobs, but rather served as fertilizer to keep creating. Jobs lived up to his name with many creative jobs.

HOMEGROWN CREATIVITY

Creative people find work and hobbies that they love. They fiddle with ways to make life more meaningful. Psychologist K. Anders Ericsson studies how people achieve the highest levels of expertise. Ericsson finds that extremely talented people across many different disciplines – music, sports, writing – engage in deliberate practice. They not only improve the skills they have, but they work to extend their skillset. With the enormous concentration required, very few spend more than four to five hours of high concentration at a time. While you need sustained periods of focus, you also need downtime. Age is less of a factor than you might guess. Research shows that musicians over 60 who continue their deliberate practice for about 10 hours a week are capable of matching the speed and technical skills of 20-year-old expert musicians. And they were tested on their ability to play a piece of unfamiliar music.[12] When you engage in creative pursuits, you are more likely to think in the present moment.

After loss, you may feel like a beginner in life. This is an opportunity to rediscover creative personality roles. First, ground yourself in self-territory. British writer Charlotte Bronte wrote about a tumultuous life filled with loss for her character, Jane Eyre. However, Jane thrives in spite of challenges because of an inner sense of herself: "I have an inward treasure born with me, which can keep me alive if all the extraneous delights should be withheld or offered only at a price I cannot afford to give." All of us can awaken to inward treasure. Creativity helps you look at your circumstances with a new twist. Creativity is not attached to any one activity, although our culture names art forms such as dancing, singing, playing a musical instrument, composing, sculpting, or painting as creative. You can sing sour notes or be a clone cook without creativity. But what would your day look like if you practiced singing and cooked with creativity? Write your own tune or cook something you never made before.

With a growth mind-set, you create newness in any activity. One simple creative action is to remake your holiday traditions. Gretchen Rubin, author of *The Happiness Project*, is up early on holidays. She even celebrates minor holidays like Leap Year. She invented a black breakfast for her children on Halloween and a red breakfast on Valentine's Day.[13] Even though she has to get up earlier than usual, seeing happiness in her children gives her extra energy. Creativity, discipline, energy – can you see links between your basic needs? I sewed my children's Halloween costumes, taking them to the fabric store to brainstorm ideas. One year my son could not find anything appealing in the McCall or Butterick pattern books. He wanted a hot dog costume! With the help of my super-creative Mom and lots of laughter, together we fashioned a costume complete with red cloth "ketchup" and green cloth "pickle relish." The real relish was seeing the look on my son's face as he tried on his hefty hot dog and bun! He loved marching as a giant hot dog, taking first place in creativity in the Boy Scouts costume parade.

Not all children move through childhood, adolescence, or young adulthood to reach midlife. Jazz saxophonist and composer Jimmy Greene and his wife, Nelba Marquez-Greene, lost their precious daughter, Ana, in the Sandy Hook Elementary School shooting tragedy that took the lives of 20 children and 6 adults. Ana was 6 years, 8 months and 10 days old. Greene was heartbroken, but he created a CD, *Beautiful Life*, as part of his grieving process. He composed *Seventh Candle* without words around the date when the family might have celebrated Ana's seventh birthday. His homegrown lyrics in *Ana's Way* capture a father's tribute to a love-inspiring daughter. Greene ends the recording with two powerful words: "Love wins."[14]

Puppeteer Jim Henson initially created his famous Muppet, Kermit the Frog, when he was grieving his grandfather's death. Fashioned out of his mother's old felt coat, Henson sewed a flexible puppet body. He *turn*ed cardboard into a pointed face in the puppet head. He glued two halves of a ping-pong ball for eyes onto the funny amphibian head. With black-inked slash marks drawn through black circles, Kermit's ping-pong eye balls demanded attention; however, Kermit did not become known as a frog until later. Of all the puppets created by Henson, Kermit was his personal favorite.[15] It may be no accident that Kermit's famous song, *It's Not Easy Bein' Green*, deals with sadness, and yet embraces acceptance. Perhaps you will write a homegrown song titled, "It's Not Easy Bein' Grievin.'"

DISTRACTION AND LOSS

Think of what happens when you cannot focus your attention on any task at hand. Distraction is rampant across activities and many kinds of jobs. Mind wandering away from normal activities is common after a loss. There are all those things you wish you would have said. Childhood memories float into consciousness after decades. And who dares to think about what the future brings? Is another calamity coming? Mark Twain quipped, "My life has been filled with terrible misfortunes most of which never happened." Actually, fears are on the minds of most midlifers. And everyone struggles with distraction at various times. Many struggle with a lack of focus on the job. While workers may have pride in a strong work ethic, a lot of nonwork time happens at work sites. A survey of 1700 white-collar workers from Boston to Beijing found that employees report spending more than half (51%) their workday simply receiving/managing information, rather than actually using the information to perform their jobs.[16] Now consider what happens in the work life of a grieving worker after loss. Unwelcome thoughts mix with the avalanche of information overload. Work to-do lists are in perpetual motion.

You may take pride in multitasking, but the reality is that multitasking has flaws. You merely split your attention, switching from one task to another very rapidly. Multitasking can diminish overall productivity as much as 40%.

Multitasking increases the stress hormone, cortisol, as well as adrenaline, the fight-or-flight-or-freeze hormone. Since your prefrontal cortex has a novelty bias, you may leap at chances to attend to something new. Yet, research findings suggest that what you may learn while multitasking causes that information to go to the wrong part of the brain for later retrieval. Psychologist Glenn Wilson's research finds that impairment to a worker's concentration is serious: "An email sitting in your inbox can reduce your effective IQ by 10 points." Wilson studies *info-mania*, the condition of too much information to process all at the same time.[17] With loss on your mind, this overstimulation seems overwhelming.

Gloria Mark, professor of *informatics* at University of California at Irvine, studies digital distraction. Mark finds that innovation and multitasking are a bad combination: "Ten and a half minutes on one project is not enough time to think in-depth about anything."[18] However, the average adult succumbs to distractions an average of every 3 minutes! After only 20 minutes of interrupted performance, people report higher stress, frustration, workload effort, and pressure.[19] Since our brains always scan the environment for safety, no one focuses with 100% concentration. Actually, it *turns* out that you cultivate creativity by a see-saw rotation of spending time in a dedicated focus period and then daydreaming. After reading for a while right now, are you getting ready to daydream a bit? Yes, this distracts you from reading, but it may lead to a creative thought or two.

- Focus (from Latin, *focus; hearth* or *fireplace*) means close or narrow attention, or concentration. Concentration focuses as a lens fixes upon sunlight on a single point to start a fire.[20]

What many people from ancient times to present time use to distract themselves from grieving is to get drunk. In 405 BC, the Greek playwright Euripedes wrote in his play, *The Baccae:* "[Dionysos] … gives to mortals the vine that puts an end to grief."[21] If you try numbing your grieving personality roles with alcohol, not only will you lose an opportunity to use creativity, but you will damage the prefrontal cortex of your brain: "Alcohol interferes with the ability of prefrontal cortex neurons to communicate with one another, by disrupting dopamine receptors … heavy drinkers also … may lose certain capabilities, such as impulse control or motor coordination or the ability to drive safely, but they aren't aware that they've lost them – or simply don't care – so they forge ahead anyway."[22] Some distractions are killers.

A further drinking complication is that excessive alcohol use causes chronic inflammation which is linked to neurodegenerative diseases like Alzheimer's disease.[23] Regardless of this dangerous inflammation link, alcohol is used frequently to medicate all kinds of losses. Funeral home visitations and memorial services often end up as drinking events. Another frequent occurrence after a death is a physician's prescription for grief-stricken family members so they can numb their pain. After my husband died suddenly, I was offered both a prescription and alcohol by well-meaning folks. I declined both. There was no *turn*ing away from what had happened. Distraction was not an answer for me. I needed to be mindful and in the present moment with my emotions and the unfolding story of my life.

TURN TIP

Be a lamp, or a lifeboat, or a ladder. Help someone's soul heal. Walk out of your house like a shepherd.

– Rumi, Persian poet and Sufi mystic

The words mindfulness and meditation scare many people. They wonder if meditation "works." To strip away any preconceived notions about how to meditate, first consider learning how to focus your awareness by slowing down your sensory intake. When you focus intently, you are in the present moment. You push all other thoughts away. Buy a small piece of chocolate of your choice. If you have an allergy to chocolate, do this exercise with one raisin.

- Take only one small piece of chocolate.
- Notice the weight of the chocolate in your hand.
- Observe the shape of this chocolate. *Turn* it over. Is it round, square or a teardrop shape?
- As you unwrap your chocolate, listen to the crinkle of the wrapper.
- Touch the chocolate. Feel its texture.
- Silently describe the chocolate: hold it up to your nose. Inhale deeply. Take deep breaths.
- Follow the scent as it travels into your nose. Be aware of what is happening in your mind.

Maybe it is anticipation or longing. Let any thoughts come and go.

- Place the chocolate in your mouth. Observe the burst of flavor. Experience the taste fully. Allow the fullness of the flavor to melt in your mouth, without biting or chewing the chocolate.
- Circle the chocolate against the roof of your mouth. Be aware of any feelings, sensations, or memories.
- Pay attention to the texture changing and molding to your tongue. Hold onto the sensation as it begins to fade.

- Be present with your feelings and sensations. Focus your attention on the taste and texture. Listen to the sound of your jaw. Feel the sensation as chocolate slides down your throat.
- You might want to reach for another chocolate. See if you can relax. Stay focused in the *present* moment.

Notice how different this experience is from your usual way of eating chocolate.[24]

MEDITATION OPENS THE CREATIVITY GATE

Creativity and mindfulness meditation are related. Both require that you suspend judgment, evaluations, or distractions. You free yourself of worrying about the past or trying to fix the future – for a time. You notice when your mind wanders. You witness your thoughts with kindness. You train your brain in calmness. Life seems possible. You may not believe that you can meditate after experiencing loss. After all, you have even more on your mind than before the loss occurred. How can you take time away from your busy thoughts to meditate? Isn't that a weird thing to do anyway? Your first thoughts demand attention, as there are many myths about meditation. The first myth is that you must completely rid your mind of thoughts. No, you do not completely empty your "monkey mind" chattering almost nonstop. You simply become aware that your mind is full of wandering thoughts. With hundred billion neurons (with hundred trillion connections),[25] thoughts are bound to rain down as fast as a summer shower! This is a good thing when you want to use more of your creativity. Researchers found that increasing your focused attention through meditation increases creativity. Specifically, meditation promotes divergent thinking, or ability to generate many ideas.[26]

Some people believe that meditation is only possible for mystics and monks. This is a fixed mind-set about prayer and/or meditation. Some meditators relate their practice to religious beliefs, others see their practice as health/ability enhancement, and still others hold both viewpoints in mind. While you may choose to focus your mind upon a religious image or thought, it is only one method for mindfulness meditation. Schools and businesses teach a secular form of meditation. As neuroscientist Andrew Newberg points out, "The neurological changes that occur during meditation disrupt the normal processes of the brain – perceptually, emotionally, and linguistically – in ways that make the experience indescribable, awe-inspiring, unifying, and indelibly real. ... But many nonreligious people have interpreted them in more secular ways."[27] While mindfulness in some form is a part of nearly every world religion, mindfulness meditation "works" regardless of any religious connotation.

Research shows that mindfulness meditation causes greater activity in the prefrontal cortex (the part of the brain just above the eyes). Mindfulness may include increased attention, as well as enhancing planning and carrying out tasks. The prefrontal cortex processes language, memory, self-reflection, and social skills, along with processing religious beliefs. "One might say that the act of prayer is a problem-solving device, designed to consciously explore a spiritual perspective or belief and to integrate that awareness into daily life."[28] French philosopher Simone Weil defines prayer in this manner: "Absolutely unmixed attention is prayer." Prayer is one form of meditation. Other common mindfulness meditation practices are the following:

Focused-attention meditation: Choose a target for your focus. Perhaps you light a candle and watch the flickering flame. You may focus on another of your senses, such as picking up all the sounds around you. Perhaps you close your eyes and listen to calming music or a CD of ocean sounds. A special focus helps you have something to anchor your awareness. Thoughts come and go, but you bring your attention back to your target of focus. You want to experience your focus rather than think about it.

Open-monitoring meditation: You do not have a particular focus other than awareness of your own breath cycles. Often, people start with focused-attention meditation and then move on to open-monitoring meditation. Your raining thoughts will enter your mind, but you do not critique them as you might on the job or in random day-to-day circumstances. You observe random thoughts and then let them pass, as rain showers inevitably pass by. You are present in the moment and in your own breathing. Your mind is calm and relaxed. You are open to your experience without making any attempt to interpret, change, reject, or ignore painful thoughts.

Compassion and loving kindness meditation: You practice having altruistic love for both yourself and others. Your focus is upon positive qualities of a person. You direct loving kindness toward someone you dearly love, a neutral person, or even toward someone in your life you are upset with currently. It is a form of unconditional love, an acceptance of yourself and others. While this ancient practice originated from Buddhist tradition, you do not have to equate the practice with religion. Beatles' singer/songwriter George Harrison has a poetic definition of compassion meditation: "When you've seen beyond yourself then you may find peace of mind is waiting there, and the time will come when you see we're all one."

Scientific studies back up Harrison's notion of gaining peace of mind from meditation. A decrease in depression was found in participants who experienced compassion meditation. Researchers found that novice meditators participating in an eight-week meditation training program had measurable effects on their brain functioning even when they were *not* meditating. The meditators decreased activation of the amygdala, the area of your brain more commonly known for its constant search for negatives and fight/flight/freeze preparation, even though they were not meditating at the time of magnetic resonance imaging (fMRI) testing.[29] Also, expert meditators experience diminished brain activity in anxiety-related areas. Meditation training increases your ability to change stress hormone levels.[30]

In considerable research on meditation conducted at the University of Wisconsin-Madison, neuroscientist Richard Davidson concluded that happiness is a skill: "It's actually something that can be cultivated. ... Everything we've learned about the brain suggests it's no different than learning the violin. ... If you practice, you'll get better at it."[31] With a growth mind-set, you can decide to *turn* your attention more frequently to happiness and creativity skill building. Like so many other topics, meditation is individual. While sitting still is not easy for many, there are other ways to practice mindfulness. A walking mindfulness practice works best for some. Others find mindfulness when they knit, sing, or use their hands for woodworking, painting, or gardening. May Sarton advises, "Everything that slows us down and forces patience, everything that sets us back into the slow cycles of nature is a help. Gardening is an instrument of grace."

YOGA MEDITATION

Yoga postures can help you develop a meditative focus. A 2012 study finds that 8.7% of U.S. adults (20.4 million people) practice yoga; 80% are women.[32] Yoga practitioners learn to elongate their breathing by using their belly, ribs, and chest to inhale/exhale. As yoga instructor Amy Weintraub advises, "The way in which you breathe is a metaphor for the way in which you are living your life. Are you taking little sips of breath as though you don't have permission to take up much space on the planet?"[33] You can change shallow breathing patterns by focusing on the present moment. The relaxation of *yoga nidra*, or a resting state where you remain fully conscious of your physical environment, can take your brain from chaotic multitasking attempts to a state of calmness.

More vigorous forms of yoga, pairing elongated breath work with energizing poses, deliver a mindful state as well. Chanting yogic meditation is another meditative path with powerful results. Helen Lavretsky, professor of psychiatry at the UCLA Semel Institute for Neuroscience and Human Behavior, finds that *Kirtan Kriya* meditation leads to stress reduction in the caretakers for the Alzheimer's patients. Practicing for just 12 minutes a day for 8 weeks was found to impact 68 of the caregivers' genes, resulting in reduced inflammation in their bodies. Approximately five million Americans care for someone with dementia today and the caregiving role is associated with higher levels of inflammation.[34] Unchecked inflammation can affect multiple organs, as well as your brain.

Another research study found a 12-week yoga intervention to have greater improvements in mood and anxiety than a matched walking exercise program. Yoga participants increased their brain chemical gamma aminobutyric acid (GABA) levels.[35] GABA increases alpha brain waves with the effects of reducing stress, nervousness, and insomnia. Alpha brain wave activity is common in people experiencing relaxing or creative endeavors. Just closing your eyes for a minute or more may increase your alpha brain wave activity. Meditation produces alpha brain waves during activities such as yoga and Tai Chi by focusing your attention on one task in the present moment. Alpha waves occur normally in the beginning stage of falling asleep. If you have low levels of GABA, there are many health consequences that you do not want; a short list of possible side effects of low GABA includes anxiety, panic disorders, depression, hypertension, and wrinkles.[36] I love both yoga and Tai Chi practices for their positive and meditative effects upon grieving.

MEDITATION AS MAINSTREAM

As meditation teacher Jon Kabat-Zinn suggests, there is nothing weird about meditation: "It is just about paying attention in your life as if it really mattered. … While it is really nothing out of the ordinary, nothing particularly special, mindfulness is at the same time extraordinarily special and utterly transformative in ways that are impossible to imagine."[37] Meditation has entered the mainstream in America. Some schools are catching meditation's impressive research drift and offer mindfulness programs in classrooms. Cancer patients meditate. Air Force reservists and their families meditate. Business leaders meditate. Prisoners meditate. Basketball players meditate. One of the more famous examples of the power of meditation is Coach Phil Jackson's winning Chicago Bulls basketball team. The Bulls trained and practiced mindfulness under George Mumford, who also taught prisoners the same techniques.[38] The Chicago Bulls won four NBA championships. When Jackson moved to Los Angeles to coach the Lakers, they practiced mindfulness too and won three NBA titles.

As Jackson coaches, "When things are going wrong, take a breath and reset yourself. You do that through mindfulness – you just come right back in and collect yourself." Meditation supports fulfillment in all areas of life.

Buddhist teacher Pema Chodron explains why a person meditates. It is not to feel good while meditating, but to have an open, compassionate awareness toward thoughts about whatever life delivers. The goal is to stay present without putting labels, good or bad, onto the meditation experience. You discover acceptance of your life: "We're so used to running from discomfort, and we're so predictable. If we don't like it, we strike out at someone or beat up on ourselves. We want to have security and certainty of some kind. ... The next time there's no ground to stand on, don't consider it an obstacle. Consider it a remarkable stroke of luck. ... Finally, after all these years, we could truly grow up."[39] The point of meditation is to slow down, notice thoughts, and accept emotions. Aware of a particular thought, you drop that thought and refocus. This brain training facilitates your ability to change your personality roles whenever you need a reset.

Some women learned to refocus their attention and change their sex drive. Psychologist and researcher Lori Brotto, associate professor of gynecology at the University of British Columbia, uses mindfulness meditation to treat sexual dysfunction in women. Brotto found that health issues and menopause are among the culprits of low sexual desire in midlife women. (Men also experience low desire; in fact, low desire in men is more common than erection problems). Brotto instructed women in an eight-week group program of mindfulness meditation to be aware of present moments. When participants redirected their thoughts back to the present moment, they stopped judging themselves. Their sexual desire, arousal, satisfaction, and pleasure increased, and their sex-related distress lessened.[40] One mindfulness technique utilized by Brotto is offered as the *Turn* Tip in this chapter (Brotto used a raisin). While your issues may not include low sexual desire, this mindfulness brain training helps reduce daily stress in general.

From championship basketball teams to the caregivers of patients with dementia, meditation practices make an incredible difference in people's lives. Meditation can provide preventive medicine, as well as healing from loss. When you grieve, you may not take good care of yourself. The unfortunate side effect of this neglect is illness. However, if your loss is of your own good health, you may not be capable of meeting your basic needs every day. Perhaps you experience chronic pain. Depression over loss of health is a concern. Meditation is one tool that provides relief. Anyone can practice meditation. There is no expensive equipment or clothing involved. When you meditate, you spend present moments in self-territory. As you practice taking deep breaths, you free yourself of your personality roles of worry and/ or loneliness, even if briefly. In the words of Buddhist monk Thich Nhat Hanh, "Real silence is the cessation of talking – of both the mouth and of the mind." He also advised against "grim" practice of meditation: "I have just two instructions for you this week. One is to breathe, and one is to smile."[41]

YOUR TURN

A ship in port is safe, but that's not what ships are built for.

> – Grace Murray Hopper, Pioneer computer scientist
> and U.S. Navy officer

If you are new to meditation, try a simple form called Breath Counting Meditation. Sit in a comfortable position with your spine straight and your head inclined forward. Close your eyes. Take a few deep breaths. Breathe without trying to influence breaths. Ideally breathing will be quiet and slow, but depth and rhythm may vary.

• To begin the exercise, count 1 to yourself as you exhale.
• The next time you exhale, count 2, and continue counting exhales up to 5.
• Then begin a new cycle, counting 1 on the next exhalation.

There is no need to count higher than 5. You will know your attention has wandered if you find yourself counting up to 8, or 19. When thoughts distract you, let them drift away like clouds in the sky. Stay neutral while noticing constant shifts in your awareness. Try ten minutes of meditating.[42] Meditation effects are cumulative. As your practice evolves, you can extend your time to 15 or even 30 minutes. However, it is better to spend a few minutes meditating every day rather than meditating for an hour once a week. Meditation provides relief from living in the past.[43] Thich Nhat Hanh views meditation with this lens: "To be still alive is a miracle. ... And when you breathe in, you touch that miracle. Therefore, your breathing can be a celebration of life." Celebration of life is a creative action.

Chapter 9

Inviting Belonging Connections

The world needs all its flowers, just as they are, and even though they bloom for only the briefest of moments. ... It is our job to find out ... what kind of flowers we are, and to share our unique beauty with the world in the precious time that we have, and to leave ... a legacy of wisdom and compassion embodied in the way we live.

> – Jon Kabat-Zinn, meditation teacher, *Coming to Our Senses*

Only in growth, reform and change, paradoxically enough, is true security to be found.

> – Anne Morrow Lindbergh, aviator and writer

Meeting your need for belonging or attachment relates to having intimate, ongoing contact with family and friends. You may ask, is belonging really a basic need? Yes, your brain develops within a social context: "One cannot develop a sense of self without a sense of the other. Humans evolved to be especially sensitive to social cues. In fact, the complexity of dealing with group social life is believed to be one of the key reasons our brains became so big."[1] The irony of our big brains and keen sense of belongingness is that some of our most cherished values – self-sacrifice, kindness, and cooperation – have been employed to help groups of people succeed in war: "Indeed, research has shown that group bonds are strengthened by conflict with outsiders. A common enemy can certainly unite people."[2] We need to increase our group belongingness ties without having to focus on "out" groups. Not only is it possible to have belongingness based upon common causes that affirm other people, it is more joyful and healing.

There is research to back up the notion that your attachments to others constitute a very important need. Psychologists Roy Baumeister and Mark Leary studied belongingness and the impact of a person's lack of belonging ties. Their research findings deviate both from Sigmund Freud's theory proposing sex and aggression as driving human behavior, and psychologist John Watson's behaviorism model of human behavior: "Give me a dozen healthy infants, well-formed, and my own specified world to bring them up in and I'll guarantee to take any one at random and train him to become any type of specialist I might select - doctor, lawyer, artist, merchant-chief and, yes, even beggar-man and thief, regardless of his talents, penchants, tendencies, abilities, vocations and the race of his ancestors."[3] Instead, Baumeister and Leary found that humans thrive and grow best when they both establish and sustain belongingness with other people.[4] Furthermore, after experiencing loss of a beloved person, an important aspect of grieving is to savor precious relationship memories.

Some loss situations are so tragic that the well-being of the following generation is affected. Rachel Yehuda, neuroscience professor and director of the Traumatic Stress Studies Division at Mount Sinai School of Medicine in New York, studied both children of Holocaust survivors and pregnant women who survived the 9/11 attacks in New York City. Yehuda found that the pregnant women who had developed posttraumatic stress disorder (PTSD) symptoms following the tragedy had significantly lower levels of the hormone cortisol (which enables the body to respond to stress) than those pregnant women who did not exhibit PTSD symptoms. A year later, the babies born to these mothers were tested. If their mother had PTSD symptoms, then the baby had lower levels of the hormone than the others. Following these youngsters, Yehuda found that they exhibited an increased stress response when shown novel stimuli. She also found reduced cortisol level results in the adult children of Holocaust survivors.[5] These important results are part of the fascinating study of epigenetics, or the study of how gene expression interacts with environmental influences. Intergenerational stress has roots.

SECURE VERSUS INSECURE ATTACHMENTS

Developmental psychologist Mary Ainsworth formed her belonging ideas from British physician John Bowlby's theory of attachment. Considered the mother of attachment theory, Ainsworth studied mother–infant pairs. She defined belongingness in terms of *secure* versus *insecure* attachment. While the labels have received revision over time, there are four general attachment styles: secure, anxious-resistant, anxious-avoidant, and disorganized-disoriented. Ainsworth's research aim was to discover the best parenting styles, but her terms also apply to adult romantic relationships. Psychologists Cindy Hazan and Phil Shaver applied these attachment terms to adults and found similarities to the mother–infant attachments categories. For example, secure infants tend to become well-adjusted youngsters, and secure adults tend to have more satisfaction with their relationships than insecure adults.[6]

However, adult relationships are complex. A strong attachment would seem best; but when adult belonging attachments are too intense, codependency develops. The best belongingness for both youngsters and adults is developing a secure base with the freedom to exercise some independence. Fortunately, insecure attachments from childhood can shift to secure attachments in an adult over time. Psychiatrist Dan Siegel provides hope for everyone by finding that a compassionate relationship with a caring adult – either a partner or a therapist – can *turn* a person in the direction of secure attachments. Furthermore, an individual with "earned security" is capable of having children who are securely attached.[7] Raising children involves intergenerational factors.[8] Three-generation households are increasing. Also, 40.2% of all U.S. births are to unmarried women.[9] Secure attachments among parents are not guaranteed in two-parent homes. Furthermore, fewer than half (46%) of children from infancy to18 years of age in the United States live in a home with two married heterosexual parents who are in a first marriage. This so-called traditional family is no longer the predominant family in the United States.[10] The takeaway message for attachment is that the particular type of family is less important than the capacity of individuals in every family unit to form secure attachments.

Perhaps English statesman and Prime Minister Benjamin Disraeli said it best: "We are *all* born for love. It is the principle of existence, and its only end." A 75-year longitudinal study, Harvard Study of Adult Development, proves the importance of secure love attachments. The health and mental well-being of 724 men (268 Harvard sophomores and 456 inner-city Boston youth) was found to depend upon the quality of their relationships. According to current director, psychiatrist Robert Waldinger, "We used to think that if you had relatives who lived to a ripe old age, that was the best predictor of a long life. … It turns out that the lifestyle choices people make in midlife are a more important predictor of how long you live."[11] Good midlife relationships are responsible for keeping you happier and healthier. Those who are isolated are more likely to have health declines beginning in midlife; they also live shorter lives. Waldinger's advice for aging is simple: "Replace workmates with playmates!"[12] Playmates are necessary at every age.

An inspiring coach, midlifer Biff Poggi at Gilman High School in Maryland, understands secure attachments. He teaches belongingness to his football teams: "The rest of the world will want to separate you by race, by socioeconomic status, by education levels, by religion, by neighborhood, by what kind of car you drive, by the clothes you wear, by athletic ability. You name it – always gonna be people who want to separate by that stuff. Well, if you let that happen now, then you'll let it happen later. Don't let it happen. If you're one of us, then you won't walk around putting people in boxes. Not now. Not ever. … I don't care if you're big or small, huge muscles or no muscles, never even played football or star of the team – I don't care about any of that stuff. … If you're here, then you're one of us, and we love you."[13] Coach Poggi further instructs his young teams never to allow anyone they see during school lunchtime to eat by themselves. How would our high schools be different places if his belongingness message reached every lunchroom? Could we eradicate the lone-wolf shooters with Coach Poggi's radical inclusiveness and kindness?

What if we extended the coach's message to workplace cafeterias? It is estimated that one in three individuals over the age of 45 suffers as chronically lonely in the United States: only a decade ago the rate was one in five.[14] Furthermore, famous people are not immune to the lonely label. Blues singer Janis Joplin said shortly before her death that she was working on a song she would title, "I just made love to 25,000 people, but I'm going home alone." In her final interview, she said, "In my insides, it really hurts if someone doesn't like me." She died of a heroin overdose when she was a rising star. Pulitzer Prize–winning poet Anne Sexton committed suicide at age 45. Her prior words express how a sense of belonging eluded her: "I am like a stone that lives … locked outside of all that's real … watching everyone fit in where I can't. … I want to belong. … I'm not a part. I'm not a member. I'm frozen."[15] Belgium-American poet May Sarton aptly differentiated loneliness from spending quality time by yourself: "Loneliness is the poverty of self; solitude is the richness of self." The goal in life is to form a secure attachment with yourself, recognizing your own uniqueness, as well as belonging to significant others.

ALL THE LONELY PEOPLE

People feel lost in loneliness when they lack belonging ties. This is one reason why loss of a friend or companion has such a big impact upon you. Just having occasional social contact does not buffer you from loneliness. Both anxiety and jealousy are common when a person feels excluded. You may have a depressed or blue role in your personality – emotions like Sexton's – that you do not belong anywhere. In fact, when you experience ostracism, rejection, or exclusion, brain scans show that you may experience the emotional rejection as physical pain; the pain occurs whether those who reject you are close friends, family, or total strangers. The rejecting behavior may be overt exclusion or merely looking away. Some individuals can shrug off a slight, but others who are socially anxious or prone to depression tend to ruminate and take longer to recover from ostracism than others.[16] As writer Rita Mae Brown reminds, "We are herd animals; we want to belong."

Disconnections are inevitable in midlife, even in the best relationships. Look at your current relationships. Notice where you have disconnections.[17] In describing a 38-year marriage, radio host Garrison Keillor dished, "They are both lost, but they are lost together!" While there are many different ways to feel lost or lonely, divorced individuals experience a loss of a dream of romantic attachment. Only a minority of divorced individuals report little distress in their divorce. More likely, divorce triggers a cascade of insecurity parts, both for the person who initiates the divorce and for the excluded partner. "Divorce produces varied forms of distress, including anger, depression, desolation, and loneliness, in nearly everyone."[18] Often the breakup of a significant relationship leaves a person grief stricken, resulting not only in psychological issues, but perhaps in physical symptoms as well. Happily married couples are less likely to experience psychological and somatic health problems than other participants.

The National Bureau of Economic Research provides marriage data.[19] Divorce rates were on the rise in the 1970s and 1980s, but in the last 25 years the divorce rate decreased. On the surface this sounds positive. However, several cultural factors are important. Today many adults in the United States are older when they first marry. Other factors include the increased longevity of people in the United States and a declining age gap between marriage partners. Cohabitation has become increasingly popular, but the increasing number of romantic breakups among cohabiting adults are not reported as divorces in spite of similar patterns of grieving that may occur. Some of the decline in divorce stems from the fact that fewer people marry. Out-of-wedlock babies today are less likely to result in too-soon weddings. Single parents raising children, as well as grandparents raising their grandchildren, are two groups with rising numbers.

Many individuals experience loneliness as children. Austrian-British philosopher Ludwig Wittgenstein was considered to be a genius. His traditional family life was filled with tension and loss: three of his four brothers committed suicide, and the fourth brother lost an arm in war. Young Ludwig was not allowed to attend school initially, as his German father was a perfectionist who did not want schooling to give his sons bad habits. Wittgenstein stuttered and was teased when he finally entered school at age 14. Many consider Wittgenstein as a gay man like one brother. This brother committed suicide after fearing that his homosexuality was going to be exposed in public. The time frame of Wittgenstein's life was not an inclusive period of acceptance and belongingness for either LGBTQ individuals or persons of Jewish descent.

In spite of his belonging struggles and his grieving challenges, Wittgenstein kept searching for knowledge. His observations are relevant today: "In philosophy one feels forced to look at a concept in a certain way. ... I suggest possibilities of which you had not previously thought. You thought that there was one possibility, or only two at most. ... It was absurd to expect ... those narrow possibilities." The one-possibility notion is an example of a fixed mind-set. Wittgenstein wisely argued for having a growth mind-set. Another one of his sage reflections describes why naming your personality roles is important: "The limits of my language are the limits of my mind. All I know is what I have words for." You need words to define what is happening in your grieving process so that you can make sense of it. Furthermore, the importance of your chosen words can lead you to creativity: "Uttering a word is like striking a note on the keyboard of the imagination,"[20] is another piece of Wittgenstein wisdom.

Wittgenstein struggled to understand the suicides of his three brothers. He wrestled with the notion that a suicidal person may not fully want to die. The explanation of such an important split decision is that "The aspect of the person who wants to end his or her life is only one part, and it has to plot against the rest of the person and circumvent objections of the rest by a sneak attack, by taking the person by surprise. What may look like an integrated person making an impulsive move might also be seen as a person in a particular mood acting quickly so as not to allow input from him- or herself in different moods."[21] It is critical to understand opposite roles in personalities.

Loneliness and/or shaming roles in those who contemplate suicide lead them to suffer in isolation. Unfortunately, many middle-aged adults took their lives in the Great Depression when they lost money in the stock market. Historian Jennifer Michael Hecht points out, "In any era, recognizing that many people are in pain may help individuals to live through their own worst times. ... The idea of collective suffering can ... bolster the idea of collectively rejecting suicide. ... It seems right to ask each other to survive, to stay on this side of the guardrail."[22] While stories of past loneliness abound, social belongingness today remains fragile. For example, sociologists found that the number of adults who said that there was no one with whom they discussed important matters has more than doubled in the United States.[23] It is a sad commentary that many midlifers do not find caring companions.

MIDLIFE NESTING CHANGES

A normal belongingness loss that midlifers may encounter is when the last child leaves home. "The transition to empty nest status has been likened to being fired from a job you never wanted to quit; it's another kind of labor, except this time it's your heart that's having contractions. ... [It's] just one of many challenges you're facing at this time. Its impact can be exacerbated by caring for aging parents, middle-age spread, menopause, male midlife crisis, root canals, or a balloon house payment."[24] While you are happy for your child as an independent and moving-toward functioning adult in their own right, your personality roles as a parent change when your children leave home. Sixty-year-old Louise describes her empty nest as bittersweet. She struggles with new roles: "[It's the] loss of day to day contact. ... [Having to] learn how to parent adult children ... how far do you go? When should you offer advice?" There is a revisiting of past belongingness with a particular child, an assessing of what worked and what might have been a better outcome if you had tried Plan B, C, or Z. There is an unknown future. When her daughter's significant other entered the scene, Louise felt worry: "It is awkward having someone come into your child's life. ... Is he going to have a say in my life when I'm really old?" Never far from awareness, Louise has a common midlife worry of wondering if she will have dementia like her father. Then she focuses on the present moment again. There is laundry waiting for attention. And there are other chores. When someone leaves the household, everyone left experiences role shifting. Who takes out the garbage now?

There are all kinds of family nests. Instead of becoming empty, some midlife households grow larger; the younger generation sometimes adds more mouths to feed and care for indefinitely. This nesting arrangement poses different loss challenges for middle-aged parents. Marisa happily planned for her future retirement. Suddenly, her bucket list rolled out of reach with the news that her teenage daughter was pregnant. Marisa no longer thinks of retiring at age 65, as she now has extra responsibilities. Marisa alternates between blaming herself and blaming the popular high schooler who is her grandchild's noncommittal father. Didn't she have enough talks with her daughter about sex? Marisa does not feel ready to be a grandparent. She certainly does not enjoy her switch to the nursing night shift so that she can care for a baby while her daughter finishes high school. How could her daughter spin the whole family upside down with her hormones and impulsivity? Marisa wants to be kind to her daughter's lover, but instead she feels lost in a maze of grieving.

As Naomi Shihab Nye says in her poem *Kindness*, "Before you know kindness as the deepest thing inside, you must know sorrow as the other deepest thing. You must wake up to sorrow. You must speak to it till your voice catches the thread of all sorrows and you see the size of the cloth."[25] One person's loss may not rate as a loss to another, as the second person may have experienced a different kind of loss and a different kind of grieving. Everyone uses different roles of his or her personality to grieve a particular loss.

RITUALS OF CONNECTION

Focusing on mindfulness, or noticing the present moment, can energize you instead of consuming your energy. Compassionate mindfulness can help on the home front. Instead of seeing your family/friend situations as having buckets with holes in them, what if you *turn* up your creative role and look for ways to appreciate another's talents? Who is best at paying the bills? Who shows promise in dealing with health issues in the family? Many in midlife face aging and/or dying grandparents and parents. What rituals might help family members know that they will be remembered? What if your partner in life receives a dubious mammogram or negative performance review at work? What are the strength roles in your personality to show kindness? Mindfulness for present moments helps to manage twists and *turns* in the midlife maze.

Today, midlifers connect with others through social media. There is good news about your gadget rituals of connection – you can stay in touch more easily with relatives and friends who live far away. The bad news is that you may have less physical presence with those who live fairly close to you. It is easier to text or talk by cell phone, but your belongingness is compromised by the distance that technology puts between you and a loved one. When you communicate with another person face-to-face, your mirror neurons can pick up nonverbal signals to let you know that you are seen, accepted, and understood. "Even a few seconds of this sharing and mirroring strengthens the resonance circuits in each (person) … allowing you to engage more easily and skillfully with other people."[26] Inspired by "National Day of Unplugging," filmmaker Tiffany Schlain suspends her family's use of texting, tweeting, emailing, and all technology connections from sunset on Friday until sunset on Saturday. She vows that Saturdays now "feel like mini-vacations … slow living. … We garden with our kids, play board games, ride our bikes and cook. … It's like a valve of pressure releases from the daily bombardment … [and] overload."[27]

In the age of information, you have an unbelievable amount of data flooding your brainwaves daily. Information scientists found that you may need to process as much as 60 bits of information per second: "In 2011, Americans took in five times as much information every day as they did in 1986 – the equivalent of 175 newspapers. During leisure time, not counting work, each individual processes 34 gigabytes or 100,000 words every day. The world's 21,274 television stations produce 85,000 hours of original programming every day as we watch an average of 5 hours of television each day, the equivalent of 20 gigabytes of audio-video images. … YouTube … uploads 6,000 hours of video every hour. … Computer gaming consumes more bytes than all other media put together, including DVDs, TV, books, magazines, and the Internet."[28] You can feel fatigue from information overload with or without experiencing a significant loss.

Psychologist Sherry Turkle researches communication in the digital age and finds that most people, children as well as adults, "have to fight the impulse to turn first to ... devices. ... We respond to every search and every new piece of information ... as though it had the urgency of a threat in the wild."[29] As Turkle points out, cell phone dependency has overtaken real communication between people: "Texting and email and posting let us present the self we want to be. We can edit and retouch. ... We can have each other at a digital distance – not too close, not too far, just right." Turkle is not antitechnology; she is pro-conversation: "Conversation cures." As Turkle reports, everyone knows that it is not OK to break up with someone by sending a text.[30] And yet, this is common today. Social media encourages individuals to show as little invulnerability as possible.

RITUALS OF CONNECTION WITH THE DECEASED

The most significant break with relationship belongingness is death. From ancient times, adults recognized that rituals commemorate their connections with the deceased. Predating modern alphabets, Nordic people wrote runes on stones and wood to convey messages to connect with others. One use of runic stones was to recognize the death of a significant person. The Klepp Runestone from Klepp Municipality in Rogaland, Norway dates to the Viking age (900–1000 AD) and has this message: "Harðr's son raised this stone in memory of his wife Ásgerðr, daughter of Gunnarr, (the) brother of Helgi of Kleppr." While a Christian cross is carved in the stone, the wife's name has two name elements from Norse paganism, including Ás, which refers to one of the Æsir, or main group of Norse gods, and the Norse goddess Gerðr.[31]

Modern rituals for grieving are diverse. Some families bury loved ones and plant gravestones. Others release ashes of their loved one to wind or waves. The lovely memorial altars created by family members for Day of the Dead community celebrations in the Latino community are wonderful reminders of the passions of a special person. Others grieve in private rituals, perhaps keeping special articles of clothing or keepsakes that once belonged to a beloved person in their life. Such items bring back precious belongingness memories.

Breaking belonging ties through a family death, and the symbolic death of a partnership through divorce/marital separation, can produce the strongest emotional reactions that a person ever faces. These life circumstances, along with a jail term of a close family member, are at the top of the stress scale.[32] Some relationships are not replaced. You have one-of-a-kind parents. You have one-of-a-kind children. The death of a child is particularly stressful, as the hope for someone to live beyond your time and possibly carry on the family's genealogy is not replaced. Julio dearly loved his oldest child. He was so proud of Juan for winning an athletic scholarship to college and he looked forward to seeing him perform on collegiate football fields. Then, the impossible happened. Calamity hit home. Julio cannot remember what he was doing at the time of the call, but he remembers the day of the week; it was a Friday. The voice on his cell phone sounded otherworldly. "There ... there ... there has been an accident. Your son is in the hospital. I think you ... you ... you better come right away."

Who was that person stuttering on the phone? Julio was angry at her for months, until one day he woke up and asked himself, "Would it have made any difference if the messenger had said it another way?" Julio's son Juan was a passenger in a car that careened off the road after a college drinking party. He had the death seat or passenger seat next to the intoxicated driver. Juan wore his seat belt, but he did not survive his injuries. He died before Julio even reached the hospital. For a very long time, Julio hated Fridays. He thought it was a shame because *before the accident* (B.A. now in his everyday speech) his favorite day of the week was Friday. He gave up on Sundays too. He stopped going to church because he was angry with God. Loss can magnify emotions.

Suzanne had difficulty getting pregnant. She married much later than her friends and became fearful that she never would have her own child. When she found out that she was pregnant, the news took her by complete surprise. Nine months into the pregnancy, Suzanne glowed with pride – until one day when she became aware that she did not feel movement from her rambunctious babe. She called her physician's office and received an appointment for the next day. Worried, she waited with restless anticipation. Her worry was warranted. "See if you can get a heartbeat," instructed the physician tersely to the attending nurse. Her beloved baby mysteriously died, but Suzanne still had to go through delivery. When the ordeal was over, Suzanne wrapped her rosary beads tightly around her empty hands. She told everyone who came to console her, "God needed Aaron more than I needed him." Some grieving midlifers are comforted by religious beliefs and they develop a stronger sense of faith; others ditch their previous beliefs. Still others do not view religion as entering into grieving. Each individual holds beliefs formed from personal stories.

TURN TIP

In my own research, I don't feel like I understand what I'm doing unless I can form a mental picture of what's going on. ... When it comes to communicating with the public, I take those mental pictures ... strip away the math, and wrap them in a story.

– Brian Greene, physicist

Imagine a loss in your life as a stone. You do not have to carve any runes in this stone, although you may if you wish. As you answer these questions, write your stone story in your Turn Journal, share answers with a friend, or do both.

* You can decide what the size of your stone should be. Is your stone a boulder, a rock garden size, or more like a doorstop stone? Is your stone made of granite, limestone, or sandstone?
* If you decided to write upon your stone, what words would you choose?
* How heavy would it be to lift your stone?
* If you cannot possibly pick up your stone, how many others would it take to lift your stone?
* How far do you plan to carry your stone?
* How long can you carry this stone?
* If you forgave someone, does that change the size of your stone?
* If your stone is ready to be planted somewhere, where would you plant it?

Perhaps you will think of your own metaphors for your grieving process. You will create your own.

RITUALS FOR GRIEVING

Belonging to oneself is a challenging task today, with or without the complication of a significant loss. Far too many adult relationships are ones where "power over" or dominance occurs. Common examples include partners or spouses, parent and children, professors and students, and employers and employees. Often, employees feel as if their boss views them as a replaceable cog in the wheel. Indeed, firings and layoffs are common in the workforce. They are a source of much grieving in midlife. In such circumstances, power erodes belongingness. In *power over* couplings, the underdog, or person without power, often fears the more powerful person. It is impossible for mutual problem solving to take place when such power differences are in place. Belongingness cannot exist for a person when that person feels at the mercy of someone else. Meaningful relating calls for *power with* relating where you are able to listen and communicate to another in a respectful manner.[33] You belong to yourself in a *power with* relationship, as well as allowing another person to have belongingness rights.

In the words of historian Theodore Zeldin, true communication hands feelings "Back and forth until an intimacy develops, and the other individual's concerns become his or her own."[34] Theologian Martin Buber's *I-Thou* relating holds that acceptance of the other person is sacred. When you discuss something with another with your "whole being," you erase arbitrary boundaries between you and the other person.[35] True dialogues focus on caring about understanding another and caring about being understood by others. In such dialogues with another, you do not feel so alone in your grieving. A modern-day man of spiritual vision, the Fourteenth Dalai Lama, calls for caring and belongingness among people. Tenzin Gyatso, born in 1935, is the first Dalai Lama to travel to the United States. His profound messages about life are followed both by Buddhist and secular audiences. The Dalai Lama counsels, "[Your] brief existence should be used in such a way that it does not create pain for others. ... Individualism means that you do not expect something from the outside or that you are waiting for orders: rather, you yourself create the initiative. ... Each individual must create her or his own positive future."[36]

Self-care, or belonging to oneself, is as necessary as having intimate and ongoing contact with family and friends.

• Care (from Old High German, *chara; to grieve or lament*) means to feel concern or interest, feel affection, or to look after and provide for the needs of someone or something.[37]

As Louise DeSalvo suggests, "By engaging in lament, we care for ourselves. For not to express grief is to put ourselves at risk for isolation, for illness."[38] You show caring both for yourself and for another when you grieve a loss with them. Such caring actions may remind you that your glass is *half-full.*

FORGIVENESS

One of the most sacred rituals to nurture belonging relationships is forgiveness. Some rush into forgiveness; others proclaim that they will never forgive. A middle ground may work best. When you withhold forgiveness, you keep yourself in a maze of disappointment, resentment, and hurt. On the other hand, forgiveness takes time. It is not a quick-fix event. You are not ready to forgive another person until you can accept your own pain in the belonging disconnection. Perhaps you have a list of people who have wronged you. Blaming and shaming another will not change the present moment, as these emotional roles are about the past. They keep you in a victim mentality. In John O'Donohue's words, "When you cannot forgive, you are a prisoner of the hurt done to you."[39] Similarly, self-blame holds you captive and makes moving forward painfully slow. The Indian leader Mahatma Gandhi claimed, "The weak can never forgive. Forgiveness is the attribute of the strong."

Navy Seal Eric Greitens understands human mistakes: "We often fail to remember that people are not great all the time. People practice greatness. They perform with greatness. People practice courage. They perform with courage. And then, one day, they don't. This does not make them cowards. It makes them human."[40] Likewise, forgiveness makes you humane. When you forgive, you are the one who experiences healing. All forgiveness issues include being capable of first forgiving yourself. Psychologist Christopher Germer advises that you first repeat to yourself a phrase like this: "I've suffered terrible loss, fear, and self-doubt. I've been lonely and confused. I forgive myself for what I've done, knowingly or unknowingly, to harm you." Only then can you move forward to forgive another: "I know that you too have suffered. You've also had times of loneliness, heartache, despair, and confusion. I forgive you for what you've done, knowingly or unknowingly, to hurt me."[41] When you can embrace these statements, you release the old story that you held onto and perpetuated. Your forgiveness role allows you to move more freely in life. Forgiveness makes space for hope.

The childhood parable of Mussa and Nagib by Brazilian writer, Malba Tahan (pen name for Julio Cesar de Mello e Souza), illustrates how forgiveness works. Two friends have an argument. Nagib slaps Mussa. While Mussa wants to slap back, he thinks about how much he cares about his friend. So, he picks up a stick and writes in the sand, "Today my best friend slapped me." The two boys watch as the desert wind blows away the words in the sand. Later, the friends swim. Mussa is dragged under by a current in the river. Nagib saves his friend. This time Mussa uses a carving knife to put a message onto a stone: "Today my best friend saved me." When Nagib asks about the two different messages, Mussa says, "When someone hurts us, we should write it down in sand where the winds of forgiveness can erase it away. This way our hearts are free from bitterness, and we can renew our friendships. But, when someone does something kind for us, we must engrave it in stone and in our hearts so that we will never forget."[42] Forgiveness leads to deeper belongingness.

YOUR TURN

The only way through pain … is to absorb, probe, understand exactly what it is and what it means. To close the door on pain is to miss the chance for growth. … Nothing that happens to us, even the most terrible shock, is unusable, and everything has somehow to be built into the fabric of the personality.

– Belgium-American writer May Sarton, *Recovering: A Journal 1978–1979*

If you want to increase your ability to have empathy with someone else, it is as easy as using your imagination. For example, when another person is speaking, imagine that you are them. Visualize their situation. Put yourself in the situation they describe. According to researchers Jean Decety and Julie Grezes, this kind of mental exercise allows your brain to form a better understanding of the other person and it doesn't matter if what you imagine is accurate![43] To increase your recovery time from distress, rehearse letting go of your stressful thoughts. John O'Donohue said it best: "It would be devastating in the autumn of your life to look back and recognize that you had created a series of haunted rooms in your heart."[44]

- Who in your life do you need to forgive?
- What can you do to forgive yourself for any part you played?

Chapter 10

Validating Ability

If you don't use your potential, it hits back at you. It strikes back, because it works on you, it wants to come out. And in order not to come out, you have to hold it back. And that is very bad for your health ... your personality ... [and] your relationships.

— Marion Rosen, German-American physical therapist, Rosen Method

The odds were a hundred to one against me, the world thought the heights were too high to climb. ... How many, many times the worm had **turn**ed. ... They all laughed at Wilbur and his brother when they said that man could fly. ... Let's at the past laugh, Ha, ha, ha."

— Ira Gershwin, songwriter, "They All Laughed," *Shall We Dance*

In his book, *Flow: The Psychology of Optimal Experience*, Hungarian-American psychologist Mihaly Csikszentmihalyi reminds us that we are at our best when we can find activities that provide us with a sense of *flow*. He defines flow as a presence, a state in which you are "so involved in some activity that nothing else seems to matter."[1] Such activities do not have to involve a competition or a masterful piece of art, although these experiences do involve a flow mentality. Having flow in your life does not require robust health or wealth.

One study interviewed a group of young paraplegics who became paralyzed as a result of tragic accidents. While these individuals talked about the negatives of their loss, they also viewed their glass *half-full* as they claimed their physical limitations were one of the most positive events in their lives. They *turn*ed their physical state into a challenge, asserting that they "felt a clarity of purpose they had lacked before. Learning to live again was in itself a matter of enjoyment and pride … to keep improving, to keep breaking through the limitations." You can find optimal performance in any dimension of experience that provides a sense of discovery/rediscovery and a present feeling that does not mind the time. An open-to-new-learning attitude embodies a growth mind-set. After experiencing a significant loss, finding your own flow activities is especially important. "Csikszentmihalyi firmly believed, 'of all the virtues we can learn, no trait is more useful, more essential for survival, and more likely to improve the quality of life than the ability to transform adversity into an enjoyable challenge.'"[2] Actually, it is your birthright to claim your potential, in whatever area(s) that you can master.

- Claim (from Latin *clamare; to call*) means to state to be true, especially when open to question, or to deserve or call for.[3]

Many different midlife events have a trauma trailer, but each individual decides how to claim their truth and ability potential. Surgeon Rhonda Cornum refused to label her Iraq prisoner of war experience as a trauma, in spite of enduring two broken arms, physical and sexual abuse, and a mock execution. Instead, Cornum labeled her loss of freedom and prisoner torture "an unfortunate accident." Reflecting upon her ordeal later, she claimed, "I became a better doctor, a better parent. … Now I could understand my patients much better when they were infirm. … I don't forget to write birthday cards, because all of these things are more precious."[4] With unbelievable odds against her, Cornum chose to live with her glass *half-full.*

You can call up or claim your potential as the rightful owner – in fact, no one else can lay claim to your talents. Yes, you do have talents and abilities. Hopefully, you have discovered some of them by midlife, but, do not assume that you have discovered *all* of your potential by a certain age. Perhaps you believe that Gen Xers can overcome adversity, but you think of baby boomers as having lived their best years already. In reality, ability still is strong in the over 50 crowd. In fact, economist David Galenson's study of old master artists highlights many examples of ability among midlifers. For example, French painter Paul Cezanne had his first one-man show at the age of 56. Cezanne created art in the decade of his 60s that ended up having a value of 15 times that of his paintings from his 20s. Galenson poses the theory that late-blooming adults show an experimental approach with a long fermentation process. In addition, midlife ability is enhanced through belongingness connections. Help came for Cezanne from another painter, Camille Pissarro, who painted with him and helped him to reach fame.[5]

MIDLIFE AND BEYOND SURPRISES

There are many stories of people who uncover a hidden talent at a time when others are surprised by their ability and achievements. One of the more popular figures in the United States to achieve more of her raw potential later in the garden of life is Anna Mary Robertson Moses, better known as Grandma Moses. Born in 1860, she died in 1961 at the ripe age of 101, so she had a few years to putter around with her potential. She began her folk artist career at age 78 after she had to give up her hobby of embroidery due to developing arthritis. Her sister made the suggestion that painting would not cause her so much pain. Moses had some experience to draw upon – she had enjoyed sketching as a child. Over 3 decades, Moses created 1500 canvasses, won awards, and received 2 honorary doctoral degrees.

While her first art sales amounted to $3 (for a large painting), it was not long before Moses' paintings earned a $10,000 price tag. One of her paintings, *Sugaring Off*, sold for $1.2 million in 2006. In her autobiography, Moses wrote, "I look back on my life like a good day's work. ... And I feel satisfied with it. I was happy ... and made the best out of what life offered. And life is what we make it, always has been, always will be."[6] Moses viewed her glass *half-full* in spite of being no stranger to loss; only five of her ten children survived infancy. Moses nurtured a growth mind-set that blossomed into the creative part of her personality.

Entrepreneur Ray Kroc bought the McDonald's franchise at age 52 after a series of itinerate jobs that included coping with war as a Red Cross ambulance driver in World War I at age 15 (he lied about his age), playing piano for a radio station, and peddling paper cups as a salesman. It was his traveling job as a milkshake machine salesman that took him to San Bernardino, California, where the McDonald brothers bought his mixers for their restaurants. Kroc sold mixers that made five milkshakes at a time, giving him the notion to use automation in a restaurant. He copied Henry Ford's assembly-line approach to speed up food orders. Whether or not you are a fan of McDonald's fast food, you cannot argue with the fact that Kroc created many jobs for people. McDonald's had 7500 locations in 31countries by the time of Kroc's death.[7]

Furthermore, his third wife, Joan Kroc, inherited his huge fortune at the age of 56 and became a generative philanthropist. When she died, she had become a major benefactor of many institutions; she created jobs and opportunities in a new way. Her bequests included giving $1.6 billion to the Salvation Army, an unprecedented gift. Joan Kroc wanted children to have opportunities to develop their talents in community centers that she did not have, as she grew up in the depression era. She also contributed $225 million to National Public

Radio, $50 million to the University of San Diego's Joan B. Kroc Institute for Peace and Justice, $50 million to the University of Notre Dame's Joan B. Kroc Institute for International Peace Studies, and $20 million to the San Diego Hospice & Palliative Care.[8] Kroc laid claim to a caring role in her personality that continues to care for people that she never met.

Scottish singer Susan Boyle became an international singing sensation at age 47 when she captured attention for performing *I Dreamed a Dream* on the reality TV show *Britain's Got Talent*. She promptly sold 700,000 copies of her first album in the first week of its debut, setting an Amazon.com record for the most advance-ordered recording. Boyle was a victim of bullying as a child and no one wanted to sit next to her in school. She suffered from learning difficulties due to a lack of oxygen in her brain at birth. Her parents were told not to expect "too much" from her. Boyle's mother did expect something and encouraged her daughter to try out for *Britain's Got Talent*. However, it seemed too scary to Boyle and she refused.

Perhaps Boyle held a fixed mind-set that she should not expect "too much" either. After her mother's death, Boyle stopped singing for two years, but eventually she gained courage and decided to sing again as a tribute to her mom. She held one job in her life before launching her professional singing career – she had a stint as a trainee cook. When she went to her audition for the TV show, she had to take six different buses. When asked later about her sudden success, Boyle reflected, "I used to be a spectator looking out at the world and now I'm a part of that world. I'm not the wee, frightened lassie I used to be. ... All I did was open my gob and sing."[9] Fortunately for those of us who love hearing a good voice singing with passion, Susan Boyle dropped her fixed mind-set along with her bucket with the loss hole in it. She developed a growth mind-set in midlife and reached for her ability potential.

MEMORY–ABILITY CONNECTIONS

Memories are an important aspect of your use of your ability. Your brain is a memory garden and is ripe for picking as well as pruning. When you consider that you have hundred billion neurons, and each one of them can make five thousand to ten thousand synaptic connections with other neurons, there is ripe potential for picking. Memories can help or hinder your use of your ability. U.S. memory champion Joshua Foer taught himself to increase his memory by becoming more mindful, to pay attention to the world around him. "Remembering can only happen if you decide to take notice."[10] Healthy memories constantly consolidate and reconsolidate. Like the classic story of the fisherman who makes the fish he caught appear larger with each telling of his fishing adventure, you touch up your memories in terms of what has happened to you. Usually this takes place in small details, but an extreme example is when NBC's Brian Williams fabricated a "memory" of being in a military helicopter. He embellished his public story of the event to imply that he was under enemy fire. Williams later said that he told the memory correctly for years, but at one point he tried to elevate his role.[11] The loss of his high profile job (NBC anchor of evening news) was a huge price Williams paid for his "memory" lie. Instead of making your ability appear larger-than-life in an embellished memory, why not use your potential to create real actions?

Your physical reality is more subjective than you may believe, according to psychologist Kelly McGonigal. Your mind-set, made up of your values and personality roles, acts as a filter for viewing your ability potential. "When a mind-set gets activated – by a memory, a situation you find yourself in, or a remark someone makes – it sets off a cascade of thoughts, emotions, and goals that shape how you respond to life. ... [Your mind-set] can influence long-term outcomes, including health, happiness, and even longevity." For example, how you view aging as a midlifer has an impact upon your will to live and thrive in life. As McGonigal suggests, your mind-set "doesn't just alter your present experience but also influences your future."[12] When you accept that your loss is stressful, but take steps to make the best of the rest of your life, you see life through the lens of a growth mind-set. Along with evolving your thought processing, you can change any negative lens of your personality.

Stress consultant Peter Levine advised NASA staff in developing the first space shuttle. What other job holds such promise – and at the same time such loss – as a space mission? No stranger to stressful memories, Levine says that when a memory is formulated, you have a period of time to change how that memory stays with you. The actual event is not what stays; it is the *new* memory that will stay. Hopefully, you can sense empowered ability in the new memory. Levine explains why eye-witnesses may give very different accounts of the very same event: "Memories are not literal records of events." Your act of remembering something is more like a mosaic, or a collection of images, sounds, smells, interpretations, and responses filled with feelings.[13] Your memories are influenced by either a fixed or growth mind-set.

Another aspect of your memory–ability connection that is fascinating is the repeat performance of certain poignant memories. How often have you heard someone say, "I married my mother (father)?" Levine suggests that memory reenactments may occur in intimate relationships, work situations, and even in repetitive accidents or psychosomatic illnesses. Just as children repeatedly recreate a stressful memory in their play, adults also replay earlier *turn*ing points if they are not addressed in a conscious manner.[14] Furthermore, memories have an impact upon many aspects of your personality functioning regardless of your consciousness of them. Once you become aware of this basic fact, you can become more conscious of present behavior and your current ability to create new memories.

REPETITIVE MEMORIES

Sometimes adults embellish their memories because they are embarrassed by what really happened in their life. But Swiss-British philosopher Alain de Botton advises, "We should not feel embarrassed by our difficulties, only by our failure to grow anything beautiful from them." According to business coach Mark Waldman, the more you repeat certain thoughts, the more these thoughts seem real to you. Your brain creates an alignment with your repeated thoughts. Any information, or any person, that interferes with your repeated thoughts may receive an almost automatic rejection. This process can sow the seeds for prejudice.[15] Families reinforce prejudice in their members – that may be carried through several generations – before someone becomes conscious of the negative repetition. Such repeated negative thoughts in a family may escalate when there has been a significant loss. Negative thinking tends to breed more negative thinking. It is difficult to make the most of your potential when most of your energy is going into distress mode. Psychotherapist Bill O'Hanlon believes that changing your depressing thoughts to the past tense gives you permission to encounter present time with more balance. Instead of saying, "I'm afraid I'll never come out of this darkness," a grieving person can say, "I've been really afraid. I've been worried that I'll never feel better."[16]

In order to make use of your potential, your first step is to reduce day-to-day distress. This is not easy when a loss shocks you to your core. For example, 45-year-old Doug loved his high-powered career with a prestigious law firm. He considered that he was set for life. He saw himself as mastering both career and partner steps. Doug believed that his marriage was solid as he was in a loving relationship. Much to his surprise, his 46-year-old wife announced one day that she was a closet lesbian, and while she felt love for him, she had to leave their marriage. This news was devastating to Doug. He teetered on the verge of depression as he struggled to grasp the details of his impending divorce. Meanwhile, Doug was in line to become a partner in his law firm. Just when he believed that he was at the pinnacle of his career, he was passed over. His longed-for promotion disappeared like a wispy cloud leaving no trace of its existence. His double loss confounded him. He searched his memories repeatedly to see what clues he had missed. The more he poured over past memories, the more confused he felt.

Elena, 44, found herself totally stressed out in her 10-year marriage to 51-year-old Martin. She questioned whether she could call her marriage loving. Marriage was far more complicated than she had realized. Elena met Martin through work. In fact, he left his second marriage to marry her. When the couple's first child was born, Elena became a stay-at-home mom, but she missed her career opportunities. She ruminated on past memories of her happiness at work when she saw more of her husband. With the arrival of her second child, Elena wavered about whether to return to a job that she had loved, but again she made the decision to stay home. As her younger child entered kindergarten, Elena felt restless and lonely, but now her earlier work no longer held appeal. The more distant her husband became, the more she felt stymied in her creative potential. She knew that she was ready to transition back into the working world, either full- or part-time, but what job did she desire? While you may argue that a loss of a career outside the home may be a choice, and therefore not a significant loss, remember that each loss and subsequent grieving process involves unique details for each individual. Awakened ability needs occur at any age when you have a growth mind-set. Actually, parents who figure out how to meet their own ability potential are strong models for teaching their children to meet their ability needs. Balancing needs is a perennial issue.

CREATING NEW MEMORIES

Many in the midlife maze share this question: Where can you find work/life balance? With a loss experience you may wonder how you can retool for engagement on the job again. Do you view your life as stuck? If the money is good but the job is not, should you ditch your first career choice to go into a better field for your current interests? For midlifers at mid-level on the career ladder, increased job responsibilities often go along with career advancement. Do you have the skillset to supervise others? Do you even want to supervise others? Psychologist Ellen Langer prefers the term "work-life integration" to work/life balance, meaning that you treat yourself at work more like you treat yourself on vacation by noticing new things about your coworkers and work.[17] I like to view this present-moment noticing as an opportunity to create new memories.

When you look at your current life, what new transitions do you envision as you plan to make use of your full potential? What have you ever dreamed of accomplishing in your life? What held you back from reaching your dream? What part of your personality can validate special memories of the past? And what role of your personality can pursue some new direction? Ability comes in many forms. When you expect yourself only to flourish in certain ways, you limit the possibilities of your own particular genius. Many achieving midlife adults have school histories in which near failures exist on their early report cards. Albert Einstein experienced early school difficulties. One of Einstein's teachers wrote in a school report, "He will never amount to anything!" John Lennon had a teacher who similarly wrote a negative critique when John was young: "Hopeless ... certainly on the road to failure."[18] Unfortunately, this teacher had a fixed mind-set about Lennon and could not imagine that someday he and fellow Beatles would roll out *Abbey Road* for *turn*tables all over the world. *Abbey Road* is considered to be one of the greatest albums of all time.

Ability and success in a career do not show up at the same age or in the same manner for everyone. Many people need time to find and follow their passion. Your creative potential does not have time or age limits. Today is a good day to begin using a special talent that you possess. The ancient Latin adage from Roman poet Horace's *Odes, Carpe diem*, applies to every day we are fortunate to have our senses. Usually translated as "seize the day," the word *carpe* means to pick or pluck. The adage more accurately translated is "pluck the day [as it is ripe]."[19]

Do not worry about success, as it is unpredictable. Radio host of *A Prairie Home Companion*, Garrison Keillor, was asked how a person might measure success. Keillor summed up ambition and success in this homey way: "Success is when you get up early and you feel ambitious, and you go and you sit at your computer with a cup of coffee and you're still in your pajamas and there is something you urgently want to do. And that's, that's the good life. Work."[20] Keillor describes work activities that have a flow or present-in-the moment quality. Follow the advice of theologian Howard Thurman: "Ask yourself what makes you come alive, and go do that, because what the world needs is people that come alive."

However, transitions to use your ability potential might provoke unforeseen loss issues. At 42, Nancy thought her search for a better job seemed uplifting; she was ready to grow new skills in another branch of law. While Nancy was the one who initiated her career change, it still took her a year to grieve the loss of that first law position. The sad role in Nancy's personality needed to have an opportunity to express her feelings of loss, but initially she did not feel that her sadness was justified because it was *her* decision to leave her firm.

TURN TIP

One can never consent to creep when one feels an impulse to soar.

– Helen Keller, deaf–blind activist

Creativity and remembering, or reconfiguring ideas, are important tools in meeting your ability needs. Gothic fiction writer Anne Rice relies on her daydreams for writing.[21] Neuroscience researcher Mark Waldman views day-dreaming as essential in brain development; in fact, he finds that employees who occasionally daydream on the job are more productive than those who never daydream when working.[22] Of course, daydreaming is troublesome if your job requires acute attention. No one wants his or her surgeon to day-dream during a complicated procedure. Pick a safe time!

A few tips may help with daydreaming to meet your potential:

- Make your daydreams positive. Allow the critical role in your personality to have some R & R time.
- Be playful in daydreaming. Add characters, costumes, sounds, and sights that encourage your imagination in novel ways. Make your own internal movie!
- Make positive daydreaming an ongoing practice even if you only devote a brief time to it each day. Your brain will make some changes from even small dreams for your bucket list.
- Create a new item from your daydreaming to add to your bucket list.
- Plan some new action(s) for the near future.

YOUR ABILITY IS "THERE," BUT WHERE?

What do you say to yourself on a regular basis? Are there more negative comments coming out of your self-directed thinking than positive ones? Psychologist John Gottman's research suggests that a 5 to 1 ratio of positives to negatives is necessary for success in relationships, business, and your own well-being.[23] This exact positivity ratio has been questioned in later research, but psychologist Barbara Frederickson maintains that the ability to flourish, or live with optimal functioning, encompasses both feeling good and doing good. This is my intention in my motto, "Make something good happen every day." I want to feel good along with making something good happen. Frederickson's definition of *positivity* includes such emotions as love, joy, gratitude, serenity, interest, and inspiration. This does not mean that you will never again experi-ence a negative thought. I admit to having my share of negative thoughts. In fact, Frederickson argues that to be 100% positive would deny the humanness of life.[24] "The data ... say that when considering negative emotions, less is bet-ter, down to a point."[25] After experiencing a loss you have a range of emotions.

However, you can awaken your consciousness to your personal ratio of positives to negatives in what you say to yourself, as well as what you say to others. Everyone has their own personal ratio, but seeing ability in glass *half-empty* terms suggests a lack of hope and eventually could lead to apathy and giving-up behaviors. If you cannot view your abilities in a positive sense, it will be difficult to use your potential. Aristotle said, "We are what we repeatedly do. Excellence, then, is not an act, but a habit." Ability habits are critical for your health. Nobel Prize winner Elizabeth Blackburn found that you can reduce stress and increase enzymes to facilitate cell division with 12 minutes of daily yoga. Her research on the *telomerase* immortality enzyme shows how in-the-moment exercise slows cellular aging.[26] You may ask how yoga can help you meet your ability needs. The beauty of a yoga habit is that you can reduce the time you spend upon negative thoughts and increase time for positive actions. Morning yoga poses bring me to the present moment and present breath. As 42-year-old writer and poet Sarah Manguso writes about suffering from a rare neurological disease, she makes it clear that you do not want to waste present moments: "The illness wasn't the real problem. Thinking about it was the problem."

Neuropsychologist and meditation teacher Rick Hansen was curious about how the world's great teachers found their deep wisdom and how all adults might also tap into their potential. He wondered what an individual needs to do to enhance a wholesome state of mind where such wisdom is possible. It *turns* out that in over 40 years of searching, Hansen found that mindfulness meditation is key to such a mind. We do not know whether Aristotle ever meditated, but meditation is an ancient practice. Hansen states that you can supercharge learning and create positive changes in the structure of your brain through mindfulness practices. When you are being mindful, you can increase the activation of your left prefrontal cortex, which is the part of your brain that has some control over negative emotions. Also, mindfulness practice decreases activation of the amygdala, your very alert alarm for any negatives and survival. Hansen presents 52 of his favorite practices in his book, *Just One Thing*.[27] Each time you practice mindfulness, you build your resilience and resourcefulness.

When you increase your ability to focus on the present moment, you are also likely to increase your ratio of positive emotions to negative emotions. In *turn*, you are likely to find more meaning and purpose in your life. A side benefit is finding that you can receive more social support, perhaps by noticing your ability to focus more, because you are more attuned to the give-and-take between people. British writer J. R. R. Tolkien began his famous book, *The Hobbit*, after he was mindful of his improvised stories to his own children. A single line from Tolkien's made-up stories was his motivation for his flow of creative writing: "In a hole in the ground there lived a hobbit."[28]

GROWTH MEANS DOING SOME
THINGS IN A DIFFERENT WAY

A truly motivated person shows energy and discipline levels that can surprise others. Similarly, meeting a basic need for creativity further dazzles.

Imagination sparks enthusiasm and discovery which can make day-to-day living fun. When you expect to engage in imagination about some topic, your learning can soar. The productions of creativity are endless when you take the time and space to tap your own resources. As astronomer and astrophysicist Carl Sagan once noted, "The use of our intelligence ... gives us pleasure. ... When we think well, we feel good. Understanding is a kind of ecstasy." Yes, this is a desired goal. However, it takes time for a grieving process to reach such an understanding. Frequently there is a misunderstanding about the nature of grieving for someone else. How many times have you heard the phrase, "it is a blessing in disguise," applied to someone else's personal misfortune? The phrase is credited to playwright Oscar Wilde who wrote, "What seems to us as bitter trials are often blessings in disguise." Such blessings do not occur for everyone. Each person who experiences a significant loss has to create his or her own journey.

Her body slammed by stage IV uterine cancer, 57-year-old Eve Ensler, author of the play, *The Vagina Monologues*, came face-to-face with grieving her own possible death. Already a survivor of trauma from her childhood – her father had sexually abused her – Eve's midlife grieving process included the need to reclaim her body and help other women in reclaiming their bodies. In her memoir, Ensler reveals her incredible story of searching in over 60 countries for other women who experienced violence and suffering similar to her own. She identifies women who tried to cope with their sexual violence like she did, being endlessly driven. She also discovers others who suffered silently or even disappeared from their families. Some were unable to find any blessings. Others found blessings beyond Ensler's imagination.

Far from the United States, Ensler found women whose tragic stories eclipsed her own losses. She especially was seared by the unspeakable violence and suffering among women in the Congo. In spite of horrific loss, many of these women inspired Ensler: "Inside the women of the Congo, was a determination and a life force I had never witnessed. There was grace and gratitude, fierce-ness and readiness. Inside this world of atrocities and horror was a red- hot energy on the verge of being born. The women had hunger and dreams, demands and a vision. They conceived of a place, a concept they called City of Joy. ... It would be a place of safety, of healing, of gathering strength, of coming together, of releasing their pain and trauma." Ensler came to view her own cancer as "an alchemist, an agent of change," and she began to rise above her previous self-pity. She credits the prayers of the women of the Congo with saving her life.[29] Ensler found blessings.

"Cancer," Ensler writes, "threw me through the window of my disassociation into the center of my body's crisis." Ensler began to use nature to sustain herself. She looked to the tree outside her hospital window. She was so weakened by her illness that it was difficult to move, but she identified with the strength of that tree: "On Tuesday I meditated on the bark; on Friday, the green leaves shimmering in late afternoon light. For hours I lost myself, my body, my being dissolving into a tree."[30] In a fascinating bit of synchronicity, Ensler received treatment from a tree root in the form of Taxol, a chemotherapy drug derived from tree bark. Ensler's instructive story is a guidebook for all who suffer from illness. She viewed the abscess in her stomach with 16 ounces of pus as the contaminated Gulf of Mexico. In a touching scene created by one of her friends, a healing ceremony was held for Ensler. Her friend baptized Ensler with flowers, honey, and water from the Gulf of Mexico. This body of water is where Ensler swam in a younger age: it is also the location where her dying parents had gazed at the horizon. While cancer threatened her very being, Ensler began to retool her personality and rediscover her energy: "I found my second wind. The second wind arrives when we think we are finished, when we can't take another step, breathe another breath. And then we do."[31] While no one wishes for a trauma or tough *turn*ing point, some rise above difficult circumstances to find grace and even gratitude.

YOUR TURN

All the strength you need to achieve anything is within you.

– Sara Henderson, Australian outback station manager and writer

- An easy exercise that takes little time is the repetition of a single word that has deep value to you throughout the day. If you choose a word with two syllables, you can say the first syllable to yourself as you inhale, and then finish the second syllable on your exhale. A word that I have found as both calming and refreshing is "ocean."
- If you can visualize an image alongside your word, there is an even stronger association in your memory. Like mindfulness meditation, this exercise of positive focusing not only can elevate your mood, but it may change gene expression.[32] What happens to your thinking during one day's practice if your word is "compassion" and your image is feeling the hugs of a friend? What about the word "acceptance" and the image of you feeling at home in your own body? You can choose your own words and images that have meaning for your life.

Chapter 11

Involving an Inner Self

What a liberation to realize that the "voice in my head" is not who
I am.
"Who am I, then?" The one who sees that.

> – Eckhart Tolle, German-Canadian writer, *A New Earth: Awakening to
> Your Life's Purpose*

Freeing yourself was one thing, claiming ownership of that freed self
was another.

> – Toni Morrison, Pulitzer Prize novelist, *Beloved*

There are meaningful being-here-now moments in your life story, although
you may not notice them as you attempt to meet your daily needs after loss.
Meanwhile, you keep rediscovering memories in your personality tool chest.
When loss happens, temporarily you may live more in the past as you try to
make sense of what happened to you. You review your past steps to understand where you traveled in the countless transitions of your life. Yet, on a
daily basis, you might feel as precarious as if you are walking through quick-
sand. You may wonder if you can find *any* particular direction for present
actions. If you believe that you cannot make any significant changes in
midlife, you are looking at life with a fixed mind-set or a glass *half-empty*.

To practice a growth mind-set and make positive choices for your life, you
become conscious more of your day than not. Holocaust survivor and neurologist Victor Frankl described conscious choices in this way: "Between stimulus
and response, there is a space. In that space lies our freedom and power to choose
our response. In our response lies our growth and freedom." It is in this silent
space that you can reset your next moves. Psychologist Martin Seligman lists

some aspects you can change in yourself; you can change panic attacks, sexual dysfunctions (frigidity, impotence, premature ejaculation), your moods (including helplessness and pessimism), depression, and your level of optimism.[1] Too many adults blame their childhoods or other people for their current behaviors rather than exercising the discipline needed for long-term change. As the Chinese proverb says, "To get through the hardest journey we need only take one step at a time, but we must keep on stepping."

WHEN SELF-TERRITORY SEEMS LOST

Change is constant and out of your control in many areas, but you do choose your next action steps. You choose how you organize your personality tool chest. Cabrina blamed her husband for their impending divorce. She had difficulty finding any internal *space* or any steps forward. Locked into grieving the loss of her marriage, and worrying about what would happen to her two children's lives through all the fighting and turmoil, she was stuck in a maze of her raw emotions. When she drew her personality map, her self-symbol was initially depicted as the round center or ovary of a daisy-like flower. Within minutes she scribbled over this flower symbol. Tearfully, she said that it was really hurt and anger that were at her core. Initially, Cabrina was unable to find *space* between any outside stimulus and her responses. She layered circles of personality roles; hurt, anger, surrender, and two layers labeled critic. Every line was red, as if her maze travels were accompanied by rings of fire. With time, Cabrina began to soften her rigid and overprotective stance. She worked on meeting her basic needs. She became more conscious of *present* moments. She welcomed loving, playful, fun, intellectual, and reasoning roles into her personality. She began to include the *space* of a calm self-territory.

An interior *space* to your personality initially may seem as elusive as abstract art. The abstract expressionist painter, Russian-American Mark Rothko (born Markus Yakovievich Rotkovich), poured out what he referred to as "dramas" onto blank canvas. Many have attempted to put certain meanings onto Rothko's stark colors or forms, but his son, psychologist Christopher Rothko, states that the paintings are not about either color or form. Instead, the younger Rothko suggests that his father's art is "tragic drama," or what his father termed the "tragedy of the human condition."[2] Some call Rothko's paintings "windows." As Christopher explains his father's art, "There is no outside. In fact, the windows have been closed off, bricked up with the most sensuous of colors. These are not windows to look out, these are windows to look *in*."[3]

The abstraction of Rothko's inward-looking art can unsettle viewers. Some are moved to tears. The poignant paint feels like something, but what is it? Rothko's art seems mysterious. As his son points out, we may fear that which we do not understand. Perhaps some viewers identify with writer Anne Lamott's fear: "My mind is like a bad neighborhood. I try not to go there alone." Rothko gave a lecture 12 years before his suicide that may convey some of his inner art processing: "There must be a clear preoccupation with death. … Tragic art, romantic art … deals with the knowledge of death… [and] hope, 10% to make the tragic concept more endurable."[4] Art can connect the viewer to unbidden emotions much like the journey of loss. But you have more than grieving parts to your personality. You have inner self-territory. Like Christopher Reeve, hold onto a hope with more than a 10% allotment. British-American poet Denise Levertov eloquently writes, "How could we tire of hope? So much is in bud."

TURN TIP

There is only one journey. Going inside yourself.

– Rainer Maria Rilke, German poet

Make space in your mind by pouring paint or words onto the page in your *Turn* Journal. Try writing a poem or putting words to whatever art you create. Words and images hold incredible meaning. Mexican-American Juan Felipe Herrera, U.S. poet laureate, wrote a stirring poem to honor nine individuals killed in their church in Charleston, South Carolina: "You have a poem to offer, it is made of action—you must search for it … run." Herrera said in an interview, "A poem can lead you through [tragedy]. … It is made of action because you're giving your whole life to it in that moment. And then … you give it to everyone. … And someone will listen."[5] Perhaps because there are few extra words, the power of poetry reaches people quickly. Often, the person most in need of being reached is the poet.

Here is a poem that I wrote after my 90-year-old father died of complications from dementia. He was wheelchair bound and could not remember that he no longer walked unassisted. When he stood up to walk, he fell:

Power of the Past, Power in *Presence*

Lingering and simmering over past hot coals,
Half-baked memories waft up my consciousness sinus.
Regrets, wounds, mistakes and mishaps mingle
Among joys, surprises, elations, and epiphanies.
What a cacophony of life experience
Sears the walls of my awareness chambers.

Coming of age 1960's curves into coming-of-aging 60's;
Boomer life smolders with the power of the past.
The collective and conscious fling boomerangs into
Moving targets of shattered dreams, as well as hopes, pursuits ...
"What if" questions burn down into mysterious ashes,
Like aboriginal art reduces landmarks into a maze of dots.
I am still here.
There is power in *presence.*

Civil rights leader Martin Luther King, Jr was a fan of Langston Hughes' poetry and used the phrase, "blasted hopes and shattered dreams" in one of his sermons just after Hughes' *A Raisin in the Sun* play opened on Broadway. King later *turn*ed the dream image into a positive goal rather than "a dream deferred." King gave many inspiring speeches, but the one he is most famous for delivering was his I Have a Dream speech.[6] Hughes' and King's words have poetry and power. Your words have poetry and power. As poet laureate of Vermont, Galway Kinnell, said, "Nobody would write poetry if the world seemed perfect."

* Since you know after loss that the world is not perfect, you do not have to write a perfect poem! Write *your* poem.
* You do not have to rhyme the lines, although you can if you so desire. Just let whatever thoughts come to you flow onto your paper or digital device.
* Perhaps you write a corrido, a ballad or folksong about your struggles. Like dream interpretation, name your poetic creation and decipher its meaning at a later time.

JUNG'S SELF DEFINITIONS

Psychologist Carl Jung had a period of intense inner turmoil in his midlife after he experienced the loss of a close and collaborative relationship with his esteemed older colleague, neurologist Sigmund Freud. The friendship-divorce occurred when Jung's developing ideas deviated from Freudian theory. During his period of emotional struggle Jung used yoga, meditation, gardening, play therapy, drawing, and imagination to find consciousness and equilibrium. His creative outpourings, sometimes in poems or artful drawings, were his version of a *Turn* Journal that he called the *Red Book*.[7] Jung drew many spontaneous circular forms (later referred to as "mandalas") that he considered as expressions of "the intuition of ordered wholeness." Jung's interpretations of his drawings, along with his understanding of a special dream of a circular wheel, led him to choose the term "self" as another word for wholeness. He viewed the self's task as unity in holding "psychic transformations" in a balanced manner.[8]

It was so important to Jung to experience this wholeness in midlife that he created his drawings regularly: "I sketched every morning in a notebook a small circular drawing, a mandala, which seemed to correspond to my inner situation at the time. With the help of these drawings I could observe my psychic transformations from day to day ... in which I saw the self ... actively at work."[9] I view Jung's mandalas as his version of a personality map. His hand-drawn colorful circles are complex, and yet they are made up of simple geometric configurations that interrelate to one another. In India, the mandala is a spiritual symbol that represents the universe. Mandala is the Sanskrit word for circle. Ancient Indian-colored circles were used as a focal point to regard the sacred space of meditation. Today, mandalas are used as coloring projects for both children and adults. Both in Egypt and India, the circle represents a snake eating its own tail. Named the *ouroboros* (Greek, *tail-devouring snake*), the symbolism behind this circle is renewal. Jung interpreted the ancient symbol to mean an integration of opposites.[10] This integration of opposites to discover renewal is the point of drawing a personality map.

When Jung coped with loss in his midlife years, he *turn*ed his attention to the present moment, creativity, and exploring the concept of self: "I began to understand that the goal of psychic development is the self [or wholeness]. There is no linear evolution; there is only a circumambulation [Latin, *around-walk*] of the self. ... Everything points toward the center. This insight gave me stability, and gradually my inner peace returned."[11] Brain research shows that you are more likely to have creative insights when your brain is in a positive mood and when you have "expansive surroundings ... conveyed by spaciousness ... relaxing outdoor colors such as blue and green contribute to this state."[12] It is no surprise that popular magazines recommend painting your bedroom walls with the "calm" colors of green and blue.

Carl Jung invited Albert Einstein to dinner several times and was highly influenced by Einstein's genius. Jung began to use Einstein's relativity theory of space and time to develop his own thinking of consciousness and how it relates to the concept of self. "When Jung was once asked by his students where the self ends and what its boundaries are, his reply is supposed to have been that it has no end, it is unbounded."[13] Jung was a nature lover and this "unbounded" notion likely relates to the unbounded universe portrayed by Einstein. Jung's nature references describe the unbounded workings of his mind: "Thoughts are like birds: they come and nest in the trees of consciousness for a little while and then they fly away. They are forgotten and disappear."[14] For Jung, human consciousness was important, but he also embraced the notion that it was not the only dimension of psychological wholeness: "For [wholeness] the indefinite extension of the unconscious is needed."[15] Like many other words, the "unconscious" and the "unbounded" mean different things to different people.

SELF AND CONSCIOUSNESS

Neuroscientist Antonio Damasio explains consciousness and unconsciousness: "Consciousness pertains to the knowing of any object or action attributed to a self. ... Consciousness is the part of the mind concerned with the apparent sense of self and knowing. There is more to mind than just consciousness and there can be mind without consciousness. ... [because] sometimes we use our minds not to discover facts but to hide them. We use part of the mind as a screen to prevent another part of it from sensing what goes on elsewhere. ... One of the things the screen hides most effectively is the body, our own body."[16] Think of a time when you may have blocked out some aspect of your body/mind. Likely, you were not aware of your blocking actions until a later time. Every person has some unconscious behaviors. As neuroscientist Christof Koch suggests, "Spelunking the caverns of your own subterranean desires, dreams, and motivations, rendering them conscious, and thereby, maybe, making them comprehensible is very difficult."[17] Unconsciousness and denial are protective in short-term uses.

However, Damasio's definition of the interaction of self and consciousness clarifies how important it is find consciousness of everyday emotions and activities: "There is indeed a self, but it is a process, not a thing, and the process is present at all times when we are presumed to be conscious. ... The mere presence of organized images flowing in a mental stream produces a mind, but unless some supplementary process is added on, the mind remains unconscious. What is missing from that unconscious mind is a self."[18] The lost-in-a-maze state occurs when it seems too difficult or painful to be conscious of your suffering after a loss. This is understandable. However, you can help yourself most by including self-territory in your awareness. Whether you realize it or not, the aspect of self remains there for you even though you may not be conscious of your ability to have inner roots.

Dick Schwartz, creator of *Internal Family Systems* therapy, describes self as the seat of consciousness.[19] There is a calm core in each person, an *I in the storm* of life.[20] When you can separate from your extreme emotions and thoughts, you can enter into a calm, centered state. With a presence of calmness, you speak *for* your emotions rather than speaking *from* a reactive emotional state.[21] As you access your inner calmness you might change the look on your face, your voice might sound softer, and you become aware that you have the ability to view the parts or roles of your personality without defensiveness or denial. There are no bad parts of you; instead, you realize that each part in your personality has a protective role. When you are conscious and self-aware, you can separate from your many personality roles – you no longer are flooded by them. You find that you can speak to others in a respectful tone of voice. You can listen to another point of view without attacking when you disagree.

As you stay curious about the real meaning of any conversation, you may experience Frankl's description of the precious *space* between a stimulus and your own response to it. Interestingly, Jung called for the development of a more spacious personality. As Jungian analyst James Hollis points out, you usually experience suffering before you find such an enlarged life. Hollis views suffering as spiritual: "It inevitably raises questions of meaning." He points out that the various religions of the world feature the suffering heritage of Jesus, Buddha, Abraham, Mohammed, and others.[22] Community advocate and minister Wayne Muller looks for the sacred in grieving and embellishes one of the blessings in the *Bible's* Sermon on the Mount: "Those who mourn are blessed … not later. Not when their trials are over. Not when they are fixed. Right here, right now."[23] Kinnell's poem picks up this theme of presence: "Reteach a thing its loveliness." In spiritual traditions, the word soul may replace the word "self." Hollis points out how ironic it is that the word "soul" has been dismissed by many in modern psychology and psychiatry, in spite of the fact that the Greek word *psyche* means soul.[24] I like both words – "self" and "soul," but to be inclusive and respectful of all people, my term for self-process is "self-territory."

INTUITION IS A FEEDER ROOT FOR SELF-TERRITORY

To begin a personal change, an important aspect of the process to obtain *wholeness* is using intuition to discover what needs to change in your life. Awareness of an intuition role can help you in your grieving process. The next step is to *turn* your attention into setting a positive intention from your intuitions. Intentions are often contemplated, but not always stretched into actions.

- Intuition (from Latin *intuitio; a looking at*) means understanding something without reasoning or proof.[25]
- Intention (from Latin *intentio; stretching)* means an aim that guides action.[26]

I see intuition as a feeder root for self-territory. Think of self-territory as the anchor root that holds a plant upright in the ground. Intuition is like a feeder root with small, hairlike networks that absorb water and nutrients to nourish a growth mind-set. You likely have your own definitions of intuitive intentions, but research shows that intuitions are more likely to come to you when you are contemplating something without negativity.[27] When you see your glass *half-full*, you generally have a more upbeat attitude. Intuitions can lead you out of the maze of emotional distress. You listen to and accept your own inner wisdom.

Whether you consider yourself to use intuitive reflection or not, you can intend to make *space* between the bossy, critical roles in your personality and the grieving, overwhelmed roles that carry with them too many worries and too much distress. Every person has opposite roles in their personality. In fact, British mathematician and philosopher Alfred North Whitehead viewed the universe as made up of opposites: "All the 'opposites' are elements in the nature of things, and are incorrigibly there."[28] These conflicting roles swirl through your day and you may feel that you are lost in a maze of confusion. To feel calm, take several deep breaths and empty your mind. A pioneer of body/mind health, Joan Borysenko, suggests that *turn*ing inward toward intuition and inner guidance can happen quite naturally.[29] Whatever words you use to describe this *space*, seat, or contemplation, it is possible to find Kinnell's self-blessing within your self-aware consciousness. Your own words for finding inner guidance are most important.

Irish philosopher John O'Donohue wrote about blessing as linked to your inner guidance: "There is a quiet light that shines in every heart. ... [It] is what enables us to recognize and receive our very presence here as blessing."[30] Physician Lissa Rankin refers to an Inner Pilot Light. This notion of inner light is popular. Often people draw a yellow lightbulb with outward rays to symbolize a reflective or intuitive role on their personality maps. When you trust your own thinking about any topic, you may feel as though a lightbulb *turns* on. Rankin views illumination as medicine for the body-mind: "It's essential to tap into and trust your Inner Pilot Light, which speaks in the voice of your intuition and sends you valuable guidance signals via your body. Although we are wired to pay attention to intuition, our culture does not value it. ... We only live in the vicinities of our bodies. We've become so caught up in our heads and dissociated from the signals our bodies send that we ignore this inner compass."[31] Rankin asks important questions: What comes between you and your intuition? In your relationships, is there always somebody wrong and somebody right? What do you consider sacred? Perhaps most importantly, are you willing to fiercely love and accept yourself?[32]

When you stretch to accept yourself, flaws and all, it is easier to increase your intuitive ability. You learn to trust that you are capable of intuitive reflections. Some midlifers find that they become more intuitive as they practice mindfulness. Others simply give themselves permission to be open to intuitive reflection. Intuitions arrive when you least expect them. German psychologist Wolfgang Kohler suggested that intuitive mind-flowing was most likely to occur in the "3 B's" – bed, bath, and bus.[33] It *turns* out that public transportation is quite conducive to intuition! In an interview with journalist Meredith Vieira, British writer J.K. Rowling of *Harry Potter* fame told of her initial intuition for a wizard child character. Rowling's creativity flowed as she rolled along train tracks. Rowling conjured up the character of Harry Potter when she was traveling on a train from Manchester to London. She said, "Ideas do come to you. But nothing had ever come ... with such [a] God, I'd love to write that [thought] ... When I got off the train I went home and started writing."

Six months later, Rowling's mother died after battling multiple sclerosis for ten years. Rowling had written in secrecy and felt enormous regret for not sharing her passionate intuition with her mother. Her grieving process became a strong influence upon her writing: "I really think from that moment on, death became a central, if not the central, theme of the seven books ... the theme of how we react to death, how much we fear it. ... In many ways, all of my characters are defined by their attitude to death and the possibility of death."[34] After her amazing about-face financial publishing success, Rowling makes *space* for time with her children, for helping single mothers, and for working to find a cure for multiple sclerosis. Her growth mind-set is growing new fibers.

SELF-TERRITORY CULTIVATION THROUGH PERSONALITY MAPPING

You can cultivate the *space* of intuition with deep breaths and mindfulness practices, but there are many different ways to access self-territory. Intuition is just one avenue to listen to self-territory. A beginning step to all listening is to recognize that the letters that make up the word "listen" can unscramble to make the word "silent". Solitude and silence are not your enemies. Think of them as your allies. Silence, along with several deep breaths, can give a go-ahead signal to your conscious awareness of the present moment. You can strengthen the intuition in your personality by sidetracking from your daily routine. You may not need a bus or train ride! Just spending free time in new surroundings can liberate intuition. Allow whatever emotions arise inside of you. Do not worry that you do not hear a voice. Writer Eckhart Tolle clarifies the notion of voice: "The 'voice in my head' is not who I am. Who am I then? The one who sees that. The awareness that is prior to thought, the *space* in which the thought – along with the emotion or sense perception – happens."[35] Yes, self-territory is the witness to your intuition and other thoughts and emotions.

One reminder to become more conscious of self-territory is to draw an image to represent this inner process in your personality (directions for a personality map are in chapter 5). Perhaps you already have drawn one personality map. You can draw another map whenever you want, as you keep discovering a new positioning of personality roles if you have a growth mind-set. As Greek philosopher Heraclitus said around 500 BC, "The only thing that is constant is change." This is both reassuring and daunting. How to take the next *turn* is the tricky aspect. Remember, you start your hand-drawn map by choosing a symbol to stand for self-territory. I suggest that you draw your self- symbol in the center of your map as a reminder that it is possible to feel centered or calm even in challenging times.

Everyone draws a self-symbol in a unique way. Some of the drawn images of self-territory that have held meaning for midlifers are the following: a blue cloud, a yellow sun with radiating rays, a yellow circle, a turquoise, and green cross-legged yoga position, two blue flowers on a green stem, a mixture of beautiful colors (in wavy lines crisscrossing each other), a multicolored dragonfly in a yin-yang circle, a red heart, a turquoise heart, a pink heart with radiating rays, an ink-drawn oval with a bisecting line going outward, and brown earth with a sun over green plants. It is fascinating to see that many symbols drawn for self-territory spontaneously *turn* out to be circular, such as clouds, suns, flowers, and an oval. Even heart-shaped drawings have a type of circularity. An interesting detail is that children draw circular scribbles as their first drawings. With no prompting from adults, three-year-old children spontaneously draw radiant suns, flowers, and "potato people" with sprouting arms and legs. French painter Francis Picabin claimed, "Our heads are round so that thoughts can change direction."

Circles appear in outer space as planets, moons, and stars; the Sun star is at the center of our life-force energy. Many report that they most often find inner space for self-territory when they are in nature. Notice how many of the above self-symbols drawn by midlife individuals depict something from nature. Looking at the spacious sky, or finding *space* in between floating thoughts by looking at a body of water, can help you locate your own inner spaciousness. Writer Alice Walker labels this internal *space* your *natural self*. Time is not the important factor; in fact, when you engage with nature, you often lose track of time. Circles are timeless, poignant symbols. There is a sense of unbounded time in self-territory.

SELF-TERRITORY CULTIVATION
THROUGH SELF-COMPASSION

British-American poet and writer David Whyte views self-connection as crucial to well-being. In fact, he characterizes adult life in terms of "3 marriages": marriage to a partner/spouse, marriage to work, and marriage to self. Of the trio, he believes that your marriage to self may be the most difficult: "We see not only the truth of our present circumstances … but we also realize how short our stay is on this earth." This interior self often is ignored when you are busy with work or juggling relationship issues. However, many midlife mistakes occur when you do not make *space* for self-compassion: "We find ourselves unable to move in these outer marriages because we have no inner foundation. ... It is as if, absent a loving relationship with this inner representation of our self, we fling ourselves in all directions in our outer lives, looking for love in all the wrong places."[36] As Schwartz says, "You can become your own healer – the special person your vulnerable parts have been waiting for."[37] When you feel self-compassion for all that you have endured, you emerge with an ability to show radical acts of kindness both to yourself and others.

A person experiencing self-compassion possesses a physiological calmness. Self-compassion is defined as having three components: (1) self-kindness, or treating yourself kindly even during difficult circumstances; (2) common humanity, or recognizing life experiences as universal to the human condition; and (3) mindfulness, or observing and balancing painful feelings rather than being consumed by them.[38] Psychologist Christopher Germer views self-compassion as essential to maintain healthy relationships: "Transforming relationships with others starts with us: it's an inside job."[39] He recommends treating yourself just as you would treat someone you love dearly: "If you're used to beating yourself up during periods of sadness or loneliness, if you hide from the world when you make a mistake, or if you obsess over how you could have prevented the mistake to begin with, self-compassion may seem like a radical idea. But why should you deny yourself the same tenderness and warmth you extend to others who are suffering?"[40] What shuts down your self-compassion? What corner can you *turn* to start treating yourself with self-compassion on a daily basis?

While you embrace others in their time of loss, you may forget about giving yourself compassion when loss strikes your family. Somehow it seems easier to have empathy for another rather than yourself. Perhaps you hold the fixed mind-set that others deserve more compassion than you deserve. Perhaps the most practiced roles of your personality include shame and blame. Usually a shaming role has its origins in early events in your lifetime. Social work researcher Brene Brown views feeling shamed, judged, and blamed as the realities of life. Too often it is easy to slip away from healthy achieving and into perfectionism, or trying to please others. As Brown sees it, "Shame is the birthplace of perfectionism. ... To overcome perfectionism we need to be able to acknowledge our vulnerabilities ... and practice self-compassion."[41]

With more self-compassion, you reach an inner sense of calmness. Brown calls such inner calmness wholehearted living. She came to the realization for herself that working hard, following the rules, and always trying to know herself in more ways were not enough if she did not wholeheartedly love herself.[42] Self-compassion will help you in your daily trek through your job and relationships. How you relate to others is connected to how you relate to yourself.

SELF-TERRITORY CULTIVATION
THROUGH CHERISHED VALUES

As Roman philosopher Seneca (4 BC – 65 AD) wisely proclaimed, "You are your choices." He also is credited with saying, "The bravest sight in the world is to see a great man [or woman] struggling against adversity." When you struggle to make sense of your loss and have a great number of decisions before you, there are many choices. However, you likely make choices based upon your past beliefs. Jerry declared, "I don't trust women," because he experienced several losses in his relationships with women. This fixed mindset of no-trust then colored all of his decision-making for future relationships. When Jerry was able to reset his thinking, to *turn* his focus toward what he valued in life, he also made a pivot in his ability to make relationship decisions that brought him joy instead of more loss. Actually, Jerry held "trust" as his most important value in life. Loss can temporarily erode your ability to connect with your value system.

British culture consultant Richard Barrett views the difference between decision-making based upon your beliefs versus your values as the difference between living in the past versus aligning yourself with a flexible future. Your past can constrain you to recreate fixed ways of making choices. You likely know how this worked for you in different scenarios. *Turn* your attention to engage in decision-making based upon your values, both at home and in the workplace. Barrett views the task of business leaders as focusing upon values in order to "liberate the corporate soul." When employees survive downsizing, they "suffer as much as those who lose their jobs. They find themselves living in a climate of fear. There is no longer any trust in the organization."[43]

As Barrett suggests, your values can transcend experiences. You have treasure within your values that you may not be conscious of on a daily basis. Rankin links values to your intuition: "The mind thinks, always chattering away, arguing with itself like a crazy person. … Your mind may steer you away from your integrity, but your intuition never will. … Learn what it feels like to behave in alignment with your values, and you'll start to sense your intuition more clearly."[44] When you are aware of your values, you are more likely to align with self-territory.

If you do not have a ready list of values to consider, review ten values that Rabbi Wayne Dosick lists as *Golden Rules* for parents to model in raising their children to have ethics: respect, honesty, fairness, responsibility, compassion, gratitude, friendship, peace, maturity (or wisdom), and faith.[45] Not only can parents have a good chance to raise healthy and moral children by living these values, but companies thrive best when they treat their employees with such values. You can form your own list of values in this *Turn* exercise.

YOUR TURN

Don't go outside your house to see flowers. My friend, don't bother with that excursion. Inside your body there are flowers.

– Kabir, poet and saint of India

Students in Mark Waldman's Executive MBA Program at Loyola Marymount University in Los Angeles have this exercise as their first assignment. You do not have to enroll in Waldman's class, but I suggest that you try his *Inner Values* assignment. Each morning for ten days, shortly after waking up, take a moment to stretch, and then ask yourself the following questions. Record your response and any accompanying reactions you might have regarding this exercise.

- Take a few deep breaths. Release your worries from the big decisions you may have to make this week.
- When you feel relaxed, ask yourself, "What is my deepest, innermost value?"
- Close your eyes for about a minute. Listen to your intuition.
- Open your eyes and jot down any word(s) that come to mind.
- Repeat the question several times and include these words in your *Turn* Journal or a piece of paper. See if there are several values that float into your awareness.
- Now look at your values and circle the one that feels most potent at this moment.
- Repeat the word several times to yourself. Notice any sensations while you say the word.

Take a few minutes at the end of ten days to record your reactions: What was your initial reaction to this exercise? Was the exercise enjoyable, boring, interesting, or annoying? Did the exercise have any effect on other aspects of your day, work, or life? How do you define the word value? Did you discover anything about yourself?

The MBA students were asked to submit their daily logs anonymously. By the end of the second week, nearly every student reported that the exercise was enlightening and enjoyable, but that was not their first impression! Initially, one CEO was blunt: "What the *#&! does this have to do with financial planning?" By the end of 10 days, he made an about-face: "I think that this exercise should be taught to every MBA student in America." Not only can you improve your body/mind health when you reflect upon your personal values, but you might experience aha moments like some of Waldman's students:

> "I realized that business is not just about numbers."

> "The exercise grounded me in the principles of goodness ... for me, work can drown out the self-talk of my own core values."

> "I used my positive word all day long. I felt calmer, less stressed. ... I loved the self-awareness it brought."[46]

Part III

BEFORE "KICKING THE BUCKET," GRAB YOUR BUCKET LIST AND ENJOY!

You now possess more consciousness to meet five basic needs. You are aware of self-territory. With a growth mind-set, you are ready to make a new bucket list of future goals.

> We must go down to the very foundations of life. For any merely superficial ordering of life that leaves its deepest needs unsatisfied is as ineffectual as if no attempt at order had ever been made.

> – Chinese *Book of Changes* or *I Ching* (circa 2500 BC)

Chapter 12

Tickling Your Fancy

And the day came when the risk to remain in a tight bud was more
painful than the risk it took to blossom.

> – Anais Nin, French novelist

A life is like a garden. Perfect moments can be had, but not preserved,
except in memory. LLAP (Live long and prosper).

> – Leonard Nimoy (his final tweet), actor, "Spock" in Star Trek

Our culture expects you to know how to take care of business in midlife.
However, in my work as a family psychologist, I find that many midlifers
feel lost as a result of experiencing significant losses. In midlife the impermanence of life confronts you: "We learn in the most painfully insulting way
that nothing, no thing or person or relationship or fortune, will ever belong
to us. It is all on loan."[1] While you wanted blossom time as ongoing in your
relationships, job, and health, the garden of life did not cooperate with your
wishes. Your cherished bucket list of dreams may have vanished. Your basic
needs piled up. When loss struck, you felt dazed and lost in a maze. While no
one wants loss to enter their life during midlife, there is a great deal to learn
from a grieving process.

As philosopher and cancer survivor Mark Nepo found out, a health crisis
and the grief that accompanies it allows you to find out what is really important in everyday living: "Health resides in restoring direct experience. ... Center yourself and think of your life as a story not yet written. ... Breathe deeply,
and imagine your path as the patch of sky a bird flies through. Now just breathe
and fly. Enter your day, and breathe and live."[2] Nepo did not shy away from
his grieving process when he was diagnosed with a rare form of lymphoma in

his 30s. He understood what Australian writer Beau Christopher Taplin meant by these words: "Your body is a forest – thick canopies of maple trees and sweet scented wildflowers sprouting in the underwood. You will grow back, over and over, no matter how badly you are devastated."

Nepo viewed his broken dreams as fertilizer for dreams that could come in the future. Midlife has enough transitions without a significant loss hitting home, but as you know now, lost dreams occur to most adults during the long developmental stage of midlife. "When you can put dead dreams to rest in peace, you free an "inner stance about to unfold."[3] Experiences after loss can sidetrack into a threshold of new beginnings. However, it is easier to write about putting the grieving process into a positive perspective than it is to make it happen. Some loss situations have extreme circumstances.

At the age of 56, the South African civil rights activist, Nelson Mandela, was sentenced to life imprisonment. He spent 27 years in prison before his release. It is difficult to imagine how he stayed positive and survived the grieving of such an ordeal. One role in his personality tickled his fancy – Mandela held onto a keen sense of humor: "I went for a long holiday for 27 years," he quipped. A more reflective role in his personality took another path: "The greatest glory in living lies not in never falling, but in rising every time you fall." And yet a third role, forgiveness, issued this wisdom: "Resentment is like drinking poison and then hoping it will kill your enemies."[4] Mandela serves as a powerful role model in turning a traumatic situation into an about-face reaction that carried him forward. He became the first democratically elected president of South Africa after his long imprisonment. You can *turn*, *turn*, and again *turn* corners in the midlife maze after loss. Whether you experienced the loss of a job, a spouse/partner/family member, your health, or some other indignity, you can dig for buried treasure in your own personality to retool and update your family/work life before it is too late.

PATCHING YOUR BUCKET'S HOLE

The phrase "to kick the bucket" has existed at least since the year 1785 as English slang and means to die. Most midlifers are not ready to kick the bucket. While the origins of the term "bucket list" are in question, I like a user-friendly definition: things to do before you kick the bucket. Another English 1700's phrase poses the real question for midlifers: "What tickles your fancy?" If something tickles your fancy, or imagination, it appeals to you and you want to try it or have it. Along with having an eye for planning financial functioning for later years, you must figure out what you really want to accomplish in the rest of your life. When you find purpose for living, you find ways to patch the holes of loss.

The O'odham Native American symbol, man (or woman) in the maze, includes stories of happiness, sadness, successes, and failure. But most of all, O'odham stories involve learning to find what tickles your fancy. The O'odham peoples' version of a maze existence includes this story: "There is a dream at the center and you reach the dream when you get to the middle of the maze. Upon reaching the center of the maze you have one final opportunity (the last *turn* in the symbol) to look back at your choices and path, before the Sun God greets you, blesses you and passes you into the next world."[5] Each person is expected to bring a gift in their final opportunity to ensure their safe return from the depths of the maze. Whatever you believe about death and religion, as a midlifer you have some precious choices to make on an everyday basis. Transitions in midlife help you define your gifts. What gift(s) do you possess that you might engage next? How can you shift directions today to accept change and make use of your talents?

B.J. Miller, a palliative care physician in San Francisco, suffered a freak accident that cost him three of his four limbs when he was in college at Princeton. Loss is one thing, but regret is a choice. Miller says that he has no regrets about his accident! "Too much good stuff has come out of it. … I was not headed toward a career in medicine before the accident." Miller's hospice work transforms grief for patients who have less than six months to live by helping them to not fear the big questions. He knows how to be in the present moment. He *turn*ed to art as a pathway to learn about perspective. He does not believe in a doctor-patient hierarchy. Miller meets each patient in the present moment: "I equate the doctor and patient because I am a patient."[6] His loss of body limbs led to a decision to retool his personality. As Miller reflected, "Let death be what takes us, not a lack of imagination." However, Miller admits that he endured "buckets of physical pain" to get to a place of gratitude in his life. He had to "come out of the closet of disability" to expand his definition of normal.[7] Miller leads family members, staff, and funeral home workers in a ritual to place flower petals on people's bodies as they leave hospice through a garden gate. "Love such moments furiously," Miller advises.[8] A perspective to stay in the present moment counts in so many everyday ways, but it is especially important in making *space* for good-bye rituals.

FROM "MISMEETING" IN LIFE TO THRIVING

Some terminations are divorce/separation good-byes. Sharing children makes saying good-bye unrealistic. Often, I heard clients say, "I married with blinders on," or "We grew apart." As poet/writer David Whyte accurately points out, "In some interior place, while the vows are being spoken out loud on the surface there is a mingling of unspoken, unresolved difficulties from the background of each partner. … [You are] marrying the mother, the father, the cousins, the whole inheritance of a family, including the exiled black sheep who hasn't even *turn*ed up for the ceremony."[9] This may be news to newly-weds, but most midlifers who are married for a few years grin at the truth of Whyte's summation. In addition to external influences of marrying a strange other family, there are relationship lessons that surface when living intimately with another individual: "Marriage is where we learn self-knowledge; where we realize that parts of our own makeup are stranger even than the stranger we have married and very difficult for another person to live with."[10] When partnerships end, the *real* good-bye is with parts of your own personality, the loss of roles that you shared with another.

If both partners in a relationship have a growth mind-set, they may have the clarity to ask themselves periodically, "In what ways do I need to do something differently?" Too many relationships lack what Austrian-born Jewish philosopher Martin Buber named *I-Thou* dialogues. Rather, Buber found that people frequently have *I-It* experiences where one person treats another as an object or by their function. In such a relationship, genuine feelings are not expressed and true sharing is compromised. An *I-Thou* relationship has both mutuality and connection; relating is considered sacred. However, for many, stories of relationships are recalled through the eyes of hurt and suffering. These stories fall into the category of *I-It* relating. If love can blind, Buber also views hate as blinding: "Hate remains blind by its very nature; one can hate only part of a being."[11] Likewise, only a part of you hates someone. A hatred role may serve an initial protective function after you experience a significant loss. But holding onto hate or anger ends up hurting you most of all. Poet and essayist Ralph Waldo Emerson had excellent advice: "You cannot do a kindness too soon, for you never know how soon it will be too late."

Buber speaks about quality relating as, "All real living is meeting." As a clue to his development of his ideas, Buber experienced loss at a very young age. His mother disappeared one day when he was only three years old. Buber suddenly was moved to live with grandparents who never brought up his mother's name. Finally, at age 14, Buber returned to live with his father who had remarried. Buber did not see his mother for 30 years. He only learned much later that his mother ran away to Russia with an army officer and had more children. He coined a new word, "mismeeting," to describe the loss of a "real meeting between people."[12] How many midlifers experience this lost-in-a-maze feeling of mismeeting when they encounter a partner/spouse/family breakup in life? In *I-Thou* relating, there is an enhancement and acceptance of the other, perhaps a missing link in Buber's early family. However, Buber *turn*ed his loss into a philosophy of living that has helped many to understand the importance of being a total participant, available and open, in relationships. Buber is widely quoted today, from religious circles to collaborative work groups.

There is no one way to work through a grieving process. Many possible paths are suggested in these chapters, but you will chart your own course. Be careful in using the critical role of your personality to think that you have taken a wrong path in your grieving process. Everyone experiences Buber's mismeetings and stumbles, or even falls down a time or two, along their journey. As social work researcher Brene Brown writes, "If we are brave enough often enough, we will fall."[13] There is no "strictly linear approach to change – it's a back-and-forth action ... an intuitive process that takes different shapes for different people."

Brown's words echo the back-and-forth notion described in the Pinwheel Model of Bereavement (chapter 2). Brown names this ability to transform yourself through your vulnerability "rising strong;" it is the same process whether you struggle with personal or professional loss. Brown's version of resiliency is viewed either as a secular or religious practice. She believes that rising strong from adversity is enhanced for some people when they celebrate "in churches, synagogues, mosques, or other houses of worship, while others find divinity in solitude, through meditation, or in nature."[14] Think of a new way in which you can be resilient after loss.

"REAL" WORK GROWS AND CHANGES

Executive leadership mentor Wayne Muller helps people who face transitions in their life and/or work: "The choice is this: Will we interpret this loss as so unjust, unfair, and devastating that we feel punished, angry, forever and fatally wounded – or, as our heart, torn apart, bleeds its anguish of sheer, wordless grief, will we somehow feel this loss as an opportunity to become more tender, more open, more passionately alive, more grateful for what remains?"[15] Sometimes midlifers throw themselves into work after experiencing a loss. The thinking goes like this: "At least I have _____ to count on."

Actually, that piece of work cannot be 100% counted on, but it is understandable that you seek something that you perceive as stable after a loss. Just remember to view your work with creativity and a growth mind-set. "We must have a relationship with our work that is larger than any individual job description we are given. A real work, like a real person, grows and changes and surprises us, asking us constantly for recommitment."[16] If you are energized by meaningful work or a project that tickles your imagination, you are well on your way to finding your gifts and a sense of balance. You never know how your creativity might in *turn* move someone else to find their gift. "Creativity is a responsibility to express and to pass on."[17]

Overwork is common for midlifers even in times when there is no loss. After all, the middle years are a time when expenses run high, especially for families with children. However, there is danger in overwork; it is a setup for *I-It* relating. In Muller's view, "In the trance of overwork, we take everything for granted. We consume things, people, and information. We do not have time to savor this life, nor to care deeply and gently for ourselves, our loved ones, or our world; rather, with increasingly dizzying haste, we use them all up, and throw them away."[18] How many people look back upon their lives after retiring and wish that they had worked in a different way?

A 2014 Gallop poll of over 80,000 adults found that less than one-third (31.5%) of workers in the United States were "engaged" in their jobs; 51% were found to be "not engaged" and 17.5% were "actively disengaged." The definition of engaged workers included feeling passion and connection to their work/workplace. Not-engaged workers were described as robotic in their actions, as sleepwalking through their workday. The actively disengaged employee actually undermined what their engaged coworkers accomplished; they also had more sick days and monopolized managers' time. The highest level of engagement (38.4%) occurred among managers and executives, while workers in manufacturing, production, transportation, and service positions had the lowest engagement levels (25.5%–28.2%). Also revealing is the generation gap in engagement levels. Millennials, or the youngest in our workforce, were the least engaged group (28.9%), while the midlife Generation X and baby boomers had a similar level of engagement (32.2%–32.7%).[19]

Most midlifers want work that is meaningful, but the definition of whether work carries with it a sense of purpose or meaning differs for each worker. As Jungian analyst James Hollis describes midlife, "Most of us live our lives backing into our future, making the choices of each new moment from the data and agenda of the old – and then we wonder why repetitive patterns *turn* up in our lives. ... As Jung once put it humorously, we all walk in shoes too small for us."[20] You may need new boots to walk in a new direction for your life. Maybe you can find those boots with bootstraps to pull yourself forward. Maybe you find a job where you wear flip-flops. Your philosophy of life may flip-flop after a significant loss. While you try to make sense of your new situation, you might ask yourself, "now what?" This is a normal reaction. Don't be surprised that a ready answer does not pop into consciousness. But do expect that you have a role in your personality that can answer your question in time.

RETIREMENT: EMPTY OR FULL BUCKET?

Individuals retire at various ages. Retirement may exist as a time of loss if you are blindsided with an early retirement not of your choosing. In a study of 2400 middle-aged U.S. adults, ages 50 or older, half were retired and half were within five years of their anticipated retirement date. For 60% of those retired, the timing of their retirement was either somewhat or completely unexpected. Another surprising finding is that 57% of retirees had unexpected challenges and stress in retirement. Nearly 80% of recent retirees (in their first five years of retirement) reported having more stress than they experienced preretirement! There were issues of health and determining how to spend free time. Another factor was financial, as pensions and benefits for retirees have reduced in recent years. Many midlifers did not have enough savings to make up for such reductions.[21] Discipline for managing personal finances is an issue across the lifespan, but it is particularly important in the midlife earning years. Is your bucket empty or full?

Shirley retired early so that she could care for her sickly mother. It was what she wanted to do at the time, but as caretaking became more strenuous, she questioned her decision. Suddenly, her 82-year-old mother needed hospitalization. Each day a new medical complication cropped up. Shirley remained stoic when her mother's physician asked her, "Do you want to do something when she flatlines [registers no brain waves or heartbeat on a monitor]?" After her mother's final transition, Shirley felt only numbness: "Tears well up, but I don't cry. I didn't even cry when my mother died. I hold my anger in. I don't show it." While anger can play an important role in people's grieving process, Shirley's anger also relates to other issues in her life. This is a common challenge in processing the many holes of loss.

Roles in your personality seldom belong to one situation. As futurist Marilyn Ferguson points out, "It's not so much that we're afraid of change or so in love with the old ways, but it's that place in between we fear. ... It's like being between trapezes. It's Linus when his blanket is in the dryer. There's nothing to hold on to." Everyone has an insecure role as part of his or her personality makeup. When you remember that all roles in your personality try to protect you in various ways, you can accept impermanence a bit easier.

While many fantasize about early retirement, the reality often is different than expected. Breyann also retired early to be a caretaker for her elderly mother. At the time, she did not question her decision about leaving her career, but she did not anticipate how many complicated emotions she would encounter later. Her now-what questions relate directly to her grieving process: "I thought I had already said goodbye to my mother. ... It was a surprise how much it hit me when she was gone." Then Breyann realized that she had never grieved the loss of her career. One loss often brings up other unresolved grieving. Without having her previous work to focus on, Breyann felt bombarded by her feelings of loss and regret. Time to grieve does make a difference. The advice offered by Elizabeth Kubler-Ross rings true: "When you learn your lessons the pain goes away."

Part of the grieving process for entering into a full-time caregiving role for a loved one is to understand both your loved one's choices and your own similar, as well as dissimilar, choices. You may shift roles in your remembering of your loved one as you progress through the years. Cultural anthropologist Mary Catherine Bateson captures the essence of how this can happen. She reports that she had a better understanding of her parents, anthropologists Margaret Mead and Gregory Bateson, as well as the life choices they made, when she reached each new decade.[22] She kept developing a greater appreciation for her parents.

ILLUSIONS OR VISITATIONS IN GRIEVING

Middle-aged adults may need a sign that it is OK to blossom in new ways after a loss. Some grieving individuals experience visual and/or other sensory illusions of their deceased loved one. If there is a message from their loved one, often it is an encouraging one: "Everything is all right." Psychotherapist Alexandra Kennedy tells of a widow experiencing a dream the night after her husband's death. The widow was amazed that her husband appeared "radiant and healthy, [and] he gently admonished her, 'I never left you.'"[23] It is this reassurance that loss carries an inner presence that paradoxically can allow you to move forward with your life. Some report that their deceased loved one encouraged them at a special time.

Neurologist Oliver Sacks interviewed people who experienced the death of a close relative. One woman reported seeing her dead mother a few hours after she had died. She stated that her mother simply wanted to check in with her. A man was awakened in the night and saw his deceased father "sitting on the corner of his bed." His father reassured him that everything was all right. Sacks had a friend who was very upset when her 20-year-old cat died. For months his friend saw the cat in the folds of curtains in her home.[24] Most people report finding these encounters comforting.

Maria's family experienced the sudden death of a beloved mother and grandmother. When family members debated whether Grandma had fallen due to a wet floor in her granddaughter's home, different opinions emerged. The grieving process for the family was complicated by fear and guilt personality roles, in spite of the fact that everyone knew that elderly people fall down for a variety of reasons that have nothing to do with the condition of floors. Then, Maria experienced a visitation. Just as the questions about her death needed some closure, Grandma "appeared" at the foot of Maria's bed. Always one to joke with her family, Grandma was laughing in the visitation. Her message was that she knew that some family members thought she fell down because of a wet floor, but actually she experienced a stroke. Everyone in the family was relieved.

It is possible that such illusions or visitations are disturbing if death comes to someone in a violent manner, or if there is a strong guilty part in one's personality functioning. Visitation encounters are described in literature and the arts. For example, in William Shakespeare's *Macbeth*, Lady Macbeth plots the murder of Duncan. Lady Macbeth cannot wash away the invisible bloodstain that she "sees" on her hands after Duncan's death. In Charles Dickens' *A Christmas Carol*, Ebenezer Scrooge "sees" his former business partner, Jacob Marley, after Jacob has died. Scrooge feels a sense of guilt for not paying his partner a decent wage to care for his family with a sickly child, Tiny Tim. The movie *The Sixth Sense* considered visitations as dealing with unfinished business.

Veterans with PTSD often have unfinished business from war trauma; some report hearing the voices of dying buddies, civilians, or even enemy soldiers. After the 9/11 attack on the World Trade Towers, some survivors continued to smell burning rubble even though the smell no longer existed. For Sacks, such unusual behaviors are normal occurrences. He experienced persistent illusions over a period of months after the death of his own mother. His experience was to see her in the street, although a part of his personality thought that he was mistaking her for other people who appeared similar in appearance to his mother. Sacks believed that grieving people have hyperalert emotions and this condition explained how such visitations and illusions may take place. Perhaps J. G. Ballard, a British novelist said it best, "What you see depends on what you are looking for."

Sacks viewed the neurology of illusion and visitation events from several angles. He questioned whether visitations might be "hallucinations:" "Something has to happen in the mind/brain for imagination to overlap its boundaries and be replaced by hallucination. Some dissociation or disconnection must occur ... quite different sorts of memory may be involved." Sacks believed that a significant loss, whether of a loved one or involving a tragic event, could have such intense emotion that the loss could "make an indelible impression on the brain and compel it to repetition. ... [Visitations] get their material from the visual experiences of a lifetime—one has to have seen people, faces, animals, landscapes to hallucinate them; one has to have heard pieces of music to hallucinate them."[25]

Finally, Sacks concluded that loss in the form of defects, disorders or illnesses "...can play a paradoxical role by bringing out latent powers, developments, evolutions, forms of life that might never be seen, or even be imaginable, in their absence."[26] For example, Sacks gave a curious account of latent powers in a surgeon. The surgeon had Tourette's syndrome, but was capable of performing complicated surgeries without even one twitch; Sacks observed this man's surgical expertise with great interest. Sacks also witnessed an autistic man's creativity soar as he perfectly mimicked every instrument of an orchestra with his voice.

THE CREATIVE SUMMONS

After a significant loss, your grieving process holds an invitation, or a creative summons. Grieving helps "to examine the places where we may have been overinvested in the lost other. ... When that energy returns to us, it is ours to carry, and ours to invest in ... [new] ways. ... To grieve the loss of an intimate relationship is to celebrate what was received as a gift, but it may also raise the question of what we were asking of the other person that we need to do for ourselves."[27] Hollis challenges midlifers to "really grow up" by recognizing that you may have entered into a relational contract with other people in your life that prevented you from growing as much as you could. Meeting earlier developmental milestones may reappear in midlife. Bateson might agree, as she sees the 50s and 60s as having some similar issues to those encountered at ages 16 and 25. Who are you in the present decade? What are you able to commit to, and how can you sustain your commitment? How will you care for yourself? Bateson speaks for many in questioning her identity: "whether I am still the person I have spent 60 years becoming and whether that is the person I want to be."[28]

Your creative summons is to decide what *really* holds meaning for you. Perhaps it is very different from the meaning that made sense when you were younger. Persian poet Rumi put it this way: "What I want is to leap out of this personality and then sit apart from that leaping. I've lived too long where I can be reached."

Perhaps you want to create some new ritual to honor a person who has died. The Mexican tradition, Dia de Muertos or Day of the Dead, is a holiday that dates back to the ninth month of the Aztec calendar. The festival honors a goddess, Queen of Mictan, as well as deceased members of the family. Families create special altars showing the interests and passions of the deceased along with special foods they enjoyed. Relatives go to cemeteries where they decorate gravesites with creativity. They take traditional foods for a picnic. One traditional holiday food is pan de muerto, a sweet bread, that may be made in the shape of a skeleton. Some people even dress up as the deceased. The sharing of stories about the loved one is part of this ritual. Other cultures – from Africa to Korea to Nepal – also have rich traditions of remembering the deceased with ancestral rituals.[29] There is no one way to grieve and the group support in these ancient traditions is very positive. Such *I-Thou* rituals give families a time and a place to share precious memories. Gratitude for the life of a loved one is expressed. However, you do not have to wait until someone has died to express gratitude for a life well lived! Who might you honor with your gratitude today?

At age 58, Camille was faced with three surgeries within a six-month time frame – two of the surgeries were due to cancer. She worried about the risks of so much general anesthesia, but she faced her medical crisis one step at a time. When she lost her hair, she celebrated that she was still alive. She meditated and lived more of her life in the present moment. While Camille's family and friends surrounded her with love, she recognized the importance of being her own strong advocate when she was wheeled into surgery each time. Camille's own strength of character was critical in her healing. When her beautiful hair grew back, Camille danced joyfully at a party she threw for her tribe of supporters. Everyone glowed with admiration for Camille's courageous journey.

Psychiatrist and Jungian analyst Jean Shinoda Bolen believes that midlife has become a "medical battlefield" where all too often doctors view disease as an enemy: "Illness is both soul-shaking and soul-evoking for the patient and for all others for whom the patient matters ... and yet this is virtually ignored and unaddressed. Instead, everything seems to be focused on the part of the body that is sick, damaged, failing, or out of control." Instead of having an opportunity to ask soul-searching questions, the patient often is bombarded with medical information or left alone. People are shocked by another's diagnosis and do not know what to say. Life may feel like a slippery slope when the borderline between life and death seems close for yourself, a family member or a cherished friend. However, the threshold that illness provides can be an opening to consciousness. "Illness can unearth love and reveal strength of character."[30]

TURN TIP

Walk as if you are kissing the Earth with your feet.

– Thich Nhat Hanh, Vietnamese Buddhist monk

- How often do you allow yourself to truly feel and express gratitude? Try this idea: go for a gratitude walk.
- Sometime soon, drop what you are doing for 15 minutes and, if you can, go outside and start walking. The discipline for your walk is that you do not think about work or daydream scenarios (real or imagined) in your head.
- First, focus only on the sensation of your feet hitting the ground, your legs stretching and your hips opening up, and your breathing getting deeper and more relaxed.

- Then turn your attention to the things in your life that you are happy about – whether it's a loving relationship, your home, or satisfying work.
- Now let those more obvious things give way to the more subtle things that you might never have thought about, but that also contribute joy to your life, that infuse you with pure gratitude. As Abraham Maslow said, "In the postmortem life everything gets precious, gets piercingly important. You get stabbed by things, by flowers and by babies and by beautiful things."
- At the end of your 15-minute (or longer) walk, return to what you were doing and notice your energy. Has it changed? How do you feel now?

Write one or two sentences in your *Turn* Journal to capture the essence of your walk.

WHAT'S ON YOUR NEW BUCKET LIST?

A scholar on aging, Jill Quadagno, suggests that American research is starting to pay attention to the baby boomers (born between 1946 and 1964) as they reach retirement age.[31] Even young boomers have diverse goals for retirement. You may think that you only have time for your bucket list of special goals in life *if* you are a certain age or retired. Aisha, a 52-year-old woman, bucks this trend. She plans to start traveling when she *turns* 60, while she feels that she still has optimum health for active plans. However, plenty of boomers choose to continue working beyond 65, albeit, in different ways for most. Make good use of your brainpower. Grab your fancied bucket and make a new list. NOW! What are you waiting for? Perhaps new learning or a new line of work is on your bucket list. Do you want to leave your life up to chance without making a conscious choice? This is taking a chance on *not* achieving what you really want to happen in the coming years.

Map your personality so it becomes easier to meet five basic needs. Meeting your daily needs will help you find your way through the midlife maze. You can find energy to tackle your bucket list and end life highly satisfied due to midlife choices you make during this crucial life phase. Perhaps you review past transitions to see how they worked for you. You may not recall every transition. There are simply too many of them, but each one helped define your current personality. Drawing a personality map has helped many middle-aged adults to face dead ends and to reset creative goals. It is possible to retool to locate treasure in your life. Perhaps you want to make more time for relating to significant others. Or, there may be a new activity that you want to pursue now. Follow Spock's parting advice; forget about having perfect activities. You figured out by now that there are no perfect careers or jobs. Just when you start dreaming of the perfect retirement, a new calamity may jolt you into having only a drop-in-the-bucket list. You do not have to wait until retirement to do something special that you always dreamed of doing. Nurture your well-being. Prosper in any way that has meaning for you.

YOUR TURN

Try to be a rainbow in someone's cloud.

– Maya Angelou, poet, *Letter to My Daughter*

Does your bucket list have any room in it for others' needs and dreams? Where might you help someone else to fulfill their dreams? Organizational psychologist Adam Grant classified workers as "givers, takers, or matchers." Givers help others without expecting anything in return. Takers want to get more than they give, while matchers attempt to balance the giving/getting scales. Interestingly, givers appear both at the bottom of the success ladder as well as at the very top. Takers fall in the middle and are busy with self-promotion, even faking data at times.[32] In order to prevent burnout, givers may become matchers in dealing with takers, as takers act competitively in most interactions.[33] A giving mentality is not confined to your work world. What can you do to share your giver talents in uplifting goals?

These questions can help you make a new bucket list. Name and claim some giver goals. Make sure that some of your goals are for *today*:

• Name a goal that sounds good, but you don't know if you can pull it off.
• Name a goal that would require you to pick up some new skills.
• Name your most ambitious goal you're willing to make sacrifices for.
• Name three goals that could have the most positive impact on other people.
• Name goals you would most like to do with a partner or a friend.
• Name a goal that is expensive.
• Name a goal that is cheap in monetary terms.
• Name a goal you could begin today.
• Name the three goals that surprised you most in this list.[34]

French mathematician, philosopher, and theologian Blaise Pascal imparted good advice: "We never care for the present moment. We are so foolish that we wander in times that are not ours, and never think of the only time that belongs to us; we are so frivolous that we dream of the days that are not, and thoughtlessly pass over the only one that exists. We never live, but hope to live; and since we are always preparing to be happy it is inevitable that we shall never be so."

Chapter 13

Yearning for Joy

If the day and the night are such that you greet them with joy, and life emits a fragrance like flowers and sweet-scented herbs, is more elastic, more starry, more immortal – that is your success.

– Henry David Thoreau, philosopher and naturalist, *Walden*

The best antidote I have found is to yearn for something. As long as you yearn, you can't congeal: there is a forward motion about yearning.

– Gail Godwin, novelist

Hotels and some office buildings avoid having a thirteenth floor. We joke about Friday the 13th as dangerous. What if danger already struck your family? Does it really matter if the date was Monday the 13th or Friday the 13th? Superstition cannot control loss and by now, you know that you have little control over loss events. Playwright Eve Ensler endured stage IV cancer and yet she found words to help others: "The wind does not *turn* away. It blows through everything. Do not be afraid. There is no more winning and losing. We have already lost. … Each one of you will know in what direction you need to move and who to take with you. … Build the circles. … Dance the circles. Sing the circles. … We are the people of the second wind."[1]

While losses are critical passages in life, they are not your only defining moments. The universe is now described as a multiverse; similarly, you are not a unitary being. Your personality is multidimensional. Look at your personality map again. Where is untapped potential or treasure? How can you evolve your personality? Can a growth mind-set give you a second wind? Where can you find joy?

- Joy (from Latin *gaudium; inward joy, gladness*; Greek *gaio; "I rejoice"*) means a source of pleasure and delight.[2]

Poet Mary Oliver asks, "What is the gift that I should bring to the world?" In *I Go Down to the Shore*, she laments about life *turn*ing points and finds this answer: "I say, oh I am miserable, what shall – what should I do? And the sea says in its lovely voice: Excuse me, I have work to do." When Mary lost her lifelong partner to cancer, she faced a *turn*ing point. She thought of two alternatives for her life: either she could buy a cabin in the woods, sequester herself with her books, and shut herself off from the world or she could see who she could meet in the world. She later concluded that taking her option to open herself up produced not only new friendships, but more *space* to be by herself and her writing.[3] Oliver found a second wind.

Fairy tales that end with "they lived happily ever after" create a fixed mindset – the false childhood belief that everything you want will work for you. Perhaps not quite everything worked out in your young adult years, but when you reached midlife perhaps you believed that you had paid some life dues. However, changes in life just keep rolling. Bucket lists of future dreams may slip away. However, you are still *here*. As journalist Norman Cousins mused, "The tragedy of life is not death but what we let die inside of us while we live." Life is precious. Every day matters.

The comedian and actress Gilda Radner, famous for role-playing Roseanne Roseannadanna on *Saturday Night Live*, experienced the death of her father when she was 14. One day her father was struck with a brain tumor that left him bedridden and unable to communicate for two years prior to his death.[4] It is no wonder that her famous TV character, Roseannadanna, made communication an art form. She was famous for her quip, "It's always something – if it ain't one thing, it's another." Another of her running commentaries was the rhetorical question, "What are ya tryin' to do, make me sick?" Unfortunately, the talented Radner died at age 42 of ovarian cancer. Yes, Roseannadanna, it is always *something*. Sometimes, *something* events *turn* out to be life enhancing. After Gilda's death, Gilda's Club was founded by her husband, Gene Wilder, her cancer psychotherapist, Joanna Bull, broadcaster Joel Siegel, and other generous individuals to provide support for cancer patients and their families. In 2009, Gilda's Club and The Wellness Community merged to create the Cancer Support Community, the largest cancer support network in the United States.[5]

FORWARD MOTION OF YEARNING

In order to really thrive, you need a purpose, a kind of self-investment. As Navy Seal Eric Greitens summarizes, "In the long run ... deprivation of purpose is as destructive as deprivation of sleep. Without purpose, we can survive — but we cannot flourish."[6] *When you rediscover a purpose for your life, you bring more joy into your life.* One late summer afternoon, I watched a young girl drop her half-eaten pretzel onto a paper plate at the community swimming pool and jump with abandon into the deep end when the lifeguard announced that a ten-minute rest period was over. What a lovely message she sent me! This is exactly the plunge that you may need to fix your midlife maze existence – what can you jump into deeply at your age?

I am reminded of writer Jean Houston's book, *Jump Time*, where she explores the fast pace of change in our world: "The only expected is the unexpected. ... Ours is an era of quantum change. ... No old formulas or stopgap solutions will suit."[7] Houston challenges adults to make use of their potential: "As we come – and more and more of us are – to the recognition that our individual destiny and the world's unfolding are linked, we must also ask ourselves, 'How best may I serve? How can I plant and nurture the seeds of a better world?'"[8] Vatican astronomer Guy Consolmagno's view of a better world includes a growth mind-set: "The big lesson everyone should learn from science is not that it's *proved* one thing or another, but that it is always open to learning more, and changing as it learns."[9] Change is not our preference, but change defines life, especially at midlife.

You may prefer a stable job, a stable relationship, stability in your health, as well as stability in the environment, but changes in all areas are common. As cultural historian Riane Eisler wisely instructs, "When you look around our world, it sometimes seems like we need to change everything. ... Actually, it comes down to one thing: relationships. ... As we relate more in partnerships to ourselves, others, and our natural habitat, we have better lives and a better world." Eisler's better world calls for shifting relationships from a domination model to a partnership model.[10] When you reach midlife, you have lived a few years, but hopefully, you also have quite a few years left to live, and I mean, to live heartily. What partnerships can you claim? What do you yearn for?

You do not have to swim the English Channel at the age of 63 like Jim Clifford, although it is an amazing feat. But what might you do to bring meaning to your life, as well as to those around you? How about writing song lyrics and finding someone to set your words to music? Or, switch that idea: perhaps you write some music, and a partner writes lyrics! Why not step away from the crowd? According to philosopher Henry David Thoreau, "The mass of men [and women] lead lives of quiet desperation and go to the grave with the song still in them." Paul McCartney of Beatles fame is wistful about songwriting: "It is amazing when someone tells me that my music helped them heal from cancer. ... Music is just a bunch of vibrations, but the feeling behind it, the meaning behind it ... it can go beyond you ... and enter people's lives. That is something that I am really happy about. ... My respect for life started to creep in my songs. A lady told me that I write about respect for females ... and there is a respect for animals. ... [I wrote] about a bird with a broken wing. I wrote that about civil rights."[11] Music is as healing for the songwriter as it is for the listener. After her mother died, songwriter Sarah McQuaid wrote a beautiful song, *Only an Emotion*, about grieving as a natural state that takes time to heal.[12] In her melodic song, McQuaid yearns for precious moments to smile again.

Neuroscientist Stephen Porges explains why music is so healing. Music stimulates the *social engagement system* in a grieving person. Grieving can shut down the social engagement system. This describes why you might experience defensive and/or aggressive behaviors after a loss, even though such personality roles are not the norm for you. Other immediate responses of social engagement shutdown are a blank stare on your face, sometimes referred to as flat facial affect. These features are hardwired into your nervous system as signs of readiness for fight, flight, or freeze actions. This is adaptive behavior. Your body knows what to do for survival. Melodic music in the frequency band of the human voice is one way you can re*turn* your social engagement system to a safe state. When a composer wants to express an emotional narrative in an orchestra, the instruments duplicating the human voice are used – violins, flutes, clarinets, trumpets, oboes, and French horns – as music in these frequencies modulate the neural regulation of muscles of your face and head without triggering defensive behavior. Positive facial expressions can *turn* you about-face to a calmer physiological state.[13] Singing can connect you to inner joy. My town has a Sing to Live community chorus, a group of singers whose lives are touched by breast cancer. Where might music enter your life?

TREASURE IS NOT A DISTANT ISLAND

The ability to live with more mindfulness to notice *treasure* in your life can help you cope with rapid changes, even with unwanted changes brought about by loss. In spite of everything you once counted on, your dreams for your future may have to shift directions. Physician Rachel Naomi Remen suggests, "We are in relationship with our expectations and not with life itself."[14] Changing how you view your life after loss feels awkward, but you can embrace your personality strength roles to follow mythologist Joseph Campbell's vision for meaning: "What we're seeking is an experience of being alive so that our life experiences on the purely physical plane will have resonances within our own innermost being and reality, so that we actually feel the rapture of being alive."[15] You can find aliveness after a lost-in-the-maze journey. *Turn* your focus to gratitude for what you do have. Be open to new ideas. Create something new with your unique potential.

My mother recalls a time when she was 12 years old and confined to bed rest for an entire year due to appendicitis and rheumatic fever. A physician told her parents in 1935, "I'm afraid there isn't anything we can do for the little lady upstairs." However, this physician did not know my mother! A fascinating detail is that my mother's middle name is Treasure. One day Lois Treasure wandered into her father's library and took a slim volume off the shelves. Intrigued with *Acres of Diamonds* by Russell Conwell, founder of Temple University, my mother remembered the kernels of truth in that allegory over 80 years later. Here is the gist of the Persian story as told by Conwell:

Ali Hafed owned a very large farm and was wealthy. However, he desired a mine of precious diamonds. He sold his farm, collected his money, and left his family to go in search of treasure. While he traveled far and wide with no luck, he eventually spent his last penny. Finding himself lost in the maze of poverty, Hafed drowned himself in the sea.

Meanwhile, the man who purchased Hafed's forsaken farm took his camel into the farm's garden to drink water from the brook. The new owner caught a flash of brightness in the water. He pulled a black stone out of the water and saw all the colors of the rainbow in one *part* of the stone. Initially, he did not comprehend his discovery, but a priest informed him that he found a diamond! Together the men rushed to the brook. It *turn*ed out that this garden held the best diamond-mine in the history of mankind. There were acres of diamonds.

Conwell delivered this message over five thousand times between 1900 and 1925. His advice holds truth for the new millennium: "If you wish to be great at all, you must begin where you are and what you are ... now."[16] Yes, there is treasure to find on your home front. You can mine your own personality to find hidden treasure and inner joy.

In spite of personal losses, you too can find treasure and joy. The message that it takes time to find treasure is an ancient one. Greek playwright Euripides (around the year 428 BC) said it this way: "Leave no stone un*turn*ed." Perhaps you have heard a modern version about two youths. A research project studied pessimists versus optimists.

One boy [or girl] was placed in a room filled with toys. An entire toy store was emptied into a single room for the sake of the study. A second boy [or girl] was given a room filled with horse manure. The children's behavior was observed behind one-way mirrors, but the results surprised the investigative team. Toy boy [or girl] seemed incapable of enjoying great fortune. Opening each successive toy box, the miserable child complained: "Where are the video games? It's hot in here. I don't have any friends to play with. I'm bored."

Meanwhile, the second boy [or girl] was busy flinging manure with much animation and excitement. With great caution one of the researchers opened the door to talk with the radiant child. The eager child exclaimed, "With all this manure I just know there is a pony in here somewhere and I'm going to find it!"[17]

The optimistic child undoubtedly returned to digging. When you are on a treasure hunt, you do not give up easily.

There is no straight path to a life of success and happiness. *Turn*ing points happen for everyone in midlife. Even people who have lost a precious child may go on to engage in nonprofit work or other helping endeavors. As one bereaved parent said, "I hate that I lost my child, but I like the person I have become ... a lot better than whom I was before."[18] Midlifers yearn for something. How much treasure can you find in your personal strengths? As you *turn* some corners after your loss, what holds meaning for you now?

TURN TIP

I am where I am because I believe in all possibilities.

– Whoopi Goldberg, actress

This exercise is not intended to put you under pressure to let go of parts of your personality. That only creates resistance. The exercise is simply to inquire and evaluate, in a relaxed way, if it is possible to let go of negative labels you use to define yourself. In the words of poet and scientist Theodore Melnechuk, "Each one of us contains a set of persons each will be: Oh, how I wish my own next self would take the place of me!" No one else can make personal choices for you. You identify who you want to be tomorrow and the next day. Letting go does not happen primarily in the mind—it happens in the body.

The next time you have an important decision to make, notice how your body is responding. Does your body feel light or heavy?[19] You want to ask yourself if it is *possible* to use different labels for yourself. In the recognition of this possibility, something may happen in your body – a deep sigh, a muscle spasm, or a release of tension you might not have even known was there. What seemed to be a prison becomes a choice again. A shift in your focus can release energy and connect you to the present moment.

Reflect on a few questions. Write your answers in your *Turn* Journal, or share the exercise verbally with someone you trust. Ask each other the questions. Make notes for each other.

- Who have you defined yourself to be at your current age? (For example, I'm a teacher. I'm intelligent. I'm educated. I'm a family man. I'm a mother.)
- Now look at your labels for yourself. For each statement, ask yourself: "If I stopped defining myself in this way, would I still exist?" "If I were no longer a teacher, would I still exist?" "If I no longer thought of myself as a father, would I still be here?" "If I no longer defined myself as intelligent, would I still exist?"
- Take your time to work through all labels you have listed. Determine if any of them can really define you or contain you. When you have considered all of your labels, discover what remains. As Pema Chodron instructs, "The future is completely open, and we are writing it moment to moment."

THE EVENING OF LIFE

You may sense that time in your life is limited. Midlife opens the transition gate to significant health challenges and/or senior citizen status, the evening of life. Life is impermanent. As you grow beyond your mid-60s, loss becomes even more common. You may ask yourself when you reach this developmental stage of integrity versus despair, "What time is *this*?" It is time to recognize that true treasure, or well-being, does not equal monetary wealth, no matter how large the portfolio. "Money is the most universally motivating, mischievous, miraculous, maligned, and misunderstood part of contemporary life. ... Wealth shows up in the action of sharing and giving, allocating and distributing, nourishing and watering the projects, people, and purpose that we believe in and care about, with the resources that flow to us and through us."[20] Like most topics, it is what you *do* with money, rather than counting it, that actually counts beyond a lifetime.

Shortly before he died of cancer, 82-year-old Oliver Sacks – the popular neurologist who wrote books about quirky brains – captured the essence of loss and death: "When people die, they cannot be replaced. They leave holes that cannot be filled, for it is the fate – the genetic and neural fate – of every human being to be a unique individual, to find his [or her] own path ... to die his [or her] own death. I cannot pretend I am without fear. But my predominant feeling is one of gratitude. I have loved and been loved: I have been given much and I have given something in return: I have read and traveled and thought and written. I have had an intercourse with the world, the special intercourse of writers and readers."[21] Who could wish for more? Poet Laureate William Stafford echoes the gratitude message from his poem, *Yes*: "It could happen any time, tornado, earthquake...no guarantees in this life. But some bonuses, like morning, like right now."[22] The beauty of living more of your life in the present moment is poignant, whether you are in the morning, afternoon, or evening of your life.

Remember, you have the ability to reset your personality for joy, gratitude, resilience, creativity, and generativity. I hope this book inspires you to evolve your personality in new directions. Some of you will live a really long life. Joan Erikson and my mother, living well into their 90s, are examples of people sharing their wisdom with a keen generative focus. When Chinese-American philosopher and social activist Grace Lee Boggs *turn*ed hundred, her sage perspective included this view: "Progress does not take place like a shot out of a pistol; it takes the labor and suffering of the negative. How to use the negative as a way to advance the positive is our challenge." Even though you may not know which way to detour after a significant loss, Boggs advised, "You have to make a way through no way."[23] Boggs made it through the midlife maze and beyond.

Research backs up Boggs' thinking. Psychologist Mark Seery tracked over two thousand Americans for four years. He challenged the notion that traumatic events in life always increase your risk of depression and/or illness. Rather, his research shows that coping with negative life events can promote your ability to develop subsequent resilience. Research participants were asked if they had ever experienced 37 different negative life events, such as the death of a friend or loved one, a serious illness or injury, a major financial difficulty, divorce, being the victim of physical or sexual violence, and/or survival of a natural disaster like a fire or flood. Participants reported eight such events in their lives on average. Only 8 % of the adults reported that they never experienced any such events.

Interestingly, the research participants with zero adversity in their lives were less happy and healthy than those who faced some hardship! Seery concluded, "People are not doomed to be damaged by adversity. Beyond recovering to past levels of functioning in the aftermath of adversity, we found evidence consistent with people actually benefiting from the experience of adversity."[24] For example, after a serious illness, other stressors may seem less important or overwhelming by comparison. My mother is fond of quoting Ralph Waldo Emerson's poetic version of dealing with adversity: "But in the mud and scum of things there alway, alway something sings." Hopefully, you can find your voice.

FINDING A VOICE

I found one midlife voice in book writing. Both *It Takes a Child to Raise a Parent* and *Midlife Maze* focus primarily on the midlife adult developmental stage that was omitted from my graduate school training. Now, 40 years later, parenting and midlife coursework still do not rate adequate coverage for psychology students. More time is devoted to studying the development of babies and adolescents than of adults. However, midlife is a critical stage. It is the longest life stage for most. Midlife is the time for raising careers and/ or children. Middle-aged adults have many taking-care-of-business responsibilities. They do not expect loss to slow them down. When loss hits home, hoped for dreams can vanish. Midlifers may neglect their basic needs and feel lost. In my writing, I want to give voice to the many tools that midlifers can use in coping with challenges and loss.

Quite by accident, I found a different voice in becoming a master gardener. One winter I saw a notice in the newspaper about classes offered by the University of Illinois Extension. The thought had not occurred to me to *study* gardening, as I grew up in the gardens of my paternal grandmother and father. I developed a greenish thumb from their good examples. As I dabbled at gardening in midlife, I found it immensely rewarding to watch the seasons *turn* to feature one plant, then another. Master gardener classes added knowledge to my love of gardening. I found out how little I knew about the many facets of plant-insect relationships. Always an admirer of nature's complexities, I began to savor gardening even more. I focused on nurturing hardiness among plants when people in my family died.

My favorite flower used to be the Bearded Iris. I love the fragrance and elegance of the flower heads. However, the lovely iris leaves the garden after a short growth spurt. When several blooms on one stalk are at their peak, the stalk falls over. Now I have many favorite flowers. I came to appreciate the hardy Lenten Rose. The evergreen leaves keep some vitality year-round, even in Zone 5 winters. The first to flower in early spring, Lenten Rose's delicate flowers curve into upside-down hammocks swinging gently in the wind. You have to focus closely on the Lenten Rose to enjoy its over*turn*ed hidden charms. The feisty blooms have color lasting for months. I love the growth lessons from the Lenten Rose: it grows in the shade, resists disease, and tolerates drought conditions. This self-seeder keeps expanding each year, forming new clumps around the parent plant.

Giving tours in the Lurie Garden in Millennium Park with other master gardeners is an uplifting experience, as we seed ideas with visitors from around the world. Some visitors know more about gardening than I do, so we share gardening tips. One summer I met Ben for the first time when he became our horticulture intern in the garden. It *turn*s out that Ben and I are from the same green thumb relatives! My grandmother, Vera, and his great-grandmother, Helen, were sisters. As cousins, my father, Bob, had a close relationship with Ben's grandmother, Josephine. I was the flower girl in Ben's grandmother's wedding! I picked red raspberries from our family garden for Ben's grandmother for several summers. She paid me in quarters for my efforts and I proudly stored those coins in my father's cigar box. Gardens hold good stories and good stores of produce. A Pueblo Indian prayer says it best: "Hold on to what is good, even if it's a handful of earth."

Whether you garden, take music lessons, tutor children, volunteer your time, or find a belly dancing class (yes, men also belly dance), discover some meaning in present moments. Find engaging free-time projects. Actress Audrey Hepburn embraced generativity: "As you grow older, you will discover that you have two hands, one for helping yourself, the other for helping others." In fact, having experienced a significant loss may make you a stronger helper than before your loss. As physician Rachel Naomi Remen understands loss, "Wounds have made me gentle with the wounds of other people, and able to trust the mysterious process by which we can heal. ... Most humbling of all, I have found that sometimes the thing that serves me best is not all my hard-earned medical knowledge but something about life I may have learned from my Russian grandmother or from a child ...a helping relationship ... like healing, is mutual. ...The wholeness in me is as strengthened as the wholeness in you."[25] This describes the essence of self-territory. When you are at peace within yourself, you strengthen your sense of wholeness. And as you rediscover wholeness, you are more sensitive to loss in others. You reach out to strengthen the wholeness in another. You embody Buber's *I-Thou* relating.

Finding a voice to face your own loss of life is a final challenge that requires a grieving process, although some individuals never reach the opportunity to grieve their own death due to sudden, accidental or tragic deaths. Midlife is the last developmental stage for many individuals. Evening or graduating senior years are not possible for everyone. Some never have the opportunity to voice palliative care physician Ira Byock's four statements that matter most: "Please forgive me," "I forgive you," "Thank you," and "I love you."[26] Consider another physician's experiences of sitting at the bedside of dying patients. She reports that her patients rarely regret not having enough control over their lives. Instead, the terminal adults have regret that they did not risk more, or pursue their passions.[27] German philosopher Johann Wolfgang von Goethe advised how to avoid regret: "What you can do, or dream you can do, begin it! Boldness has genius, power and magic in it. Begin it now."

THE SEASON TO *TURN, TURN, TURN* IS NOW!

From ancient times to the present, everyone has his or her own notions of what might bring a sense of well-being in life, but it boils down to how you spend your time: "The easiest way to increase happiness is to control your use of time."[28] Improv professor Patricia Ryan Madson emphasizes moving more of the time: "Kick-start your life – walk, run, crawl, fly, bicycle: move in the direction of your purpose."[29] In the PBS documentary, *The Boomer List,* Steve Wozniak, cofounder of Apple Computers, offered his formula for happiness, H = F cubed: "Happiness equals food, fun, and friends!" Deepak Chopra, Indian-American physician in holistic health, recommended spiritual growth as a formula for happiness. Still another version of looking at wholesome well-being is the advice of the CEO of IBM, Virginia Rometty: "Never let anyone else define you." And without apology, she added, "Growth and comfort never co-exist."[30] I will keep my motto, "Make something good happen every day."

Do I really mean *every day*? Yes, every day. The word for good in Aramaic means ripe. I like the reference to nature. Making something good *happen* means to take action at the ripe or right time and place. How you spend time matters. But you will choose your own treasured words for a motto. Perhaps a song will inspire a motto for you to *turn* your life in the direction of a growth mind-set and the capacity to see your glass *half-full.* Pete Seeger wrote the song, *Turn! Turn! Turn! (To Everything There is a Season)* in the late 1950s, but the lyrics are timeless. In fact, Seeger borrowed his lyrics from these ancient words in Ecclesiastes (3: 1–8) in the *Bible*: "For everything there is a season, and a time for every matter under heaven: a time to be born, and a time to die; a time to plant, and a time to pluck up what is planted … a time to weep, and a time to laugh; a time to mourn, and a time to dance."[31] Find lyrics that resonate with you.

As I gather final thoughts about writing this book, I am grateful for the experience. Writing has been part of my grieving process, whether in writing a gratitude journal for two different years, keeping a dream journal, or book writing. Perhaps some form of writing will help you. Here are two more entries from my two *Turn* (to gratitude) Journals:

> Today was Parenthesis consultation group. Issues? The van driver for the teen moms' program died. Both the executive director and a social worker resigned. I am grateful there is a core group who remain on staff! I enjoy volunteering supervision time for support staff, as their casework is so difficult. It was a social worker's 51st birthday, but a child care worker's one year anniversary of her infant's death. Life!
>
> I am grateful for the opportunity to have a free morning in the garden. I weeded, planted, and dug up extra plants to give away – my Tai Chi teacher, Bea, has a special plant for a poison ivy cure, so I traded my corydalis lutea for her jewelweed.

As Irish philosopher John O'Donahue eloquently wrote in his foreword to the *The Infinite Thread: Healing Relationships Beyond Loss*, "Grief [is] not a desert but … a slow garden of remembrance, surprise, and unexpected novelty." You are not destined to stay in a bereft state after a significant loss.

You can create a personality map to find the hope and treasure you need to retool for a highly satisfying life.

You will gather your own healing strategies that help you in grieving loss, as there is no one pathway for processing grief. And when you see others who are stuck in a maze of emotions, encourage them along their journey. *Turn*ing points happen in everyone's life. Remember that the verb *turn* comes from the Greek word *tomos* which means *circular movement* around an axis or center in order to achieve a result. Poet Maya Angelou understood circularity in life: "As soon as healing takes place, go out and heal someone else." Joan Erikson's words are another reminder of the importance of tending and befriending others: "The important thing is to share what you know. ... Be generative and pass it on." When you harvest something from a vegetable garden, you save the seeds from what grew best for the next growing season. Time has a way of bending into a circle.

Notes

INTRODUCTION

1. Daniel K. Mroczek, "Positive and Negative Affect in Midlife," in *How Healthy Are We? A National Study of Well-being at Midlife*, eds. Orville Gilbert Brim, Carol D. Ryff, and Ronald C. Kessler (Chicago, IL: University of Chicago, 2004), 213–214.

2. "MIDUS II, MIDUS Refresher," accessed April 29, 2015. http://midus.colectica.org/.html.

3. "MIDUS II," accessed April 29, 2015. http://www.ncbi.nlm.nih.gov/pmc/articles/PMC3827458/.html.

4. Dan P. McAdams and Philip J. Bowman, "Narrating Life's Turning Points: Redemption and Contamination," in *Turns in the Road; Narrative Studies of Lives in Transition*, eds. Dan P. McAdams, Ruthellen Josselson, and Amia Lieblich (Washington, DC: American Psychological Association, 2001), 12.

5. *American Heritage Dictionary*, 5th ed., s. v. "turn."

6. "O'odham People," accessed April 28, 2015. https://en.wikipedia.org/wiki/I%27itoi.html.

7. "O'odham Values," accessed April 28, 2015. http://www.mothertongues.com/catalog.php/mothertongues/ct12925.html.

8. "Man in the maze," accessed July 29, 2015. http://www.forwardwalking.com/2013/11/25/man-in-the-maze/.html.

9. Carl G. Jung, *Modern Man in Search of a Soul* (New York: Harcourt, Brace and World, 1933), 108.

10. Tara Brach, *True Refuge: Finding Peace and Freedom in Your Own Awakened Heart* (New York: Bantam, 2012), 7–8.

11. Richard C. Schwartz, *Internal Family Systems* (New York: Guilford, 1995), 48–50.

12. "Christopher Reeve," accessed April 30, 2015. http://www.biography.com/people/christopher-reeve-9454130#synopsis.html.

CHAPTER 1

1. Hans-Werner Wahl and Andreas Kruse, "Historical Perspectives of Middle Age within the Life Span," in *Middle Adulthood: A Lifetime Perspective*, eds. Sherry Willis and Mike Martin (Thousand Oaks, CA: Sage, 2005), 15.

2. "Steps of Life," accessed May 5, 2015. https://commons.wikimedia.org/wiki/Category:Steps_of_life.html.

3. Wahl and Kruse, *Middle Adulthood*, 6.

4. Barbara Strauch, *The Secret Life of the Grown-up Brain: The Surprising Talents of the Middle-Aged Mind* (New York: Viking, 2010), 92 –94.

5. "IQ increase," accessed March 25, 2015. http://www.allpsychologycareers.com/topics/middle-adulthood-development.html.

6. Adam Grant, *Originals: How Non-conformists Move the World* (New York: Viking, 2016), x.

7. "Living," accessed September 3, 2015. https://pdotberry.wordpress.com/about/.html.

8. "Midlife," accessed March 19, 2015. http://dictionary.reference.com/browse/midlife.html.

9. Orville Gilbert Brim, Carol D. Ryff, and Ronald C. Kessler, eds. *How Healthy Are We? A National Study of Well-being at Midlife* (Chicago, IL: University of Chicago, 2004).

10. Margie E. Lachman, "Development in Midlife," *Annual Review of Psychology*, 55 (2004): 307.

11. "Grieving," accessed September 3, 2015. https://sarahmcquaid.bandcamp.com/track/only-an-emotion.html.

12. Brene Brown, *Daring Greatly: How the Courage to be Vulnerable Transforms the Way We Live, Love, Parent, and Lead* (New York: Avery, 2012), 33.

13. Erik Erikson, *Childhood and Society,* 2nd ed. (New York: W. W. Norton, 1963).

14. Erikson, *Childhood and Society,* 247–269.

15. Dan P. McAdams, "The psychology of life stories," *Review of General Psychology,* 5 (2001): 100.

16. Dan P. McAdams, *The Stories We Live By: Personal Myths and the Making of the Self* (New York: William Morrow, 1993), 95.

17. Joan Anderson, *A Walk on the Beach: Tales of Wisdom from an Unconventional Woman* (New York: Broadway, 2004), 103–104.

18. Joan M. Erikson. *The Life Cycle Completed: Extended Version* (New York: W. W. Norton, 1997), 106–114.

19. *American Heritage Dictionary*, 5th ed., s. v. "versus."

20. Dan P. McAdams and Philip J. Bowman, "Narrating Life's Turning Points: Redemption and Contamination," in *Turns in the Road: Narrative Studies of Lives in Transition,* eds. Dan P. McAdams, Ruthellen Josselson, and Amia Lieblich (Washington, DC: American Psychological Association, 2001), 19–28.

21. "Mid-Life Crisis," accessed April 15, 2015. http://articles.latimes.com/2003/mar/23/local/me-jacques23.html.

22. Margie E. Lachman and Rosanna M. Bertrand, "Personality and the Self in Midlife," in *Handbook of Midlife Development,* ed. Margie E. Lachman (New York: Wiley, 2001), 279–309.

23. "Middle Age," accessed June 17, 2015. http://www.apa.org/monitor/2011/04/mind-midlife.aspx.html.

24. Carol Dweck, *Mindset: The New Psychology of Success: How We Can Learn to Fulfill our Potential* (New York: Random House, 2006), 6–13.

25. "PTSD," accessed June 16, 2015. http://www.aaos.org/news/aaosnow/may11/clinical8.asp.html.

26. Eric Greitens, *Resilience: Hard-won Wisdom for Living a Better Life* (New York: Houghton Mifflin, 2015), 11–12.

27. Bessel Van der Kolk, *The Body Keeps the Score: Brain, Mind and Body in the Healing of Trauma* (New York: Viking, 2014), 79.

28. Schwartz, *Internal Family,* 9.

29. "PTSD," accessed June 18, 2015. http://ptsdtreatmenthelp.com/emdr-for-soldiers-with-ptsd/.html.

30. Donald Capps, *Understanding Psychosis: Issues and Challenges for Sufferers, Families, and Friends* (Lanham, MD: Rowman and Littlefield, 2010), 57.

31. "Depression," accessed September 3, 2015.http://www.cdc.gov/nchs/data/databriefs/db172.pdf.

32. "Anxiety," accessed September 3, 2015. http://www.adaa.org/about-adaa/press-room/facts-statistics.html.

33. "Suicide," accessed June 10, 2015..http://www.washingtonpost.com/local/baby-boomers-are-killing-themselves-at-an-alarming-rate-begging-question-why/2013/06/03/d98acc7a-c41f-11e2-8c3b-0b5e9247e8ca_story.html.

34. "Suicide," accessed June 10, 2015. http://thenationshealth.aphapublications.org/content/45/4/E21.ful.html.

35. "Suicide," accessed June 15, 2015. http://www.nytimes.com/2013/05/19/opinion/sunday/douthat-loneliness-and-suicide.html?_r=0.html.

36. Dan P. McAdams, Holly M. Hart, and Shadd Maruna, "The Anatomy of Generativity," in *Generativity and Adult Development: How and Why We Care for the Next Generation,* eds. Dan P McAdams and Ed de St. Aubin (Washington, DC: American Psychological Association, 1998), 18–22.

37. McAdams, Hart, and Maruna, *Generativity,* 30–33.

38. Greitens, *Resilience,* 17.

39. Schwartz, *Internal Family,* 33–38.

40. Richard C. Schwartz, *You Are the One You've Been Waiting For: Bringing Courageous Love to Intimate Relationships* (Oak Park, IL: Trailheads, 2008), 11.

41. Matthew Desmond, *Evicted: Poverty and Profit in the American City* (New York: Crown, 2016), 4.

42. James W. Pennebaker, *The Secret Life of Pronouns: What Our Words Say About Us* (New York: Bloomsbury, 2011), 128.

43. "Journaling," accessed August 23, 2015. http://uudb.org/articles/ralphwaldo-emerson.html.

44. Louise DeSalvo, *Writing as a Way of Healing: How Telling Our Stories Transforms Our Lives* (New York: HarperSanFrancisco, 1999), 70.

45. Teresa M. Amabile, *Nurturing a Lifetime of Creativity* (New York: Crown, 1989), 12–13.

CHAPTER 2

1. Kelly McGonigal, *The Upside of Stress: Why Stress is Good for You, and How to Get Good at It* (New York: Avery, 2015), xii.

2. Kelly McGonigal, "Losing Our War on Stress: It's Time to Reconsider Our Approach," *Psychotherapy Networker,* 40 (2016): 57–58.

3. Fred H. Gage, "Brain, Repair Yourself," *Scientific American,* September 2003, 47–53.

4. "Physical Exercise," accessed November 21, 2015. http://www.salk.edu/scientist/rusty-gage/.html.

5. David Whyte, *The House of Belonging* (Langley, WA: Many Rivers, 1996), 23.

6. "Gratitude," accessed January 21, 2016. http://www.onbeing.org/program/david-steindl-rast-anatomy-of-gratitude/transcript/8366.

7. Nancy J. Moules, et.al., "Making Room for Grief: Walking Backwards and Living Forward," *Nursing Inquiry,* 11 (2004): 99–107.

8. Ruth Davis Konigsberg, *The Truth about Grief: The Myth of its Five Stages and the New Science of Loss* (New York: Simon and Schuster, 2011), 22.

9. "Grieving," accessed July 2, 2015. http://www.ncbi.nlm.nih.gov/pmc/articles/PMC2898114/.html.

10. Christine Clifford, *Cancer Has Its Privileges: Stories of Hope and Laughter* (New York: Perigee, 2002), 24.

11. Michaela Haas, *Bouncing Forward: Transforming Bad Breaks into Breakthroughs* (New York: Enliven/Atria, 2015), 111–112.

12. "Stillbirth," accessed June 23, 2015. http://www.nytimes.com/video/science/100000003745151/silence-of-stillbirth.html?emc=edit_th_20150623&nl=todaysheadlines&nlid=23039635.html.

13. "Child Death," accessed June 23, 2015. http://www.hopexchange.com/Statistics.html.

14. "Miscarriage," accessed July 31, 2015. http://www.slate.com/blogs/xx_factor/2015/07/31/while_looking_to_the_future_zuckerberg_s_pregnancy_announcement_also_acknowledges.html .

15. "Infant death," accessed February 25, 2016. http://www.theolympian.com/news/nation-world/national/article61963667.html.

16. Christof Koch, *Consciousness: Confessions of a Romantic Reductionist* (Cambridge, MA: MIT Press, 2012), 76.

17. Lea Winerman, "The Mind's Mirror," *APA Monitor on Psychology* 36 (2005): 48–50.

18. "Money stress," accessed August 19, 2015. http://apa.org/news/press/releases/2015/02/money-stress.aspx.html.

19. Geneen Roth, *Lost and Found: One Woman's Story of Losing Her Money and Finding Her Life* (New York: Viking, 2011), 73.

20. Louise Hay and David Kessler, *You Can Heal Your Heart: Finding Peace after a Breakup, Divorce, or Death* (Carlsbad, CA: Hay House, 2014), 3–8.

21. Andrew Newberg and Mark Robert Waldman, *Words Can Change Your Brain: Twelve Conversation Strategies to Build Trust, Resolve Conflict, and Increase Intimacy* (New York: Plume, 2013), 24.

22. Hay and Kessler, *You Can Heal*, 11–15.

23. Vicky Whipple, *Lesbian Widows: Invisible Grief* (Binghamton, NY: Harrington Park, 2006), 197–198.

24. Frank S. Pittman, III, *Turning Points: Treating Families in Transition and Crisis* (New York: W. W. Norton, 1987), 30.

25. Pittman, *Turning Points*, xi–xvii.

26. Elisabeth Kubler-Ross and David Kessler, *On Grief and Grieving: Finding the Meaning of Grief through the Five Stages of Loss* (New York: Scribner, 2005), 17–18.

27. Elisabeth Kubler-Ross, *On Death and Dying: What the Dying Have to Teach Doctors, Nurses, Clergy and Their own Families* (New York: Macmillan, 1969), 38–113.

28. Paul K. Maciejewski, et al., "An Empirical Examination of the Stage Theory of Grief," *JAMA*, 297 (2007): 716–123.

29. Susan L. Carter, "Themes of Grief," *Nursing Research*, 38 (1989): 354–358.

30. Phyllis Ann Solari-Twadell, et al., "The Pinwheel Model of Bereavement," *Journal of Nursing Scholarship*, 27 (1995): 323–326.

31. DeSalvo, *Writing*, 4–8.

32. Judith Viorst, *Necessary Losses: The Loves, Illusions, Dependencies, and Impossible Expectations That All of Us Have to Give Up in Order to Grow* (New York: Ballantine, 1986), 15.

33. Silvan S. Tomkins, "Script Theory," in *The Emergence of Personality*, eds. Joel Aronoff, Albert I. Rabin, and Robert A. Zucker (New York: Springer, 1987), 147–216.

34. McAdams and Bowman, *Turns*, 16.

35. "Heart patients," accessed July 4, 2015. http://www.apa.org/pubs/journals/releases/scp-0000050.pdf.html.

36. Martin E. Seligman, et al., "Positive Psychology in Progress: Empirical Validation of Interventions," *American Psychologist*, 60 (2005): 410–421.

CHAPTER 3

1. McAdams and Bowman, *Turns*, 19–28.

2. J. Allan Hobson, foreword to *Breakthrough Dreaming: How to Tap the Power of Your 24-hour Mind*, by Gayle Delaney (New York: Bantam, 1991), xiv.

3. "Dream research," accessed August 6, 2015.http://articles.chicagotribune.com/2001-02-18/features/0102180498_1_dreaming-sleep-disorder-service-rosalind-cartwright.html.

4. Rosalind Cartwright, "The Contribution of the Psychology of Sleep and Dreaming to Understanding Sleep-Disordered Patients," *Sleep Medicine Clinics*, 3 (2008): 157–166.

5. T. J. Wray, *Grief Dreams: How They Help Us After the Death of a Loved One* (San Francisco, CA: Jossey-Bass, 2005), 2.

6. "Dream normality," accessed April 21, 2015. http://www.umsonline.org/PrinterFriendly/dreamssamplelesson.htm.

7. Robert J. Hoss, *Dream Language: Self-understanding through Imagery and Color* (Ashland, OR: Innersource, 2005), 46.

8. "Invention dreams," accessed April 21, 2015. http://www.neuroscientificallychallenged.com/blog/history-of-neuroscience-otto-loewi.html.

9. Jeremy P. Taylor, *The Wisdom of Your Dreams: Using Dreams to Tap into your Unconscious and Transform your Life* (New York: Jeremy P. Tarcher/Penguin, 2009), 27.

10. J. Allan Hobson, *Dreaming: An Introduction to the Science of Sleep* (New York: Oxford University, 2002), ix.

11. "Magnetism," accessed April 21, 2015. http://van.physics.illinois.edu/QA/listing.php?id=225.html.

12. "Carl Jung," accessed August 17, 2015.https://adamcmadison.wordpress.com/tag/carl-jung/page/4/.html.

13. Hobson, *Dreaming,* 171.

14. "Nightmares," accessed September 22, 1015. http://www.webmd.com/sleep-disorders/guide/nightmares-in-adults?page=2.html.

15. Atul Gawande, *Being Mortal: Medicine and What Matters in the End* (New York: Metropolitan, 2014), 7.

16. Oliver Sacks, *Hallucinations* (New York: Vintage, 2012), 227–228.

17. Barry Krakow and Antonio Zadra, "Clinical Management of Chronic Nightmares: Imagery Rehearsal Therapy," *Behavioral Sleep Medicine,* 4 (2006): 45–70.

18. "Night terrors," accessed September 22, 1015. http://www.webmd.com/sleep-disorders/night-terrors.html.

19. Carl G. Jung, *Memories, Dreams, Reflections,* ed. Aniela Jaffe, trans. Richard and Clara Winston (New York: Random House, 1965), 96–97.

20. Wray, *Grief Dreams,* 2–4.

21. Taylor, *Dreams,* 66.

22. "Message dreams," accessed August 17, 2015. http://www.learningstrategies.com/blog/index.php/archives/1290.

23. Taylor, *Dreams,* 61–71.

24. Gayle Delaney, *Breakthrough Dreaming: How to Tap the Power of Your 24-Hour Mind* (New York: Bantam Books, 1991), 9–10; 20.

25. Taylor, *Dreams,*165; 194–195; 211.

26. David K. Randall, *Dreamland: Adventures in the Strange Science of Sleep* (New York: W. W. Norton, 2012), 88.

27. Taylor, *Dreams,* 184–187.

28. "Bible dreams," accessed April 21, 2015. http://overviewbible.com/infographic-dreams-bible/.html.

29. *The Holy Bible, Revised Standard Version* (New York: Thomas Nelson and Sons, 1952), Genesis 41: 17–27.

30. Delaney, *Breakthrough Dreaming,* 3–8; 35.
31. Hoss. *Dream Language,* 227–232.
32. Taylor, *Dreams,* 118–119.

CHAPTER 4

1. Alexandra Kennedy, *The Infinite Thread: Healing Relationships beyond Loss* (Hillsboro, OR: Beyond Words, 2001), xv.

2. Antonio Damasio, *Looking for Spinoza: Joy, Sorrows, and the Feeling Brain* (Orlando, FL: Harcourt, 2003), 85.

3. Janis Clark Johnston, *It Takes a Child to Raise a Parent: Stories of Evolving Child and Parent Development* (Lanham, MD: Rowman and Littlefield, 2013), 21–22.

4. "Midlife loss," accessed May 18, 2015.http://www.dailyfinance.com/2011/02/12/simple-abundance-author-bounces-back-from-financial-brink.html.

5. Sarah Ban Breathnach, *Moving On: Creating Your House of Belonging with Simple Abundance* (New York: Meredith, 2006), xiii.

6. "Pain in loss," accessed July 29, 2015. https://en.wikipedia.org/wiki/Rose_Kennedy.html.

7. Lissa Rankin, *Mind Over Medicine: Scientific Proof That You Can Heal Yourself* (Carlsbad, CA: Hay House, 2013), 26–27.

8. Jeffrey A. Kottler, *Change: What Really Leads to Lasting Personal Transformation* (New York: Oxford University, 2014), 118.

9. "Resilience," accessed June 3, 2015. http://www.apa.org/monitor/oct02/pp.aspx.html.

10. *American Heritage Dictionary,* 5th ed., s. v. "resilient."

11. "Creative resilience," accessed June 3, 2015. http://www.npr.org/2015/09/11/439236972/after-sandy-katrina-and-sept-11-this-sculptor-finds-art-in-survival.html.

12. Patricia B. Allen, *Art Is a Way of Knowing: A Guide to Self-knowledge and Spiritual Fulfillment through Creativity* (Boston, MA: Shambala, 1995), 103.

13. "Death Café," accessed February 10, 2016. http://www.theguardian.com/life-andstyle/2014/mar/22/death-cafe-talk-about-dying.html.

14. "Resilience tips," accessed June 3, 2015.http://www.apa.org/helpcenter/road-resilience.aspx.html.

15. Antonio Sausys, *Yoga for Grief Relief: Simple Practices for Transforming Your Grieving Mind and Body* (Oakland, CA: New Harbinger, 2014), 1.

16. Abraham H. Maslow. *Toward a Psychology of Being.* 3rd ed. (New York: John Wiley, 1999), 168–169.

17. Abraham H. Maslow. *Motivation and* Personality. 2nd ed. (New York: Harper and Row, 1970), 35–51.

18. Maslow, *Motivation,* 128.

19. "Handprints," accessed August 30, 2015. http://www.warpaths2peacepipes.com/native-american-symbols/handprint-symbol.html.

CHAPTER 5

1. William Bridges, *Managing Transitions: Making the Most of Change,* 3rd ed. (New York: Da Capo, 2009), 3–5; 27.

2. Juan Enriquez and Steve Gullans, *Evolving Ourselves: How Unnatural Selection and Nonrandom Mutation are Changing Life on Earth* (New York: Penguin, 2015), 60–63.

3. McCrae and Costa Jr., "Personality," 515.

4. Sanjay Srivasstava, et al., "Development of Personality in Early and Middle Adulthood: Set Like Plaster or Persistent Change?" *Journal of Personality and Social Psychology,* 84 (2003): 1041–1053.

5. Dan P. McAdams and Jennifer L. Pals, "A New Big Five: Fundamental Principles for an Integrative Science of Personality," *American Psychologist,* 61 (2006): 204–217.

6. "Midlife students," accessed February 3, 2016. http://source.southuniversity.edu/making-a-successful-midlife-career-change-27131.aspx.html.

7. Daniel J. Siegel and Tina Payne Bryson, *The Whole-Brain child: 12 Revolutionary Strategies to Nurture Your Child's Developing Mind* (New York: Delacorte, 2011), 27–29.

8. *Random House Dictionary,* s. v. "emotion."

9. *American Heritage Dictionary,* 5th ed., s. v. "emotion."

10. *American Heritage Dictionary,* 5th ed., s. v. "role."

11. Maslow, *Psychology of Being,* 172–173.

12. Barbara M. Byrne, *Measuring Self-concept across the Life Span: Issues and Instrumentation* (Washington DC: American Psychological Association, 1996), 141.

13. *Random House Dictionary, s. v.* "self."

14. *Random House Dictionary, s. v.* "territory."

15. Johnston, *It Takes a Child,* 24.

16. Kottler, *Change,* 29.

17. Schwartz, *Internal Family,* 37–38.

18. Johnston, *It Takes a Child,* 259.

19. Schwartz, *Internal Family,* 27–28.

20. Marvin Minsky, *The Emotion Machine: Commonsense Thinking, Artificial Intelligence, and the Future of the Human Mind* (New York: Simon and Schuster, 2006), 306.

21. Minsky, *Emotion,* 74.

22. Hal Stone and Sidra Stone, *Partnering, A New Kind of Relationship: How to Love Each Other Without Losing Yourselves* (Novato, CA: New World, 2000), 49.

23. Julia Cameron, *The Artist's Way: A Spiritual Path to Higher Creativity* (New York: Jeremy P. Tarcher/Putnam, 1992), 9–10.

24. "Ancient maps," accessed February 4, 2016. https://en.wikipedia.org/wiki/Here_be_dragons.html.

25. McAdams and Pals, "Personality," 204–217.

26. Stephen Levine, *Healing into Life and Death* (New York: Anchor, 1987), 232.

27. Arieh Y. Shalev, et al., "Prevention of Posttraumatic Stress Disorder by Early Treatment," *Archives of General Psychiatry,* 69 (2012): 166–176.

28. Minsky, *Emotion*, 321.
29. Johnston, *It Takes a Child*, 269–270.

CHAPTER 6

1. "Lifestyle and disease," accessed August 6, 2015. http://www.lifestylemedicine.org/LMMB0312.html.
2. Robert Scaer, *The Trauma Spectrum: Hidden Wounds and Human Resiliency* (New York: W. W. Norton, 2005), 2.
3. Martin E. P. Seligman, *Authentic Happiness: Using the New Positive Psychology to Realize Your Potential for Lasting Fulfillment* (New York: Free Press, 2002), 215.
4. "Humor," accessed August 5, 2015. http://www.ted.com/talks/robert_wright_on_optimism?language=en.html.
5. *American Heritage Dictionary*, 5th ed., s. v "inspiration."
6. "Sex and sleep," accessed May 20, 2015. http://bettersleep.org/better-sleep/the-science-of-sleep/sleep-statistics-research/infographic-lack-of-sleep-a-public-health-epidemic/.html.
7. David K. Randall, *Dreamland: Adventures in the Strange Science of Sleep* (New York: W. W. Norton, 2012), 62.
8. David B. Agus, *The End of Illness* (New York: Free Press, 2011), 240–250.
9. Randall, *Dreamland*, 62.
10. "Naps," accessed August 11, 2015. http://www.webmd.com/balance/features/the-secret-and-surprising-power-of-naps.html.
11. Mason Currey, *Daily Rituals: How Artists Work* (New York: Knopf, 2013), 45.
12. "Sleep deprivation," accessed April 2, 2016. http://www.dailymail.co.uk/home/you/article-3513699/Arianna-Huffington-importance-slowing-sleeping-well.html.
13. "Sleep study," accessed June 17, 2015. http://www.howmuchisit.org/sleep-study-cost/.html.
14. "Trauma," accessed August 18, 2015. http://www.nicabm.com/peterlevine-trauma/confirmed/?del=8.19.15PeterLevineLMtoall.html.
15. Peter A. Levine, *In an Unspoken Voice: How the Body Releases Trauma and Restores Goodness* (Berkeley, CA: North Atlantic, 2010), 291.
16. Levine, *Unspoken Voice*, 127–129.
17. Randall. *Dreamland*, 32–36.
18. "Smoking," accessed November 22, 2015. http://www.everydayhealth.com/sleep/101/improve-sleep.aspx.html.
19. "Meditation," accessed June 18, 2015. http://archinte.jamanetwork.com/article.aspx?articleid=2110998.html.
20. "Diet," accessed August 13, 2015. http://newsroom.cumc.columbia.edu/blog/2015/07/29/junk-food-may-increase-depression-risk/.html.
21. "Comfort food," accessed December 15, 2015. http://www.news.cornell.edu/stories/2007/01/food-and-mood-sad-are-twice-likely-eat-comfort-food.html.
22. Minsky, *Emotion*, 80.

23. Geneen Roth, *Women, Food, and God: An Unexpected Path to Almost Everything* (New York: Scribner, 2010), 2–13.

24. Susan Albers, *Eat, Drink, and Be Mindful: How to End your Struggle with Mindless Eating and Start Savoring Food with Intention and Joy* (Oakland, CA: New Harbinger, 2008), 13; 30–32.

25. "Runners," accessed December 14, 2015. http://www.mahotamagazine.com/en/lee-sok-lian/health-wellness/item/10-little-known-benefits-of-walking-backwards.html.

26. Agus, *End of Illness*, 219.

27. "Exercise," accessed August 10, 2015. http://www.ncbi.nlm.nih.gov/pmc/articles/PMC1402378/.html.

28. Agus, *End of Illness*, 230–234.

29. Sian Beilock, *How the Body Knows Its Mind: The Surprising Power of the Physical Environment to Influence How You Think and Feel* (New York: Atria, 2015), 170–175.

30. Carl W. Cotman and Nicole C. Berchtold, "Exercise: A Behavioral Intervention to Enhance Brain Health and Plasticity," *Trends in Neuroscience* 25 (2002): 295–301.

31. Strauch, *Grown-Up Brain,* 140.

32. Beilock, *Body Knows its Mind*, 194; 212–213.

33. "Exercise and skin," accessed August 11, 2015. http://well.blogs.nytimes.com/2014/04/16/younger-skin-through-exercise/.html.

34. Roth, *Women, Food and God,* 39.

CHAPTER 7

1. "Cave art," accessed November 1, 2015. https://en.wikipedia.org/wiki/Chauvet_Cave.html.

2. Gregory Curtis, *The Cave Painters: Probing the Mysteries of the World's First Artists* (New York: Knopf, 2006), 114–132.

3. "Cave movies," accessed February 15, 2015. https://www.youtube.com/watch?v=al3-Kl4BDUQ.html.

4. "Handprint protection," accessed November 1, 2015. http://www.academia.edu/11203963/Handprints_in_the_Rock_Art_and_Tribal_Art_of_Central_India.html.

5. "Memory," accessed June 12, 2015. http://www.rickhanson.net/how-your-brain-makes-you-easily-intimidated/.html.

6. Norman Doidge, *The Brain's Way of Healing: Remarkable Discoveries and Recoveries from the Frontiers of Neuroplasticity* (New York: Viking, 2015), 7–9.

7. Sara J. White, "Using Self-talk to Enhance Career Satisfaction and Performance," *American Journal of Health-System Pharmacy,* 65 (2008): 514–519.

8. James W. Pennebaker, *Writing to Heal: A Guided Journal for Recovering from Trauma and Emotional Upheaval* (Oakland, CA: New Harbinger, 2004), 4–8.

9. Pennebaker, *Writing,* 9–12.

10. Joan Didion, *The Year of Magical Thinking* (New York: Knopf, 2005), 132–161.

11. Naomi Epel, *Writers Dreaming: 26 Writers Talk about Their Dreams and the Creative Process* (New York: Vintage, 1994), 12.

12. DeSalvo, *Writing*, 36–39.

13. Isabel Allende, *Maya's Notebook: A Novel* (New York: HarperCollins, 2013), 362.

14. "Discipline," accessed October 18, 2015. https://soundcloud.com/onbeing/mary-oliver-listening-to-the-world-1.html

15. "Delight," accessed June 9, 2015.http://kriscarr.com/blog-video/how-to-find-happiness-with-delight/.html.

16. "Email breakups," accessed January 16, 2016.http://breakupemail.com/dump.php.html.

17. Doidge, *Brain's Way*, 109.

18. William Stafford, *The Way It Is: New & Selected Poems* (Minneapolis, MN: Graywolf, 1998), 161.

19. Sausys, *Yoga for Grief*, 2.

20. Minsky, *Emotion*, 69.

21. Bridges, *Managing Transitions*, 42.

22. *American Heritage Dictionary*, 5th ed., s.v. "change."

23. Adam Gopnik, *The Table Comes First: Family, France, and Meaning of Food* (New York: Vintage, 2011), 11.

24. "Fast food," accessed November 15, 2005.http://www.ask.com/food/many-pounds-food-average-adult-eat-day-3f49d34cd3d872cd?qo=questionPageSimilarContent.html.

25. "Male cooks," accessed October 19, 2015. http://eatocracy.cnn.com/2010/09/30/more-men-manning-the-family-meal-making/.html.

26. Home cooking," accessed October 19, 2015. http://www.washingtonpost.com/news/wonkblog/wp/2015/03/05/the-slow-death-of-the-home-cooked-meal/.html.

27. "Devalued cooking," accessed October 19, 2015. http://michaelpollan.com/resources/cooking/.html.

28. "Food marketing," accessed October 19, 2015.https://www.youtube.com/watch?v=lVyo712BBRk.html.

29. *American Heritage Dictionary*, 5th ed., s.v. "imagination."

30. *American Heritage Dictionary*, 5th ed., s.v. "insight."

31. Gary Klein, *Seeing What Others Don't: the Remarkable Way We Gain Insights* (Philadelphia, PA: Public Affairs, 2013), 24.

32. Klein, *Seeing*, 244.

33. "Resilience," accessed June 3, 2015. http://www.apa.org/helpcenter/road-resilience.aspx.html.

34. Michael Michalko, *Cracking Creativity: The Secrets of Creative Genius* (Berkeley, CA: Ten Speed, 2001), 13

35. John O'Donohue, *Anam Cara: A Book of Celtic Wisdom* (New York: HarperCollins, 1997), 92.

36. Pennebaker, *Writing, 55.*
37. DeSalvo, *Writing*, 74.

CHAPTER 8

1. Maslow, *Psychology of Being*, 172–173.
2. "Dementia," accessed June 10, 2015. http://www.nlm.nih.gov/medlineplus/news/fullstory_151918.html.
3. Keith Sawyer, *Zigzag: The Surprising Path to Greater Creativity* (San Francisco, CA: Jossey-Bass, 2013), 106.
4. J. Allan Hobson, *13 Dreams Freud Never Had: The New Mind Science* (New York: Pi Press, 2005), 15; 21–22.
5. Sonia Sotomayer, *My Beloved World* (New York: Knopf, 2013), 1.
6. "Play importance," accessed June 17, 2015. http://www.ted.com/talks/stuart_brown_says_play_is_more_than_fun_it_s_vital.html.
7. Michalko, *Cracking Creativity*, 4.
8. Bill O'Hanlon, *Do One thing Different: Ten Simple Ways to Change Your Life* (New York: Quill, 2000), 44–45.
9. Patrician Ryan Madson, *Improv Wisdom: Don't Prepare, Just Show Up* (New York: Bell Tower, 2005), 30.
10. "Inventors," accessed February 4, 2016. http://www.one.org/us/2015/05/27/10-female-inventors-you-should-know-about/.html.
11. "Steve Jobs," accessed July 1, 2015. http://abcnews.go.com/Technology/steve-jobs-fire-company/story?id=14683754&page=2.html.
12. "Musicians," accessed August 8, 2015. https://hbr.org/2007/07/the-making-of-an-expert.html.
13. "Holiday creativity," accessed June 12, 2015. https://gretchenrubin.com/happiness_project/2012/03/celebrate-leap-day-or-any-other-minor-holiday/.html.
14. "School shooting," accessed February 15, 2016. http://somethingelsereviews.com/2014/11/14/jimmy-greene-beautiful-life-review/.html.
15. Brian Jay Jones, *Jim Henson: The Biography* (New York: Ballantine, 2013), 46–48.
16. "Work time management," accessed June 25, 2015. http://www.lexisnexis.com/en-us/about-us/media/press-release.page?id=128751276114739.html.
17. Daniel J. Levitin, *The Organized Mind: Thinking Straight in the Age of Information Overload* (New York: Dutton, 2014), 97.
18. Levitin, *Organized Mind*, 169–171.
19. "Distractions," accessed July 30, 2015. http://www.ics.uci.edu/~gmark/chi08-mark.pdf.html.
20. *American Heritage Dictionary*, 5th ed., s.v. "focus."
21. "Alcohol and grieving," accessed August 8, 2015. http://www.theoi.com/Olympios/DionysosGod.html.
22. Levitin, *Organized Mind*, 165–168.
23. "Alcohol and inflammation," accessed July 7, 2015. http://www.ncbi.nlm.nih.gov/pmc/articles/PMC2842521/.html.
24. Albers, *Eat, Drink and Be Mindful*, 76–77.

25. "Brain neurons," accessed July 5, 2015. http://www.scientificamerican.com/article/100-trillion-connections/.html.

26. Lorenza S. Colzato, Ayca Ozturk, and Bernhard Hommel, "Meditate to Create: The Impact of Focused-Attention and Open-Monitoring Training on Convergent and Divergent Thinking," *Frontiers in Psychology*, 3 (2012): 116.

27. Andrew Newberg and Mark Robert Waldman, *Why We Believe What We Believe: Overcoming our Biological Need for Meaning, Spirituality, and Truth* (New York: Free Press, 2006), 169.

28. Newberg and Waldman, *Why We Believe*, 175.

29. "Meditation," accessed July 2, 2015. http://www.massgeneral.org/about/press-release.aspx?id=1520.html.

30. Matthieu Ricard, Antoine Lutz, and Richard J. Davidson, "The Mind of the Meditator," *Scientific American*, November, 2014, 39–45.

31. "Meditation and happiness," accessed July 5, 2015.http://www.huffingtonpost.com/2015/01/23/richard-davidson-davos_n_6529652.html.

32. "Meditation and yoga," accessed July 5, 2015.http://www.yogajournal.com/uncategorized/new-study-finds-20-million-yogis-u-s/.html.

33. Amy Weintraub, *Yoga for Depression: A Compassionate Guide to Relieve Suffering Through Yoga* (New York: Broadway, 2004), 125.

34. "Caregivers' health," accessed July 1, 2015. http://www.sciencedaily.com/releases/2012/07/120724144538.htm.

35. "Yoga versus walking," accessed July 1, 2015. http://www.ncbi.nlm.nih.gov/pmc/articles/PMC3111147/.html.

36. "Alpha waves," accessed July 1, 2015. http://www.vitalityandwellness.com.au/health-blog/low-gaba-levels-increase-gaba-naturally.html.

37. Jon Kabat-Zinn, *Coming to Our Senses: Healing Ourselves and the World Through Mindfulness* (New York: Hyperion, 2005), 11.

38. Kabat-Zinn, *Coming to Our Senses*, 36.

39. Pema Chodron, *When Things Fall Apart: Heart Advice for Difficult Times* (Boston, MA: Shambhala, 2000), 117.

40. "Meditation and sexual desire," accessed June 24, 2015. http://www.theglobeandmail.com/life/health-and-fitness/health-advisor/how-a-raisin-can-save-your-sex-life-and-other-lessons-in-mindfulness-meditation/article22950111/.html.

41. Brach, *True Refuge*, 34.

42. "Meditation and breath," accessed July 6, 2015. http://www.drweil.com/drw/u/ART00521/three-breathing-exercises.html.

43. van Der Kolk, *Body Keeps the Score*, 67.

CHAPTER 9

1. Maia Szalavitz and Bruce D. Perry. *Born for Love: Why Empathy Is Essential – and Endangered* (New York: William Morrow, 2010), 104.

2. Szalavitz and Perry, *Born for Love*, 110.

3. John B. Watson, *Behaviorism, Revised ed* (Chicago, IL: University of Chicago, 1930), 82.

4. Roy F. Baumeister and Mark R. Leary, "The Need to Belong: Desire for Interpersonal Attachments as a Fundamental Human Motivation," *Psychological Bulletin,* 117 (1995): 497-529.

5. http://onbeing.org/program/rachel-yehuda-how-trauma-and-resilience-cross-generations/7786 (accessed August 2, 2015).

6. Cindy Hazan and Philip R. Shaver. "Romantic Love Conceptualized as an Attachment Process," *Journal of Personality and Social Psychology,* 52 (1987), 511–524.

7. Daniel J. Siegel. *The Mindful Therapist: A Clinician's Guide to Mindsight and Neural Integration* (New York: W. W. Norton, 2010), 68.

8. Johnston, *It Takes a Child,* 4.

9. "Unmarried mothers," accessed December 15, 2015. http://www.cdc.gov/nchs/fastats/unmarried-childbearing.hteml.

10. "Traditional family," accessed December 15, 2015. http://www.pewresearch.org/fact-tank/2014/12/22/less-than-half-of-u-s-kids-today-live-in-a-traditional-family/.html.

11. "Male wellbeing," accessed February 16, 2016. http://news.harvard.edu/gazette/story/2012/02/decoding-keys-to-a-healthy-life/.html.

12. "Midlife relationships," accessed February 16, 2016. http://www.businessinsider.com/robert-waldinger-says-3-things-are-the-secret-to-happiness-2015-12.html.

13. Jeffrey Marx. *Season of Life: A Football Star, a Boy, a Journey to Manhood* (New York: Simon and Schuster, 2003), 43; 48–49.

14. "Loneliness," accessed August 2, 2015. http://www.nytimes.com/2013/05/19/opinion/sunday/douthat-loneliness-and-suicide.html?_r=0.html.

15. Anne Sexton, *Anne Sexton: A Self Portrait in Letters,* ed. Lois Ames (New York: First Mariner, 2004), 251.

16. Kipling D. Williams, "The Pain of Exclusion," *Scientific American Mind,* January/February, 21 (2011): 30–37.

17. Christopher K. Gerrmer, *The Mindful Path to Self-compassion: Freeing Yourself from Destructive Thoughts and Emotions* (New York: Guilford, 2009), 163.

18. Baumeister and Leary, "Need to Belong," 507.

19. "Divorce rate," accessed May 11, 2015. http://www.nber.org/papers/w12944.html.

20. "Ludwig Wittgenstein," accessed September 18, 2015. https://en.wikiquote.org/wiki/Ludwig_Wittgenstein.html.

21. Jennifer Michael Hecht, *Stay: A History of Suicide and the Philosophies against It* (New Haven, CT: Yale University, 2013), 187.

22. Hecht, *Stay,* 214–215.

23. "Social isolation," accessed September 18, 2015. https://today.duke.edu/2006/06/socialisolation.html.

24. Lauren Schaffer and Sandy Fleischl Wasserman. *133 Ways to Avoid Going Cuckoo When the Kids Fly the Nest: A Parent's Guide for Surviving Empty Nest Syndrome* (New York: Three Rivers, 2001), 9–11.

25. Naomi Shihab Nye, *Words Under the Words: Selected Poems* (Portland, OR: Far Corner, 1995).

26. Linda Graham, *Bouncing Back: Rewiring Your Brain for Maximum Resilience and Well-Being* (Novato, CA: New World Library, 2013), 140.

27. "Technology vacation," accessed August 2, 2015. https://hbr.org/2013/03/techs-best-feature-the-off-swi.html.

28. Levitin, Organized Mind, 6–7.

29. SherryTurkle, *Reclaiming Conversation: The Power of Talk in a Digital Age* (New York: Penguin, 2015), 77.

30. Turkle, *Reclaiming Conversation, 21–25.*

31. "Runes," accessed August 2, 2015. https://en.wikipedia.org/wiki/Klepp_I_Runestone.html.

32. Thomas H. Holmes and Richard H. Rahe, "The social readjustment rating scale," *Journal of Psychosomatic Research,* 11 (1967): 213–218.

33. Jean Baker Miller and Irene Pierce Stiver, *The Healing Connection: How Women Form Relationships in Therapy and in Life* (Boston, MA: Beacon, 1997), 11

34. Theodore Zeldin, *An Intimate History of Humanity* (New York: HarperCollins, 1994), 32.

35. Martin Buber, *I and Thou,* trans. Walter Kaufmann (New York: Charles Scribner's Sons, 1970), 62

36. Dalai Lama, *Advice on Dying: And Living a Better Life, Trans. and ed, Jeffrey Hopkins* (New York: Atria, 2002), 41–44.

37. *American Heritage Dictionary,* 5th ed., s. v. "care."

38. DeSalvo, *Writing,* 54.

39. John O'Donohue, *Eternal Echoes: Exploring our Yearning to Belong* (New York: Cliff Street, 1999), 134.

40. Greitens, *Resilience,* 28.

41. Gerrmer, *Mindful Path,* 176.

42. "Forgiveness," accessed September 24, 2015. http://www.uua.org/re/tapestry/children/tales/session5/123298.shtml.

43. Jean Decety and Julie Grezes, "The Power of Simulation: Imagining One's Own and Other's Behavior," *Brain Research,* 1079 (2006): 4–14.

44. O'Donohue, *Eternal Echoes,* 120.

CHAPTER 10

1. Mihaly Csikzentmihalyi, *Flow: The Psychology of Optimal Experience* (New York: Harper and Row, 1990), 4.

2. Csikzentmihalyi, *Flow,* 193–200.

3. *American Heritage Dictionary,* 5th ed., s. v. "claim."

4. Haas, *Bouncing Forward,* 19.

5. "Late-blooming adults," accessed August 20, 2015. http://www.newyorker.com/magazine/2008/10/20/late-bloomers-2?currentPage=1.html.

6. "Art at any age," accessed August 19, 2015.https://en.wikipedia.org/wiki/Grandma_Moses.html.

7. "Success at any age," accessed August 19, 2015.http://www.biography.com/people/ray-kroc-9369349#early-life.html.

8. "Joan Kroc," accessed August 19, 2015. https://en.wikipedia.org/wiki/Joan_Kroc.

9. "Job creation," accessed August 19, 2015.http://www.imdb.com/name/nm3409164/bio.html.

10. Joshua Foer, *Moonwalking with Einstein: The Art and Science of Remembering Everything* (New York: Penguin, 2011), 268.

11. http://www.today.com/news/brian-williams-opens-first-interview-suspension-t27276 (Accessed October 15, 2015).

12. McGonigal, *Upside of Stress*, 11–14.

13. Peter A. Levine, *Waking the Tiger: Healing Trauma* (Berkeley, CA: North Atlantic, 1997), 207–210.

14. Peter A. Levine, *Healing Trauma: A Pioneering Program for Restoring the Wisdom of Your Body* (Boulder, CO: Sounds True, 2008), 19–20.

15. "Memory distortion," accessed October 15, 2015. http://launchmoxie.com/wp-content/uploads/downloads/1-NeuroWisdom-Ebook.pdf.html.

16. Bill O'Hanlon, *Out of the Blue: Six Non-Medication Ways to Relieve Depression* (New York: W. W. Norton, 2014), 30–31.

17. "Work-life integration," accessed September 13, 2015. http://www.onbeing.org/program/ellen-langer-science-of-mindlessness-and-mindfulness/transcript/6335.html.

18. "John Lennon," accessed October 14, 2015. http://www.theguardian.com/education/2005/jan/11/schools.uk1.html.

19. "*Carpe diem*," accessed January 12, 2016. https://en.wikipedia.org/wiki/Carpe_diem.html.

20. "Garrison Keillor," accessed January 12, 2016.http://www.startribune.com/on-cnn-garrison-keillor-looks-ahead-to-retirement/364768491/.html.

21. Phil Cousineau, *Stoking the Creative Fires: 9 Ways to Rekindle Passion and Imagination* (San Francisco, CA: Conari, 2008), 53–54.

22. "Daydreaming," accessed August 20, 2015. http://launchmoxie.com/wp-content/uploads/downloads/1-NeuroWisdom-Ebook.pdf.html.

23. "Positive relating," accessed January 6, 2016. https://www.gottman.com/blog/the-positive-perspective-dr-gottmans-magic-ratio/.html.

24. Barbara L. Fredrickson, *Positivity: Groundbreaking Research Reveals How to Embrace the Hidden Strength of Positive Emotions, Overcome Negativity, and Thrive* (New York: Crown, 2009), 16–32.

25. Barbara L. Frederickson, "Updated Thinking on Positivity Ratios," *American Psychologist*, 68 (2013): 814–822.

26. "Cellular aging," accessed October 15, 2015. http://www.bloomberg.com/news/articles/2013-11-22/harvard-yoga-scientists-find-proof-of-meditation-benefit.html.

27. Rick Hansen, *Just One Thing: Developing a Buddha Brain One Simple Practice at a Time* (Oakland, CA: New Harbinger, 2011), 4–6.

28. Cousineau, *Stoking the Creative*, 52.

29. Eve Ensler, *In the Body of the World: A Memoir* (New York: Metropolitan, 2013), 3–8.

30. Enssler, *In the Body*, 101.

31. Ensler, *In the Body*, 213.

32. "Positive focus," accessed October 15, 2015. http://www.sciencedaily.com/releases/2013/12/131208090343.html.

CHAPTER 11

1. Martin E. P. Seligman. *What You Can Change...and What You Can't: The Complete Guide to Successful Self-Improvement* (New York: Vintage, 2007), 5.

2. Christopher Rothko, *Mark Rothko: From the Inside Out* (New Haven, CT: Yale University, 2015), 18.

3. Rothko, *Mark Rothko*, 8–9.

4. "Mark Rothko," accessed September 15, 2015. https://en.wikipedia.org/wiki/Mark_Rothko.html.

5. "Poetry and grieving," accessed September 15, 2015. http://www.npr.org/2015/09/15/438630601/poet-laureates-migrant-childhood-was-like-living-in-literature-every-day.html.

6. "Martin Luther King," accessed January 10, 2016. https://news.ncsu.edu/2015/01/5q-mlk/.html.

7. Joan Chodorow, ed., *Encountering Jung: Jung on Active Imagination* (Princeton, NJ: Princeton University, 1997), 1–3.

8. Murray Stein, *Jung: Map of the Soul* (Chicago, IL: Open Court, 1998), 153–159.

9. Jung, *Memories, Dreams, Reflections*, 195–196.

10. "Renewal symbolism," accessed January 14, 2016. http://mu6.com/uroboros.html.

11. Chodorow, *Encountering Jung*, 39.

12. John Kounios and Mark Beeman, *The Eureka Factor: AHA Moments, Creative Insight, and the Brain* (New York: Random House, 2015), 204–205.

13. Stein, *Jung*, 203–204.

14. Stein, *Jung*, 208.

15. Carl Jung, *Psychological Reflections: A New Anthology of His Writings 1905–1961*, eds. Jolande Jacoby and R.F.C. Hull. (Princeton, NJ: Princeton University, 1978), 334.

16. Antonio Damasio, *The Feeling of What Happens: Body and Emotion in the Making of Consciousness* (New York: Harcourt Brace, 1999), 27–28.

17. Koch, *Consciousness*, 77.

18. Damasio, *The Feeling*, 8–10.

19. Schwartz, *Internal Family*, 57–58.

20. "Self description," accessed August 30, 2015. http://www.selfleadership.org/about-internal-family-systems.html.

21. Schwartz, *You Are the One*, 13–14.

22. James Hollis, *Finding Meaning in the Second Half of Life: How to Finally, Really Grow Up* (New York: Gotham, 2005), 33; 210.

23. Wayne Muller, *Sabbath: Finding Rest, Renewal, and Delight in Our Busy Lives* (New York: Bantam, 2000), 42–43.

24. Hollis, *Finding Meaning,* 5.

25. *American Heritage Dictionary,* 5th ed., s. v. "intuition."

26. *American Heritage Dictionary,* 5th ed., s. v. "intention."

27. Kounios and Beeman, *Eureka Factor,* 131–140.

28. Alfred North Whitehead, *Process and Reality: An Essay in Cosmology* (New York: Free Press, 1978), 350.

29. Joan Borysenko, *A Woman's Journey to God: Finding the Feminine Path* (New York: Riverhead, 1999), 84.

30. John O'Donohue, *To Bless the Space Between Us* (New York: Doubleday, 2008), xiii.

31. Lissa Rankin, *The Fear Cure: Cultivating Courage as Medicine for the Body, Mind, and Soul* (Carlsbad, CA: Hay House, 2015), 225.

32. Rankin, *Mind Over Medicine,* 196–203.

33. "Intuition," accessed September 18, 2015. http://patmartin.typepad.com/literacy_is_all/2008/02/bus-bath-and-be.html.

34. "J.K. Rowlings," accessed September 18, 2015. http://www.nbcnews.com/id/20001720/ns/dateline_nbc-harry_potter/t/harry-potter-final-chapter/#.VfySIpcsD8U.html.

35. Eckhart Tolle, *A New Earth: Awakening to Your Life's Purpose* (New York: Penguin, 2006), 22.

36. David Whyte, *The Three Marriages: Reimagining Work, Self, and Relationship* (New York: Riverhead, 2009), 31– 35.

37. Schwartz, *You Are the One,* 12.

38. Asle Hoffart, Tuva Oktedalen, and Tomas F. Langkaas, "Self-compassion Influences PTSD Symptoms in the Process of Change in Trauma-focused Cognitive-behavioral Therapies: A Study of Within-person Processes," *Frontiers in Psychology,* 6 (2015): 1–11.

39. Germer, *Mindful Path,* 161.

40. Gerrmer, *Mindful Path,* 2.

41. Brene Brown, *The Gifts of Imperfection: Let Go of Who You Think You're Supposed to Be and Embrace Who You Are* (Center City, MN: Hazelden, 2010), 55–57.

42. Brown, *Gifts of Imperfection,* xi.

43. Richard Barrett, *Liberating the Corporate Soul: Building a Visionary Organization* (New York: Routledge, 2013), 5.

44. Rankin, *Fear Cure,* 231–232.

45. Wayne Dosick, *Golden Rules: The Ten Ethical Values Parents Need to Teach Their Children* (New York: HarperCollins, 1995).

46. Newberg and Waldman, *Words Can Change,* 103–107.

CHAPTER 12

1. Wayne Muller, *A Life of Being, Having, and Doing Enough* (New York: Harmony, 2010), 101.

2. Mark Nepo, *The Book of Awakening: Having the Life You Want by Being Present to the Life You Have* (San Francisco, CA: Conari, 2011), 396–397.

3. Nepo, *Book of Awakening,* 145.

4. "Nelsen Mandela," accessed August 19, 2015. http://www.purposefairy. com/71089/22-life-changing-lessons-to-learn-from-nelson-mandela/.html.

5. "Maze symbol," accessed April 28, 2015. http://www.warpaths2peacepipes. com/native-american-symbols/symbol-of-life.htm.

6. "Doctor-patient hierarchy," accessed September 15, 2015. https://paw.princeton.edu/issues/2014/02/05/pages/3274/index.xm.html.l

7. "Disability and gratitude," accessed January 31, 2016. http://www.onbeing. org/program/bj-miller-reframing-our-relationship-to-that-we-dont-control/8380.html.

8. "Hospice rituals," accessed September 15, 2015. http://www.geripal. org/2015/09/redesigning-dying.html.

9. Whyte, *Three Marriages*, 244.

10. Whyte, *Three Marriages*, 265.

11. Buber, *I and Thou,* 63–68.

12. Maurice Friedman, *Encounter on the Narrow Ridge: A Life of Martin Buber* (New York: Paragon House, 1991), 4–6.

13. Brene Brown, *Rising Strong: The Reckoning. The Rumble. The Revolution* (New York: Spiegel and Grau, 2015), 5.

14. Brown, *Rising Strong*, 7–11.

15. Muller, *A Life of Being*, 98.

16. Whyte, *Three Marriages*, 29.

17. Cousineau, *Stoking the Creative Fires*, 2008, 213.

18. Muller, *Sabbath*, 4–5.

19. "Worker engagement," accessed August 31, 2015. http://www.gallup.com/ poll/181289/majority-employees-not-engaged-despite-gains-2014.aspx.html.

20. Hollis, *Finding Meaning*, 31.

21. "Retirement," accessed October 30, 2015. http://www.voya.com/sites/unit. voya.com/files/Retirement_Experience_Study.pdf.html.

22. Mary Catherine Bateson, *Composing a Further Life: The Age of Active Wisdom* (New York: Knopf, 2010), 99.

23. Kennedy, *The Infinite Thread*, 7.

24. Sacks, *Hallucinations*, 235.

25. Sacks, *Hallucinations,* 229–242; 277.

26. Oliver Sacks, *An Anthropologist on Mars* (New York: Vintage, 1995), xvi.

27. Hollis, *Finding Meaning*, 73.

28. Bateson, *Composing a Further Life*, 87.

29. "Mexican ritual," accessed November 2, 2015. https://en.wikipedia.org/wiki/ Day_of_the_Dead.html.

30. Jean Shinoda Bolen, *Close to the Bone: Life-Threatening Illness and the Search for Meaning* (New York: Schribner, 1996), 14–19.

31. Jill S. Quadago, *Aging and Life Course: An Introduction to Social Gerontology,* 3rd ed. (Boston, MA: McGraw-Hill, 2005).

32. Adam Grant, *Give and Take: Why Helping Others Drives Our Success* (New York: Penguin, 2013), 4–39.

33. Grant, *Give and Take,*198.

34. Michael Ogden and Chris Day, *2 Do Before I Die: The Do-It-Yourself Guide to the Rest of Your Life* (New York: Little, Brown, 2005), 194–195.

CHAPTER 13

1. Ensler, *In the Body,* 216.

2. "Joy," accessed May 15, 2016. http://www.etymonline.com/index.php?term=joy.

3. "Mary Oliver," accessed October 18, 2015. http://www.oprah.com/entertainment/Maria-Shriver-Interviews-Poet-Mary-Oliver.html.

4. "Gilda Radner," accessed September 4, 2015. https://en.wikipedia.org/wiki/Gilda_Radner.html.

5. "Cancer support," accessed September 4, 2015. http://gildasclubnyc.org/our-history-mission/.html.

6. Greitens, *Resilience*, 16.

7. Jean Houston, *Jump Time: Shaping Your Future in a World of Radical Change* (New York: Jeremy P. Tarcher/Putnam, 2000), 1–2.

8. Houston, *Jump Time*, 41.

9. "Change," accessed August 16, 2015.http://www.freep.com/story/news/local/michigan/2014/11/10/jesuit-brother-wins-carl-sagan-medal/18774213.html..

10. Riane Eisler, *The Power of Partnership: Seven Relationships that Will Change Your Life* (Novato, CA: New World, 2002), 176.

11. "Paul McCartney," accessed September 13, 2015. http://summit.foodrevolution.org/replays.html.

12. "Sarah McQuaid," accessed September 13, 2015. https://sarahmcquaid.bandcamp.com/album/i-won-t-go-home-til-morning.html.

13. Stephen W. Porges, "Music Therapy and Trauma: Insights from the Polyvagal Theory," in *Music Therapy and Trauma: Bridging Theory and Clinical Practice,* ed. Kristen Stewart (New York: Satchnote, 2008), 1–10.

14. Rachel Naomi Remen, *Kitchen Table Wisdom* (New York: Riverside, 1996), 66.

15. "Aliveness," accessed September 3, 2015. http://www.goodreads.com/quotes/10442-people-say-that-what-we-re-all-seeking-is-a-meaning.

16. Russell H. Conwell, *Acres of Diamonds* (New York: Harper and Row, 1915), 4–59.

17. "Optimism," accessed October 7, 2015. https://www.salesgravy.com/sales-articles/attitude/attitude-is-everything.html.

18. Haas, *Bouncing Forward*, 39.

19. Rankin, *Mind Over Medicine*, 218.

20. Lynne Twist, *The Soul of Money: Reclaiming the Wealth of Our Inner Resources* (New York: W. W. Norton, 2003), 7; 105.

21. "Oliver Sacks," accessed September 3, 2015. http://www.nytimes.com/2015/02/19/opinion/oliver-sacks-on-learning-he-has-terminal-cancer.html.

22. Stafford, *The Way It Is*, 247.

23. "Long life," accessed August 10, 2015. http://www.onbeing.org/program/becoming-detroit/transcript/5836.html.

24. Mark D. Seery, E. Alison Holman, and Roxane Cohen Silver, "Whatever Does Not Kill Us: Cumulative Lifetime Adversity, Vulnerability, and Resilience," *Journal of Personality and Social Psychology*, 99 (2010): 1025–1041.

25. Rachel Naomi Remen, *My Grandfather's Blessing: Stories of Strength, Refuge, and Belonging* (New York: Riverhead, 2000), 198–199.

26. "Dying words," accessed May 15, 2016. http://irabyock.org/books/the-four-things-that-matter-most/.

27. Rankin, *The Fear Cure*, 266.

28. Daniel Kahneman, *Thinking, Fast and Slow* (New York: Farrar, Straus and Giroux, 2011), 396–397.

29. Madson, *Improv Wisdom*, 46.

30. "Happiness formula," accessed August 10, 2015. http://www.pbs.org/wnet/americanmasters/the-boomer-list-watch-full-film-the-boomer-list/3492/.html.

31. *The Holy Bible*, Ecclesiastes 3: 1–8.

References

Agus, David B. *The End of Illness.* New York: Free Press, 2011.

Albers, Susan. *Eat, Drink, and Be Mindful: How to End your Struggle with Mindless Eating and Start Savoring Food with Intention and Joy.* Oakland, CA: New Harbinger, 2008.

Allen, Patricia B. *Art Is a Way of Knowing: A Guide to Self-knowledge and Spiritual Fulfillment through Creativity.* Boston, MA: Shambala, 1995.

Allende, Isabel. *Maya's Notebook: A Novel.* New York: HarperCollins, 2013.

Amabile, Teresa M. *Nurturing a Lifetime of Creativity.* New York: Crown, 1989.

American Heritage Dictionary of the English Language, 5th ed. Boston, MA: Houghton Mifflin Harcourt, 2016.

Anderson, Joan. *A Walk on the Beach: Tales of Wisdom from an Unconventional Woman.* New York: Broadway, 2004.

Barrett, Richard. *Liberating the Corporate Soul: Building a Visionary Organization.* New York: Routledge, 2013.

Bateson, Mary Catherine. *Composing a Further Life: The Age of Active Wisdom.* New York: Knopf, 2010.

Baumeister, Roy F. and Mark R. Leary. "The Need to Belong: Desire for Interpersonal Attachments as a Fundamental Human Motivation," *Psychological Bulletin* 117 (1995): 497–529.

Beilock, Sian. *How the Body Knows Its Mind: The Surprising Power of the Physical Environment to Influence How You Think and Feel.* New York: Atria, 2015.

Bolen, Jean Shinoda. *Close to the Bone: Life-Threatening Illness and the Search for Meaning.* New York, Schribner, 1996.

Borysenko, Joan. *A Woman's Journey to God: Finding the Feminine Path.* New York: Riverhead, 1999.

Brach, Tara. *True Refuge: Finding Peace and Freedom in Your Own Awakened Heart.* New York: Bantam, 2012.

Breathnach, Sarah Ban. *Moving On: Creating Your House of Belonging with Simple Abundance.* New York: Meredith, 2006.

Bridges, William. *Managing Transitions: Making the Most of Change,* 3rd ed. New York: Da Capo, 2009.

Brim, Orville Gilbert, Carol D. Ryff, and Ronald C. Kessler, eds. *How Healthy Are We? A National Study of Well-being at Midlife.* Chicago, IL: University of Chicago, 2004.

Brown, Brene. *Daring Greatly: How the Courage to be Vulnerable Transforms the Way We Live, Love, Parent, and Lead.* New York: Avery, 2012.

Brown, Brene. *Rising Strong: The Reckoning, The Rumble, The Revolution.* New York: Spiegel and Grau, 2015.

Brown, Brene. *The Gifts of Imperfection: Let Go of Who You Think You're Supposed to Be and Embrace Who You Are.* Center City, MN: Hazelden, 2010.

Buber, Martin. *I and Thou,* trans.Walter Kaufmann. New York: Charles Scribner's Sons, 1970.

Byrne, Barbara M. *Measuring Self-concept across the Life Span: Issues and Instrumentation.* Washington DC: American Psychological Association, 1996.

Cameron, Julia. *The Artist's Way: A Spiritual Path to Higher Creativity.* New York: Jeremy P. Tarcher/Putnam, 1992.

Capps, Donald. *Understanding Psychosis: Issues and Challenges for Sufferers, Families, and Friends.* Lanham, MD: Rowman and Littlefield, 2010.

Carter, Susan L. "Themes of Grief," *Nursing Research* 38 (1989): 354–358.

Cartwright, Rosalind. "The Contribution of the Psychology of Sleep and Dreaming to Understanding Sleep-Disordered Patients," *Sleep Medicine Clinics* 3 (2008): 157–166.

Chodorow, Joan, ed. *Encountering Jung: Jung on Active Imagination.* Princeton, NJ: Princeton University, 1997.

Chodron, Pema. *When Things Fall Apart: Heart Advice for Difficult Times.* Boston, MA: Shambhala, 2000.

Clifford, Christine. *Cancer Has Its Privileges: Stories of Hope and Laughter.* New York: Perigee, 2002.

Colzato, Lorenza S., Ayca Ozturk, and Bernhard Hommel. "Meditate to Create: The Impact of Focused-Attention and Open-Monitoring Training on Convergent and Divergent Thinking," *Frontiers in Psychology* 3 (2012): 116.

Conwell, Russell H. *Acres of Diamonds.* New York: Harper and Row, 1915.

Cotman, Carl W. and Nicole C. Berchtold. "Exercise: A Behavioral Intervention to Enhance Brain Health and Plasticity," *Trends in Neuroscience* 25 (2002): 295–301.

Cousineau, Phil. *Stoking the Creative Fires: 9 Ways to Rekindle Passion and Imagination.* San Francisco, CA: Conari, 2008.

Csikzentmihalyi, Mihaly. *Flow: The Psychology of Optimal Experience.* New York: Harper and Row, 1990.

Currey, Mason. *Daily Rituals: How Artists Work.* New York: Knopf, 2013.

Curtis, Gregory. *The Cave Painters: Probing the Mysteries of the World's First Artists.* New York: Knopf, 2006.

Damasio, Antonio. *Looking for Spinoza: Joy, Sorrows, and the Feeling Brain.* Orlando, FL: Harcourt, 2003.

Damasio, Antonio. *The Feeling of What Happens: Body and Emotion in the Making of Consciousness.* New York: Harcourt Brace, 1999.

Decety, Jean W. and Julie Grezes. "The Power of Simulation: Imagining One's Own and Other's Behavior," *Brain Research* 1079 (2006): 4–14.

Delaney, Gayle. *Breakthrough Dreaming: How to Tap the Power of Your 24-Hour Mind.* New York: Bantam, 1991.

DeSalvo, Louise. *Writing as a Way of Healing: How Telling Our Stories Transforms Our Lives.* New York: HarperSanFrancisco, 1999.

Matthew Desmond. *Evicted: Poverty and Profit in the American City.* New York: Crown, 2016.

Didion, Joan. *The Year of Magical Thinking.* New York: Knopf, 2005.

Doidge, Norman. *The Brain's Way of Healing: Remarkable Discoveries and Recoveries from the Frontiers of Neuroplasticity.* New York: Viking, 2015.

Dosick, Wayne. *Golden Rules: The Ten Ethical Values Parents Need to Teach Their Children.* New York: HarperCollins, 1995.

Dweck, Carol. *Mindset: The New psychology of Success: How We Can Learn to Fulfill our Potential.* New York: Random House, 2006.

Eisler, Riane. *The Power of Partnership: Seven Relationships that Will Change Your Life.* Novato, CA: New World, 2002, 176.

Enriquez, Juan, and Steve Gullans. *Evolving Ourselves: How Unnatural Selection and Nonrandom Mutation are Changing Life on Earth.* New York: Penguin, 2015.

Ensler, Eve. *In the Body of the World: A Memoir.* New York: Metropolitan, 2013.

Epel, Naomi. *Writers Dreaming: 26 Writers Talk about Their Dreams and the Creative Process.* New York: Vintage, 1994.

Erikson, Erik. *Childhood and Society, 2nd* ed. New York: W. W. Norton, 1963.

Erikson, Joan M. *The Life Cycle Completed: Extended Version.* New York: W. W. Norton, 1997.

Foer, Joshua. *Moonwalking with Einstein: The Art and Science of Remembering Everything.* New York: Penguin, 2011.

Fredrickson, Barbara L. *Positivity: Groundbreaking Research Reveals How to Embrace the Hidden Strength of Positive Emotions, Overcome Negativity, and Thrive.* New York: Crown, 2009.

Frederickson, Barbara L. "Updated Thinking on Positivity Ratios," *American Psychologist* 68 (2013): 814–822.

Friedman, Maurice. *Encounter on the Narrow Ridge: A Life of Martin Buber.* New York: Paragon House, 1991.

Gage, Fred H. "Brain, Repair Yourself," *Scientific American*, September (2003): 47–53.

Gawande, Atul. *Being Mortal: Medicine and What Matters in the End.* New York: Metropolitan, 2014.

Germer, Christopher K. *The Mindful Path to Self-compassion: Freeing Yourself from Destructive Thoughts and Emotions.* New York: Guilford, 2009.

Gopnik, Adam. *The Table Comes First: Family, France, and Meaning of Food.* New York: Vintage, 2011.

Graham, Linda. *Bouncing Back: Rewiring Your Brain for Maximum Resilience and Well-Being.* Novato, CA: New World Library, 2013.

Grant, Adam. *Give and Take: Why Helping Others Drives Our Success.* New York: Penguin, 2013.

Grant, Adam. *Originals: How Non-conformists Move the World.* New York: Viking, 2016.

Greitens, Eric. *Resilience: Hard-won Wisdom for Living a Better Life.* New York: Houghton Mifflin, 2015.

Haas, Michaela. *Bouncing Forward: Transforming Bad Breaks into Breakthroughs.* New York: Enliven/Atria, 2015.

Hansen, Rick. *Just One Thing: Developing a Buddha Brain One Simple Practice at a Time.* Oakland, CA: New Harbinger, 2011.

Hay, Louise, and David Kessler, *You Can Heal Your Heart: Finding Peace after a Breakup, Divorce, or Death.* Carlsbad, CA: Hay House, 2014.

Hazan, Cindy, and Philip R. Shaver. "Romantic Love Conceptualized as an Attachment Process," *Journal of Personality and Social Psychology* 52 (1987): 511–524.

Hecht, Jennifer Michael. *Stay: A History of Suicide and the Philosophies against It.* New Haven, CT: Yale University, 2013.

Hobson, J. Allan. *Dreaming: An Introduction to the Science of Sleep.* New York: Oxford University, 2002.

Hobson, J. Allan. *13 Dreams Freud Never Had: The New Mind Science.* New York: Pi Press, 2005.

Hobson, J. Allan. *Foreword to Breakthrough Dreaming: How to Tap the Power of Your 24-hour Mind,* by Gayle Delaney. New York: Bantam, 1991.

Hoffart, Asle, Tuva Oktedalen, and Tomas F. Langkaas. "Self-compassion Influences PTSD Symptoms in the Process of Change in Trauma-focused Cognitive-behavioral Therapies: A Study of Within-person Processes," *Frontiers in Psychology* 6 (2015): 1–11.

Hollis, James. *Finding Meaning in the Second Half of Life: How to Finally, Really Grow Up.* New York: Gotham, 2005.

Holmes, Thomas H., and Richard H. Rahe. "The social readjustment rating scale," *Journal of Psychosomatic Research* 11 (1967): 213–218.

Hoss, Robert J. *Dream Language: Self-understanding through Imagery and Color.* Ashland, OR: Innersource, 2005.

Houston, Jean. *Jump Time: Shaping Your Future in a World of Radical Change.* New York: Jeremy P. Tarcher/Putnam, 2000.

Johnston, Janis Clark. *It Takes a Child to Raise a Parent: Stories of Evolving Child and Parent Development.* Lanham, MD: Rowman and Littlefield, 2013.

Jones, Brian Jay. *Jim Henson: The Biography.* New York: Ballantine, 2013.

Jung, Carl G. *Memories, Dreams, Reflections,* ed. Aniela Jaffe, trans. Richard and Clara Winston. New York: Random House, 1965.

Jung, Carl G. *Modern Man in Search of a Soul.* New York: Harcourt, Brace, 1933.

Jung, Carl. *Psychological Reflections: A New Anthology of His Writings 1905–1961,* eds. Jolande Jacoby and R.F.C. Hull. Princeton, NJ: Princeton University, 1978.

Kabat-Zinn, Jon. *Coming to Our Senses: Healing Ourselves and the World through Mindfulness.* New York: Hyperion, 2005.

Kahneman, Daniel. *Thinking, Fast and Slow.* New York: Farrar, Straus and Giroux, 2011.

Kennedy, Alexandra. *The Infinite Thread: Healing Relationships beyond Loss.* Hillsboro, OR: Beyond Words, 2001.

Klein, Gary. *Seeing What Others Don't: the Remarkable Way We Gain Insights.* Philadelphia, PA: Public Affairs, 2013.

Koch, Christof. *Consciousness: Confessions of a Romantic Reductionist.* Cambridge, MA: MIT Press, 2012.

Konigsberg, Ruth Davis. *The Truth about Grief: The Myth of its Five Stages and the New Science of Loss.* New York: Simon and Schuster, 2011.

Kottler, Jeffrey A. *Change: What Really Leads to Lasting Personal Transformation.* New York: Oxford University, 2014.

Kounios, John, and Mark Beeman. *The Eureka Factor: AHA Moments, Creative Insight, and the Brain.* New York: Random House, 2015.

Krakow, Barry and Antonio Zadra. "Clinical management of chronic nightmares: Imagery rehearsal therapy," *Behavioral Sleep Medicine* 4 (2006): 45–70.

Kubler-Ross, Elisabeth. *On Death and Dying: What the Dying Have to Teach Doctors, Nurses, Clergy and Their own Families.* New York: Macmillan, 1969.

Kubler-Ross, Elisabeth and David Kessler. *On Grief and Grieving: Finding the Meaning of Grief through the Five Stages of Loss.* New York: Scribner, 2005.

Lachman, Margie E. "Development in Midlife," *Annual Review of Psychology* 55 (2004): 305–331.

Lachman, Margie E., and Rosanna M. Bertrand, "Personality and the self in midlife," in *Handbook of Midlife Development,* ed. Margie E. Lachman. New York: Wiley, 2001.

Lama, Dalai. *Advice on Dying: And Living a Better Life,* trans. and ed. Jeffrey Hopkins. New York: Atria, 2002.

Levine, Peter A. *Healing Trauma: A Pioneering Program for Restoring the Wisdom of Your Body.* Boulder, CO: Sounds True, 2008.

Levine, Peter A. *In an Unspoken Voice: How the Body Releases Trauma and Restores Goodness.* Berkeley, CA: North Atlantic, 2010.

Levine, Peter A. *Waking the Tiger: Healing Trauma.* Berkeley, CA: North Atlantic, 1997.

Levine, Stephen. *Healing into Life and Death.* New York: Anchor, 1987.

Levitin, Daniel J. *The Organized Mind: Thinking Straight in the Age of Information Overload.* New York: Dutton, 2014.

Maciejewski, Paul K., Baohui Zhang, Susan D. Block, and Holly G. Pringerson. "An empirical examination of the stage theory of grief," *JAMA* 297 (2007): 716–123

Madson, Patrician Ryan. *Improv Wisdom: Don't Prepare, Just Show Up.* New York: Bell Tower, 2005.

Marx, Jeffrey. *Season of Life: A Football Star, a Boy, a Journey to Manhood.* New York: Simon and Schuster, 2003.

Maslow, Abraham H. *Motivation and Personality,* 2nd ed. New York: Harper and Row, 1970.

Maslow, Abraham H. *Toward a Psychology of Being,* 3rd ed. New York: John Wiley, 1999.

McAdams, Dan P. "The psychology of life stories," *Review of General Psychology* 5 (2001): 100–122.

McAdams, Dan P. *The Stories We Live By: Personal Myths and the Making of the Self.* New York: William Morrow, 1993.

McAdams, Dan P., Holly M. Hart, and Shadd Maruna, "The Anatomy of Generativity," in *Generativity and Adult Development: How and Why We Care for the Next Generation,* eds. Dan P McAdams and Ed de St. Aubin. Washington, DC: American Psychological Association, 1998.

McAdams, Dan P. and Jennifer L. Pals. "A New Big Five: Fundamental Principles for an Integrative Science of Personality," *American Psychologist* 61 (2006): 204–217.

McAdams, Dan P. and Philip J. Bowman. "Narrating Life's Turning Points: Redemption and Contamination" in *Turns in the Road; Narrative Studies of Lives in Transition,* eds. Dan P. McAdams, Ruthellen Josselson, and Amia Lieblich. Washington, DC: American Psychological Association, 2001.

McCrae, Robert R., and Costa Jr, Paul T. "Personality Trait Structure as a Human Universal," *American Psychologist* 52 (1997): 509–516. McGonigal, Kelly. "Losing Our War on Stress: It's Time to Reconsider Our Approach," *Psychotherapy Networker* 40 (2016): 57–58.

McGonigal, Kelly. *The Upside of Stress: Why Stress is Good for You, and How to Get Good at It.* New York: Avery, 2015.

Michalko, Michael. *Cracking Creativity: The Secrets of Creative Genius.* Berkeley, CA: Ten Speed, 2001.

Miller, Jean Baker, and Irene Pierce Stiver, *The Healing Connection: How Women Form Relationships in Therapy and in Life.* Boston, MA: Beacon, 1997.

Minsky, Marvin. *The Emotion Machine: Commonsense Thinking, Artificial Intelligence, and the Future of the Human Mind.* New York: Simon and Schuster, 2006.

Moules, Nancy J., Karl Simonson, Mark Prins, Paula Angus, and Janice M. Bell. "Making Room for Grief: Walking Backwards and Living Forward," *Nursing Inquiry* 11 (2004): 99–107.

Mroczek, Daniel K. "Positive and Negative Affect in Midlife" in *How Healthy Are We? A National Study of Well-being at Midlife,* eds. Orville Gilbert Brim, Carol D. Ryff, and Ronald C. Kessler. Chicago, IL: University of Chicago, 2004.

Muller, Wayne. *A Life of Being, Having, and Doing Enough.* New York: Harmony, 2010.

Muller, Wayne. *Sabbath: Finding Rest, Renewal, and Delight in Our Busy Lives.* New York: Bantam, 2000.

Nepo, Mark. *The Book of Awakening: Having the Life You Want by Being Present to the Life You Have.* San Francisco, CA: Conari, 2011.

Newberg, Andrew and Mark Robert Waldman. *Why We Believe What We Believe: Overcoming our Biological Need for Meaning, Spirituality, and Truth.* New York: Free Press, 2006.

Newberg, Andrew and Mark Robert Waldman. *Words Can Change Your Brain: Twelve Conversation Strategies to Build Trust, Resolve Conflict, and Increase Intimacy.* New York: Plume, 2013.

Nye, Naomi Shihab. *Words Under the Words: Selected Poems.* Portland, OR: Far Corner, 1995.

O'Donohue, John. *Anam Cara: A Book of Celtic Wisdom.* New York: HarperCollins, 1997.

O'Donohue, John. *Eternal Echoes: Exploring our Yearning to Belong.* New York: Cliff Street, 1999.

O'Donohue, John. *To Bless the Space between Us.* New York: Doubleday, 2008.

Ogden, Michael and Chris Day. *2 Do Before I Die: The Do-It-Yourself Guide to the Rest of Your Life.* New York: Little, Brown, 2005.

O'Hanlon, Bill. *Do One thing Different: Ten Simple Ways to Change Your Life.* New York: Quill, 2000.

O'Hanlon, Bill. *Out of the Blue: Six Non-Medication Ways to Relieve Depression.* New York: W. W. Norton, 2014.

Quadago, Jill S. *Aging and Life Course: An Introduction to Social Gerontology,* 3rd ed. Boston, MA: McGraw-Hill, 2005.

Pennebaker, James W. *The Secret Life of Pronouns: What Our Words Say About Us.* New York: Bloomsbury, 2011.

Pennebaker, James W. *Writing to Heal: A Guided Journal for Recovering from Trauma and Emotional Upheaval.* Oakland, CA: New Harbinger, 2004.

Pittman, III, Frank S. *Turning Points: Treating Families in Transition and Crisis.* New York: W. W. Norton, 1987.

Randall, David K. *Dreamland: Adventures in the Strange Science of Sleep.* New York: W. W. Norton, 2012.

Rankin, Lissa. *Mind Over Medicine: Scientific Proof That You Can Heal Yourself.* Carlsbad, CA: Hay House, 2013.

Rankin, Lissa. *The Fear Cure: Cultivating Courage as Medicine for the Body, Mind, and Soul.* Carlsbad, CA: Hay House, 2015.

Remen, Rachel Naomi. *Kitchen Table Wisdom.* New York: Riverside, 1996.

Remen, Rachel Naomi. *My Grandfather's Blessing: Stories of Strength, Refuge, and Belonging.* New York, Riverhead, 2000.

Ricard, Matthieu, Antoine Lutz, and Richard J. Davidson. "The Mind of the Meditator," *Scientific American,* November (2014): 39–45.

Roth, Geneen. *Lost and Found: One Woman's Story of Losing Her Money and Finding Her Life.* New York: Viking, 2011.

Roth, Geneen. *Women, Food, and God: An Unexpected Path to Almost Everything.* New York: Scribner, 2010.

Rothko, Christopher. *Mark Rothko: From the Inside Out.* New Haven, CT: Yale University, 2015.

Sacks, Oliver. *An Anthropologist on Mars.* New York: Vintage, 1995.

Sacks, Oliver. *Hallucinations.* New York: Vintage, 2012.

Sawyer, Keith. *Zigzag: The Surprising Path to Greater Creativity.* San Francisco, CA: Jossey-Bass, 2013.

Schwartz, Richard C. *Internal Family Systems.* New York: Guilford, 1995.

Schwartz, Richard C. *You Are the One You've Been Waiting for: Bringing Courageous Love to Intimate Relationships.* Oak Park, IL: Trailheads, 2008.

Seery, Mark D., E. Alison Holman, and Roxane Cohen Silver. "Whatever Does Not Kill Us: Cumulative Lifetime Adversity, Vulnerability, and Resilience," *Journal of Personality and Social Psychology* 99 (2010): 1025–1041.

Seligman, Martin E. P. *Authentic happiness: Using the New Positive Psychology to Realize Your Potential for Lasting Fulfillment.* New York: Free Press, 2002.

Seligman, Martin E. P. *What You Can Change...and What You Can't: The Complete Guide to Successful Self-Improvement.* New York: Vintage, 2007.

Seligman, Martin E., Tracy A. Steen, Nansook Park, and Christopher Peterson. "Positive Psychology in Progress: Empirical Validation of Interventions," *American Psychologist* 60 (2005): 410–421.

Sausys, Antonio. *Yoga for Grief Relief: Simple Practices for Transforming Your Grieving Mind and Body.* Oakland, CA: New Harbinger, 2014.

Scaer, Robert. *The Trauma Spectrum: Hidden Wounds and Human Resiliency.* New York: W. W. Norton, 2005.

Schaffer, Lauren and Sandy Fleischl Wasserman. *133 Ways to Avoid Going Cuckoo When the Kids Fly the Nest: A Parent's Guide for Surviving Empty Nest Syndrome.* New York: Three Rivers, 2001.

Sexton, Anne. *Anne Sexton: A Self Portrait in Letters,* ed. Lois Ames. New York: First Mariner, 2004.

Shalev, Arieh Y., Yael Ankri, Yossi Israeli-Shalev, Tamar Peleg, Rhonda Adessky, and Sara Freedman. "Prevention of Posttraumatic Stress Disorder by Early Treatment," *Archives of General Psychiatry* 69 (2012): 166–176.

Siegel, Daniel J. *The Mindful Therapist: A Clinician's Guide to Mindsight and Neural Integration.* New York: W. W. Norton, 2010.

Siegel, Daniel J., and Tina Payne Bryson. *The Whole-Brain child: 12 Revolutionary Strategies to Nurture Your Child's Developing Mind.* New York: Delacorte, 2011.

Solari-Twadell, Phyllis Ann, Sandra Schmidt Bunkers, Chin-Eng Wang, and Dona Snyder. "The Pinwheel Model of Bereavement," *Journal of Nursing Scholarship* 27 (1995): 323–326.

Sotomayer, Sonia. *My Beloved World.* New York: Knopf, 2013.

Srivasstava, Sanjay, Oliver P. John, Samuel D. Gosling, and Jeff Potter. "Development of Personality in Early and Middle Adulthood: Set Like Plaster or Persistent Change?" *Journal of Personality and Social Psychology* 84 (2003): 1041–1053.

Stafford, William. *The Way It Is: New & Selected Poems.* Minneapolis, MN: Graywolf, 1998.

Stein, Murray. *Jung: Map of the Soul.* Chicago, IL: Open Court, 1998.

Strauch, Barbara. *The Secret Life of the Grown-up Brain: The Surprising Talents of the Middle-Aged Mind.* New York: Viking, 2010.

Stone, Hal, and Sidra Stone. *Partnering, A New Kind of Relationship: How to Love Each Other Without Losing Yourselves.* Novato, CA: New World Library, 2000.

Szalavitz, Maia, and Bruce D. Perry. *Born for Love: Why Empathy is Essential – and Endangered.* New York: William Morrow, 2010.

Tolle, Eckhart. *A New Earth: Awakening to Your Life's Purpose.* New York: Penguin, 2006.

Tomkins, Silvan S. "Script Theory," in *The Emergence of Personality,* eds. Joel Aronoff, Albert I. Rabin, and Robert A. Zucker. New York: Springer, 1987.

Taylor, Jeremy P. *The Wisdom of Your Dreams: Using Dreams to Tap into your Unconscious and Transform your Life.* New York: Jeremy P. Tarcher/Penguin, 2009. *The Holy Bible, Revised Standard Version.* New York: Thomas Nelson, 1952.

Turkle, Sherry. *Reclaiming Conversation: The Power of Talk in a Digital Age.* New York: Penguin, 2015.

Twist, Lynne. *The Soul of Money: Reclaiming the Wealth of Our Inner Resources.* New York: W. W. Norton, 2003.

Van der Kolk, Bessel. *The Body Keeps the Score: Brain, Mind and Body in the Healing of Trauma.* New York: Viking, 2014.

Viorst, Judith. *Necessary Losses: The Loves, Illusions, Dependencies, and Impossible Expectations That All of Us Have to Give Up in Order to Grow.* New York: Ballantine, 1986.

Watson, John B. *Behaviorism, Revised ed.* Chicago, IL: University of Chicago, 1930.

Weintraub, Amy. *Yoga for Depression: A Compassionate Guide to Relieve Suffering through Yoga.* New York: Broadway, 2004.

Whipple, Vicky. *Lesbian Widows: Invisible Grief.* Binghamton, NY: Harrington Park, 2006.

White, Sara J. "Using Self-talk to Enhance Career Satisfaction and Performance," *American Journal of Health-System Pharmacy* 65 (2008): 514–519.

Whitehead, Alfred North. *Process and Reality: An Essay in Cosmology.* New York: Free Press, 1978.

Whyte, David. *The House of Belonging.* Langley, WA: Many Rivers, 1996.

Whyte, David. *The Three Marriages: Reimagining Work, Self, and Relationship.* New York: Riverhead, 2009.

Williams, Kipling D. "The Pain of Exclusion," *Scientific American Mind* 21 (2011): 30–37.

Winerman, Lea. "The Mind's Mirror," *APA Monitor on Psychology* 36 (2005): 48–50.

Wray, T. J. *Grief Dreams: How They Help Us After the Death of a Loved One.* San Francisco, CA: Jossey-Bass, 2005.

Zeldin, Theodore. *An Intimate History of Humanity.* New York: HarperCollins, 1994.

Index